WEST BRITONS

West Britons provides a fresh interpretation of the bloodiest, most devastating years in Cornwall's history and a wholly new perspective on the history of the far South West of Britain. The book explores the unprecedented series of rebellions which took place in Cornwall between 1497 and 1648, traces the connections which existed between those revolts and the contemporary Cornish perception of themselves as a separate people, and argues that Cornish history must be viewed within a British, rather than a purely English context.

Mark Stoyle is Senior Lecturer in Early Modern History at the University of Southampton. He is the author of *Loyalty and Locality: Popular Allegiance in Devon during the English Civil War* (Exeter, 1994) and *From Deliverance to Destruction: Civil War and Rebellion in an English City* (Exeter, 1996).

CHARLES R.

 E are fo highly fenfible of the extraordinary merit of Our County of *Cornwall*, of their zeale for the Defence of Our Perfon, and the juft Rights of Our Crowne, (in a time when We could contribute fo little to Our owne Defence or to their Afsiftance; in a time when not only no Reward appeared, but great and probable dangers were threatned to Obedience and Loyalty;) of their great and eminent Courage and Patience in their indefatigable Profecution of their great Work againft fo potent an Enimy, backt with fo ftrong, Rich, and Populous Citties, and fo plentifully furnifhed and fupplied with Men, Armes, Mony, Ammunition, and Provifion of all kinds; And of the wonderfull fucceffe with which it hath pleafed Almighty God (though with the loffe of fome moft eminent Perfons, who fhall never be forgotten by Vs) to Reward their Loyalty and Patience by many ftrange Victories over their and Our Enimies, in defpight of all humane Probability, and all imaginable difadvantages; That as We cannot be forgetfull of fo great deferts, fo We cannot but defire to publifh to all the World, and perpetuate to all Time the Memory of thefe their merits, and of Our acceptance of the fame. And to that end, We doe hereby render Our Royall thankes to that Our County, in the moft publike and moft Lafting manner We can devife, commanding Copies hereof to be Printed and publifhed, and one of them to be read in every Church and Chappell therein, and to be kept for ever as a Record in the fame, That as long as the Hiftory of thefe Times, and of this Nation fhall continue, the memory of how much that County hath merited from Vs and Our Crowne, may be derived with it to Pofterity. *Given at Our Campe at* Sudeley *Caftle, the Tenth of September,* 1643.

Printed at *Oxford*, by *Leonard Lichfield*, Printer to the *Univerfity*. 1643.

Charles I's letter to the Cornish, 1643.

WEST BRITONS

Cornish Identities and the
Early Modern British State

MARK STOYLE

UNIVERSITY
of
EXETER
PRESS

First published in 2002 by
University of Exeter Press
Reed Hall, Streatham Drive
Exeter EX4 4QR
UK
www.exeterpress.co.uk
Printed digitally since 2011
© Mark Stoyle 2002

British Library Cataloguing in Publication Data
A catalogue record for this book is available
from the British Library.

ISBN : 978-0-85989-688-7

Typeset in 11½pt Monotype Garamond
by XL Publishing Services, Tiverton

For Kate and Scott

Contents

List of Illustrations   ix
List of Abbreviations   xi
Acknowledgements   xiii

Introduction   1
Chronology   7

1 'The Dissidence of Despair': Rebellion and Identity in
  Early Modern Cornwall   9

2 'Knowest Thou My Brood?': Locating the Cornish in
  Tudor and Stuart England   29

3 'England No England, but Babel': English 'Nationalism',
  Welsh and Cornish Particularism and the English Civil War   50

4 'Pagans or Paragons?': Images of the Cornish during the
  English Civil War   66

5 'The Last Refuge of a Scoundrel': Sir Richard Grenville
  and Cornish Particularism, 1644–1646   91

6 'The Gear Rout': The Cornish Rising of 1648 and
  the Second Civil War   113

7 William Scawen: A Seventeenth-century Cornish Patriot   134

8 'A Monument of Honour': The Cornish Royalist Tradition
  after 1660   157

Conclusion   181

Appendices

1 'A Gratulacion to Cornish Men': A letter sent by a group of
  Cornish Royalist gentlemen to the parish constables, 1642   185
2 The Parliamentarian Summons to Cornwall: A letter to
  the Sheriff of Cornwall from Sir Thomas Fairfax and
  Oliver Cromwell, 1645   187
3 Extract from William Scawen's *Antiquities Cornu-Brittanic*,
  c.1688   190
4 Officers of the King's Cornish Infantry Regiments, 1642–1646 193

Notes   213
Index   253

Illustrations

Maps

1. Cornwall: Major Towns and Villages — 11
2. The Retreat of the Cornish Language — 15
3. The Hundreds of Cornwall — 22
4. Marches of the New Cornish Tertia, 1645 — 100
5. The Cornish Rising of 1648 — 119
6. The Parish of St Germans and its Surroundings — 135
7. The World of William Scawen — 137
8. Cornish Trained Band Regiments of the Royalist Army — 192

Frontispiece and jacket illustration

Charles I's letter to the Cornish, 1643: original broadside version
By permission of the Devon Record Office and Mr J. W. Tremayne. Photograph by D. Garner.

Plates (between pages xvi and 1)

1 Holbein: 'Reskemeer, a Cornish Gent'
  The Royal Collection copyright 2001, Her Majesty Queen Elizabeth II.

2 Extract from the articles of the Prayer Book rebels, 1549
  By permission of Lambeth Palace Library.

3 Cornish hurling balls
  By permission of the Royal Institute of Cornwall. Photograph by W.J. Watton.

4 Colonel Thomas St Aubyn
  By permission of Pencarrow House.

5   Sir Richard Grenville
    Reproduced from R. Granville, The History of the Granville Family
    Exeter, 1895, p. 275.

6   Painted board, Camborne Church
    Photograph by B. Stuart-White.

7   Decorated screen and door, Philleigh Church
    Photograph by Lynn Stoyle.

8   Charles I and his chief supporters
    By permission of the Ashmolean Museum, Oxford.

9   Anthony Payne
    By permission of the Royal Institute of Cornwall Photographic Collection.

10 'The Cornish followed the lad up the hill'
    Reproduced from A.H. Norway, Highways and Byways in Devon and
    Cornwall, *London, 1911, p. 197).*

Abbreviations

AHR	*American Historical Review.*
APC	J.R. Dasent et al. (eds), *Acts of the Privy Council.*
BIHR	*Bulletin of the Institute of Historical Research.*
BL	British Library, London.
Bod.	Bodleian Library, Oxford.
CCAM	M.A.E. Green (ed.), *Calendar of the Committee for Advance of Money, 1643–56*, (three volumes, 1881).
CCC	M.A.E. Green (ed.), *Calendar of the Committee for Compounding, 1643–60*, (five volumes, 1882–92).
CJ	*Commons Journals.*
CRO	Cornish Record Office, Truro.
CS	*Cornish Studies.*
CSPD	*Calendar of State Papers Domestic.*
CSPV	*Calendar of State Papers Venetian.*
DCNG	*Devon and Cornwall Notes and Gleanings.*
DCNQ	*Devon and Cornwall Notes and Queries.*
DNB	*Dictionary of National Biography.*
DRO	Devon Record Office, Exeter.
E.	Thomason Tracts, kept at the British Library.
ECAB	Exeter Chamber Act Book, kept at the Devon Record Office.
EHR	*English Historical Review.*
EQSOB	Quarter Sessions Order Books for the City of Exeter, kept at the Devon Record Office.
FSL	Folger Shakespeare Library, Washington DC.
HJ	*Historical Journal.*
HMC	*Historical Manuscripts Commission.*

HR	*Historical Research.*
HT	*History Today.*
IO	*A List of Officers claiming to the Sixty Thousand Pounds . . . Granted by his Sacred Majesty for the relief of His Truly Loyal and Indigent Party* (London, 1663).
JBS	*Journal of British Studies.*
JRIC	*Journal of the Royal Institute of Cornwall.*
KAO	Kent Archives Office.
LJ	*Lords Journals.*
L & P	J.S. Brewer et al. (eds), *Letters and Papers, Foreign and Domestic, of the reign of Henry VIII* (1862–1920).
MSP	Maimed Soldiers' Petitions, kept at the Devon Record Office.
n.d.	No date of publication.
NLW	National Library of Wales, Aberystwyth.
OC	*Old Cornwall.*
OED	*Oxford English Dictionary.*
P & P	*Past and Present.*
PRO	Public Record Office, London.
RO	P.R. Newman, *Royalist Officers in England and Wales 1642–1660: A Biographical Dictionary* (London, 1981).
RTPI	*Report and Transactions of the Plymouth Institution.*
SH	*Southern History.*
SP	State Papers.
TDA	*Report and Transactions of the Devonshire Association.*
TRHS	*Transactions of the Royal Historical Society.*
WCSL	West Country Studies Library, Exeter.
WDRO	West Devon Record Office, Plymouth.
WSL	William Salt Library, Stafford.

Acknowledgements

This book has been some six years in the making. Over that time I have benefited immeasurably from the help of others, and it is a great pleasure to be able to record my gratitude to them now. First, I would like to thank Paul Brough, John Draisey and the staff of the Cornish and Devon Record Offices. The service which they provide is second to none. Second, I would like to thank my students, past and present, for the energy and enthusiasm with which they have approached the study of Cornwall's past. I am especially grateful to Tasha Allen, Kirstein Cheyne, Stephen Dean, Mike Hunkin and Karina Manos in this respect. Third, I would like to thank all of the generous scholars who have, at various times, discussed the question of Cornish identity with me, most notably Cliff Davies, Rhys Davies, R.J. Evans, Todd Gray, Joanna Mattingly, Amos Miller, Oliver Padel, J.G.A. Pocock, Ivan Roots, Ian Roy, David Underdown, Greg Walker, Andy Wood, Joyce Youings, and—among my colleagues in the History Department at Southampton—David Brown, Alistair Dougall, Brian Golding, Peter Gray, Marjorie Huntley, Tony Kushner, John Oldfield, John Rule and Kevin Sharpe.

I have a number of other, particularly important, debts: to Jannine Crocker, who provided me with a great deal of technical assistance, and without whom this book could not have been written; to George Bernard and Alastair Duke, who have constantly supported and encouraged me in this, as in all my other intellectual endeavours; to Simon Baker, Ronald Hutton and John Morrill, who read and commented on the original text, and who have helped me in so many other ways besides; to Philip Payton, who also read the text, and who has welcomed me so generously to the field of Cornish history; and, last but not least, to my late supervisor, Gerald Aylmer, whose death this year was such a tragic loss to his family, to his friends and to the world of historical scholarship as a whole. I salute his memory. My greatest debt, as always, is to my wife and to my parents, for their selfless and unstinting support. Finally, I would like to thank my sister and my brother-in-law for the remarkable patience and good humour with which they have tolerated my constant irruptions into their daily lives over the past seven years. This book is dedicated to them, with love and gratitude.

Mark Stoyle
Caeriske, November 2001

We are grateful to the following copyright holders for permission to reproduce articles by Mark Stoyle: the University of Chicago Press and the editor of the *Journal of British Studies* for 'The Dissidence of Despair: Rebellion and Identity in Early Modern Cornwall', first published in the *Journal of British Studies*, 38, no. 4 (1999), pp. 423–44; Cambridge University Press and the editors of *The Historical Journal* for 'English Nationalism, Celtic Particularism, and the English Civil War', first published in *The Historical Journal*, 43, no. 4 (2000), pp. 1113–28; Addison Wesley Longman Ltd, Oxford University Press and the editors of *The English Historical Review* for 'Pagans or Paragons?: Images of the Cornish during the English Civil War', first published in *The English Historical Review*, 111, no. 441 (1996), pp. 299–323; Blackwell Publishers Ltd and the editor of *Historical Research* for 'The Last Refuge of a Scoundrel: Sir Richard Grenville and Cornish Particularism, 1644–6', first published in *Historical Research*, 71, no. 174 (1998), pp. 31–51; North American Conference on British Studies and the editor of *Albion* for 'The Gear Rout: The Cornish Rising of 1648 and the Second Civil War', first published in *Albion*, 32, no. 1 (2000), pp. 37–58.

Within the image: Reskemeer a çorni[sh]   Gent:

Plate 1. 'Reskemeer, a Cornish Gent': A drawing of either John or William Reskimer, of Merthen, by Hans Holbein, *c.* 1530.

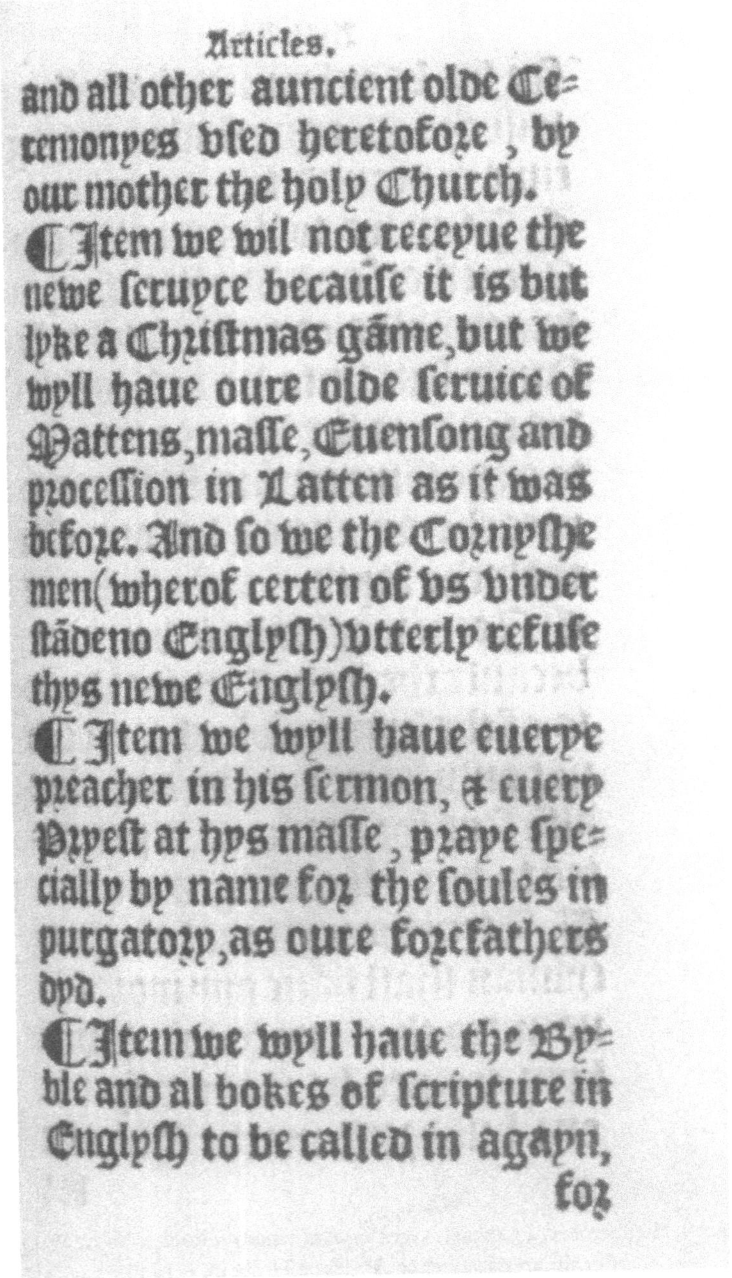

and all other auncient olde Ce=
remonyes vsed heretofoze , by
our mother the holy Church.

¶ Item we wil not receyue the
newe scrupce becaufe it is but
lyke a Chzistmas game,but we
wyll haue oure olde seruice of
Mattens,maffe,Euensong and
procession in Latten as it was
befoze. And so we the Cozpshe
men(wherof certen of vs vnder
stådeno Englysh)vtterly refuse
thys newe Englysh.

¶ Item we wyll haue euerye
pzeacher in his sermon, & euery
Pzyest at hys maffe , pzaye spe=
ciallp by name foz the soules in
purgatozy,as oure fozefathers
dyd.

¶ Item we wyll haue the By=
ble and al bokes of scripture in
Englysh to be called in agayn,
foz

Plate 2. Extract from the articles of the Prayer Book rebels, 1549. Note the
uncompromising declaration on lines 10–13 that 'we the Cornyshe men . . . utterly
refuse thys newe Englysh'.

Plate 3. Cornish hurling balls, date unknown. The central ball is engraved with the words 'God Save the King' at the top. The motto on the lower part of the ball reads 'Play Fare bee merry and wise, that of your sport noe harm arise'.

Plate 4. Colonel Thomas St Aubyn, of Clowance, 1641. St Aubyn was one of the regimental commanders of the Old Cornish tertia.

Plate 5. Sir Richard Grenville: 'The King's General in the West'.

Plate 6. Painted board, Camborne Church. Hung in a prominent position on the church wall, this board reproduces Charles I's commendation of the Cornish people for their loyalty.

Plate 7. (*above and below*) Decorated screen and door, Philleigh Church. Here, painted wooden boards featuring the King's declaration have been placed on either side of a royal coat-of-arms dated 1635 in order to create a little shrine to Cornish royalism.

Plate 8. Charles I and his chief supporters, from an early eighteenth-century edition of Clarendon's *History of the Rebellion*. 'Sir Bevil Greenvile' appears second from right on the bottom row.

Plate 9. Anthony Payne, from a late seventeenth-century portrait attributed to Sir Godfrey Kneller.

The Cornish followed the lad up the hill.

[*To face p.* 196.

Plate 10. 'The Cornish followed the lad up the hill': an Edwardian impression of the Battle of Lansdown, inspired by the romantic vision of the Reverend R.S. Hawker. The Fotherington-Thomas-like figure at the centre of the action is intended to represent Sir John Grenville.

Introduction

Are the Cornish English? At the beginning of the new millennium, as for centuries before, opinion on this question remains sharply divided. To the east of the Tamar, the great majority of people continue to take it for granted that Cornwall is an English county much like any other. To the west of that historic boundary, on the other hand, matters are very different as the advocates and opponents of Cornish nationalism, respectively energized and alarmed by the devolutionary *Zeitgeist*, engage in an increasingly heated debate as to whether or not a distinctive Cornish ethnic identity still persists. The essays contained in the present volume do not seek to participate directly in this contemporary political debate, or to comment on the precise status enjoyed by Cornish people in modern-day British society. Instead, they set out to explore the nature of Cornishness in the past, and particularly during the troubled years of the sixteenth and seventeenth centuries. Together, the essays make three major claims. The first is that a separate sense of Cornish ethnic identity did indeed exist during the early modern period. The second is that that sense of identity endured for much longer than has often been assumed. The third is that that same sense of identity exerted a powerful influence on Cornish politico-religious behaviour throughout the Tudor and Stuart periods—and that it helped to underpin the violent series of rebellions which took place in Cornwall between 1497 and 1648.

* * *

A Devonshire man writing about Cornish history is, perhaps, peculiarly obliged to declare his motives. I should therefore stress, from the very beginning, that—whatever else this book may be—it is not an attempt to perpetuate traditional county rivalries or to assert the innate superiority of Devonshire folk to their Cornish neighbours, whether on or off the sporting field. Although relationships across the Tamar have frequently been strained over the past 500 years—and on occasions bitterly hostile—there is also a venerable tradition of affection and respect for the Cornish people in Devon; one which stretches at least as far back as the sixteenth century. Marriages between the gentry families of Devon and Cornwall were commonplace during the early modern period;[1] in Stuart Oxford, undergraduates from Devon and Cornwall banded together against the rest of the world,[2] and in 1671 the Devon minister John Hickes wrote with great pride of 'Devon and Cornwall being so nearly conjoynd and such fri[e]ndly neighbours'.[3] It is in the spirit of Hickes, rather than that of some of his more jaundiced fellow countrymen, that the essays contained in this book have been written.

To confess to a sense of affinity with the Cornish, however, is not to deny an awareness of Cornish difference. On the contrary, it could be argued that, right up until our own day, Devonians have always—thanks to their unique geographical propinquity to Cornwall—been especially conscious of the various subtle, and not so subtle, signifiers which serve to set the Cornish apart. Certainly, I have appreciated for as long as I can remember that the river Tamar marks a frontier, in a way that the boundaries between Devon, Dorset and Somerset do not. Yet it was not until I started to delve into the pre-modern history of my own county, as a postgraduate student, that I began to realize just how different that history had been from the history of its western neighbour. My doctoral thesis was a study of popular allegiance in Devon during the English Civil War.[4] Naturally enough, this study was primarily focused on the experiences and attitudes of ordinary Devonians—but, as my work progressed, I became increasingly aware of the fact that the patterns of popular political behaviour which had been discernible to the east of the Tamar during the 1640s were quite unlike those which had been discernible to the west. Whereas Devon, Dorset and Somerset had been torn apart by the events of the Civil War, Cornwall had, after some initial hesitation, reacted to that conflict as a more or less united community. Whereas those counties had exhibited a great deal of support for both King and Parliament, Cornwall had been overwhelmingly Royalist. And whereas the soldiers drawn from those three counties had fought at least as bravely as those from any other English shire, the Cornish troops had possessed a valour and a martial éclat which was uniquely their own.

What could explain these striking contrasts?

Turning to the standard histories of the Civil War, I found that they had little to say on the subject. Most writers agreed that the Cornish had been quite exceptionally Royalist, but few offered any convincing explanation as to why this should have been so. Few, indeed, seemed especially to care: popular royalism has never been a fashionable subject among historians of the 1640s.[5] There was a general assumption that, in Cornwall as elsewhere, it must have been a combination of deference to local leaders and innate religious conservatism which had led ordinary people to support the King, but scholars had seldom troubled to ask themselves why the self-same ingredients should have created a more fervent strain of royalism in Cornwall than they did anywhere else. The single alternative explanation which was occasionally, if very tentatively, advanced, was that the strength of Cornish support for the King might somehow have been linked to Cornwall's unique cultural heritage: to what was variously described as an intense 'local patriotism' and an abiding sense of 'racial difference'.[6] I first began to investigate this theory while in the process of converting my thesis into a book (*Loyalty and Locality*, published in 1994). My initial thoughts on the connections between 'Cornishness' and wartime allegiance were published there.[7] Yet as I devoted more attention to the subject over the following years, it became increasingly clear to me that the study of Cornish ethnic identity had not only been neglected by historians of the Civil War, but by historians of the British Isles as a whole.

Amidst the plethora of books and articles on 'British history' which had appeared since the early 1980s, there had been very little discussion of Cornwall's claim to be considered as one of the discrete constituent parts of these islands. Many of the key works of the new British historiography had paid no attention whatsoever to Cornwall,[8] while even those which had had limited themselves to observing that Cornwall's case deserved more detailed examination.[9] The paucity of writing on Cornish ethnic identity during the early modern period seemed especially puzzling, for—as M.J. Hechter had observed—it was during this critical period that Cornwall had finally become 'assimilated to English culture',[10] or—as Adrian Hastings rather more bluntly put it—that the Cornish themselves had 'become English'.[11]

A succession of distinguished Cornish historians—most notably, perhaps, T.Q. Couch, A.L. Rowse and Philip Payton—had long been arguing that the events of the Tudor period in the South-west had possessed an ethnic dimension, and that 'the rebellions of 1497 and 1549 were to Cornwall what those of 1715 and 1745 were to the Highlands of Scotland'.[12] Yet even these scholars had paid little attention to the events of the seventeenth century[13]—and their findings had not, in any case, received the recognition they deserved from the new breed of early modern British historians. It was a desire to fill this historiographical gap, and to carry out a more detailed analysis of the complicated series of interactions which had taken place between the English and the Cornish during the sixteenth and seventeenth centuries, which inspired the pieces in the present collection. The earliest of them was written in 1995, the latest in 2000—and five of them have previously appeared in scholarly journals. Obviously, some of my opinions have developed since these pieces were first published, but not to such an extent as to alter my basic view of the subject, nor—I hope—as to affect the coherence of the collection as a whole. The previously published journal articles have been left as I originally wrote them, apart from the removal of one or two questionable statements and factual inaccuracies, and the conversion of the footnotes into a standard format. As a result there is a certain amount of 'overlap' in the central section of the book and several important themes repeat themselves, but I hope that this will not detract unduly from the reader's enjoyment.

The first chapter in the collection surveys the current debate on 'Britishness', notes that Cornwall has so far been largely ignored in that debate and argues that this is a serious oversight which needs to be addressed. It goes on to make the case for the Cornish as a separate 'people', and to argue that the six major rebellions which occurred in Cornwall during the Tudor and early Stuart periods were partly fuelled by Cornish conviction that their separate cultural identity was under attack. Chapter 2, written especially for this volume, explores the shifting nature of English attitudes towards Cornwall and the Cornish between c.1497 and 1642. It suggests that, in the wake of the Tudor risings, the Cornish came to be seen by their neighbours as an inherently 'rebellious' people—and that this in turn served to hasten the decline of the very ethnic identity which the rebels had sought to protect. The third chapter is, perhaps, the most ambitious in the entire collection. Building on one of the central claims advanced in the first essay—that Cornish support for the King during the Civil War had been partly founded on the belief that Charles I respected the 'Celtic' inhabitants of his kingdoms as the Parliamentarians did not—it argues that the same had also been true in

Wales, and that, to the west of Offa's Dyke, just as in Cornwall, ubiquitous popular royalism had been a product of deep-rooted ethnic fears. Cornish and Welsh behaviour had been founded on the conviction that Parliament was the party of Englishness, in other words, and this in turn, the essay contends, helps to illuminate a hitherto neglected truth: that English nationalism lay at the very heart of the English Civil War.

The creation of a Cornish Royalist army in 1642, a force which was to remain in being for the next three and a half years, ensured that during the Civil War Cornwall would play a more influential role in national events than it had ever done before. Chapters 4 and 5 explore two different aspects of Cornwall's wartime experience. Chapter 4 shows how Parliamentarian propagandists, infuriated by Cornwall's wholehearted support for the King, launched a series of vitriolic attacks upon the Cornish people, while Chapter 5 re-examines the wartime career of the Cornish Royalist leader Sir Richard Grenville (1600–59), and shows how he exploited Cornish particularist sentiment in order to bolster his own position within the Royalist hierarchy. More specifically, the essay reveals that—in a desperate attempt to persuade ordinary Cornish people to fight on against the Parliamentarians—Grenville briefly floated the prospect of a semi-independent Cornish state.

The concluding chapters are concerned with the aftermath of the Civil War, and with shifting perceptions of Cornish identity in the period after 1646. Chapter 6 analyses the causes and consequences of the last Cavalier rising in Cornwall, in May 1648, and argues that the rebels' defeat marked the *coup de grâce* for traditional Cornishness. Chapter 7 investigates the life and writings of William Scawen (1600–89), the Cornish antiquarian who did more than anyone else to encourage scholarly interest in the Cornish tongue, and argues that his royalism and his sense of Cornish patriotism were inextricably intertwined. The final chapter traces the way in which memories of Cornwall's wartime royalism helped to transform views of Cornish identity in the post-Restoration era and beyond, and examines the process by which the Cornish—so long suspected by the English of being inveterate rebels—came to be celebrated, in High Tory and Anglican circles at least, as the most loyal of subjects.

The appendices which appear at the end of the collection are designed to illustrate, and to reinforce, some of the book's main themes. Thus the letter reproduced in Appendix 1 shows the jubilation with which local Royalist leaders reacted to Cornwall's mass rising for the King in 1642, while the summons reproduced in Appendix 2 reveals the bitterness which Cornwall's wartime behaviour had stirred up in the hearts of English Parliamentarians by 1645. Appendix 3—an extract from William Scawen's *magnum opus*, the *Antiquities Cornu-Brittanic* (*c.*1688)— affords a vivid insight into views of Cornish identity towards the end of the seventeenth century. Finally, Appendix 4, a list of the Cornish infantry regiments which served the King between 1642 and 1646, demonstrates the vital contribution which Cornwall made to the Royalist war effort.

* * *

The title of this book—West Britons—may possibly raise a few eyebrows. I am well aware that the sobriquet is one which historians more commonly associate with the people of Ireland than with the people of Cornwall.[14] The fact that William Camden was using this term to refer to the Cornish as early as the 1580s, however, must surely justify its reappropriation here[15]—and it should not be forgotten that for almost two centuries *The West Briton* has been the title of Cornwall's leading weekly newspaper.[16] That this particular name should have been chosen for that publication in the first place—and retained ever since— is no coincidence, of course. Throughout the modern era, many Cornish men and women have continued to regard themselves, not as English provincials, but as British originals: descendants of a distinct Celtic people and inhabitants of a 'land set apart'. Many of their early modern ancestors felt the same way, viewing the cultural, political and religious world in which they had their being as a British, rather than as a purely English, one. This book attempts to see the turbulent events of the sixteenth and seventeenth centuries through *their* eyes, as well as through those of their English neighbours.

Chronology

1485   Accession of King Henry VII.

1497   *May*, insurrection at St Keverne. First Cornish rising.
June, defeat of the rebels at Blackheath.
September, arrival of Perkin Warbeck. Second Cornish rising.
October, Henry VII oversees the pacification of the West.

1509   Accession of King Henry VIII.

1537   Rumours of fresh disturbances in Cornwall.

1539   Creation of the Council of the West.

1547   Demonstration against confiscation of church goods at Penryn.

1548   Murder of Archdeacon Body at Helston. Third Cornish rising.

1549   *June*, 'Prayer Book Rebellion'. Fourth Cornish rising.
August, defeat of the rebels at several battles in Devon.
September, Cornwall subdued by the Royal army.

1558   Accession of Queen Elizabeth I.

1594   Affair of the Duchy suit. New suspicions of the Cornish are aroused.

1599   Publication of Shakespeare's *Henry V*.

1600   Birth of Richard Grenville and William Scawen.

1603   Accession of King James I.
Publication of Richard Carew's *Survey of Cornwall*.

1617   Publication of Middleton and Rowley's play, *A Fair Quarrel*.

1625   Accession of King Charles I.

1632 Publication of Richard Brome's play, *The Northern Lasse.*

1642 *August*, outbreak of the English Civil War.
October, Cornwall secured for the King. Fifth Cornish rising.
November, creation of the Cornish Army.

1643 Cornish Army conquers South-west England for the King.
July, death of Sir Bevill Grenville.
September, Charles I publishes his 'Declaration' to the Cornish.

1644 *July*, invasion of Cornwall by Essex's Parliamentary army.
September, defeat of Essex at Lostwithiel.
October–December, creation of the New Cornish Tertia.

1645 Charles, Prince of Wales and Duke of Cornwall, is sent into the West by the King.

1646 *January*, arrest of Sir Richard Grenville.
March, Treaty of Millbrook: Cornwall submits to the Parliament.
End of the First Civil War.

1648 Rebellions at Penzance and the Lizard. Sixth Cornish rising.

1649 Execution of King Charles I.

1659 Death of Sir Richard Grenville.

1660 Restoration of the Monarchy.

1688 Completion of William Scawen's *Antiquities Cornu-Brittanic.*

1689 Death of William Scawen.

1704 Publication of Edward Hyde's *History of the Rebellion.*

1715 Abortive Jacobite rising at St Columb.

1723 Memorial to Sir Bevill Grenville erected on Lansdown Hill.

1777 Death of Dolly Pentreath (reputedly the last person who could converse in the Cornish language).

1

'The Dissidence of Despair'

Rebellion and Identity in Early Modern Cornwall

In May 1648 a group of Cornishmen who had rebelled against Parliament in the name of Charles I met with comprehensive defeat at 'the Gear', near Helford, and were then pursued back across the Lizard peninsula to the sea-coast beyond. Surrender seemed inevitable, yet a number of the fugitives refused to submit. Instead they 'joyned hand-in-hand' and hurled themselves bodily into the water: 'a desperate expedient on that rocky coast' as one later writer remarked.[1] What can have driven them to such despair? No convincing answer can be given by looking at the events of 1648 alone. The rebels' despairing plunge can only be understood if it is seen as the final act in a long-running drama, a story of repeated popular protest in western Cornwall which spanned over 150 years. It is a story which has gone largely unrecognized by previous historians, most of whom have portrayed the Cornish revolts of 1497, 1548, 1549, 1642 and 1648 as isolated events, rather than as part of a continuum.[2] Yet it is a story which deserves to be told, not only because it provides a dramatic new explanation for many of the most important rebellions of the Tudor and Stuart periods, but also because it serves as an enduring monument to a forgotten people and their struggle to preserve a separate identity for themselves in the face of overwhelming odds.

I

A fierce sense of distinctiveness has always characterized the inhabitants of Cornwall. That this is so owes much to physical conditions, for Cornwall is 'a land apart': an isolated peninsula, some ninety miles long,

9

which is (in the words of a Stuart visitor) 'enwrapt with the sea on all sides, except toward Devonshire, and there bounded by the River Tamar, which . . . runs almost from sea to sea' (see Map 1).[3] These natural defences had served the Celtic inhabitants of the peninsula well during the Dark Ages, permitting them to withstand the Saxon tide which submerged the indigenous populations to the east. As a result, Cornwall had remained an independent, British entity until well into the tenth century. By 937, however, the so-called 'West Britons' had at last been brought firmly under Saxon rule.[4]

Cornwall was the first part of the Celtic periphery to be incorporated within the English state, therefore, and a thousand years of political and cultural subordination lay ahead. Needless to say, the effects of this uniquely long period of subjection were to be profound. Of all the Celtic peoples of the British Isles, the Cornish are those whose voices have been most effectively drowned out by traditional, Anglocentric historiography. For centuries, speakers and writers of English have gone out of their way to pour cold water on the suggestion that Cornwall might be anything other than an integral part of England.[5] And although a number of Cornish scholars have attempted to challenge this orthodoxy,[6] their arguments have, so far, failed to penetrate the mainstream of historical thought, at least as far as the early modern period is concerned.

Despite the *nouvelle vague* for 'British history', and the flood of books and articles on 'the British Problem' which has appeared over the past few years, Cornish history continues to be widely regarded as just another aspect of English local history, while Cornwall's claim to be considered as a discrete entity within the early modern British state continues to be virtually ignored. One or two historians have admittedly been prepared to acknowledge that Cornwall's case might be worthy of closer inspection.[7] None of the key works of the new British historiography deal with Cornwall in any depth, however, while the prevailing scholarly attitude towards Cornwall and its inhabitants is well summed up by John Morrill's recent comment that Cornish history is 'best accommodated within the traditional "national" framework'.[8]

In the past it might have been possible to retort that the Cornish were themselves 'a nation'.[9] But appeals to the concept of nationhood carry less conviction today. As the work of Benedict Anderson, Ernest Gellner, and many others has shown, 'nations' are more or less artificial

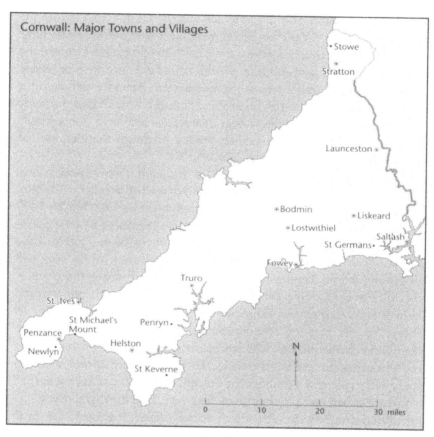

Map 1

constructs, brought together by a particular combination of circumstances, and susceptible to alteration (or even collapse) as those circumstances change over time.[10] More controversially, 'nationalism' in its proper sense has now been claimed to be an exclusively modern phenomenon, a habit of thought which simply did not exist before the eighteenth century.[11] Yet even as nations (like 'races' before them) have swum and disappeared before our eyes, Anthony Smith has stressed the persistence in the pre-modern world of ethnic groups, or *ethnie*: 'collective cultural units' whose members were bound together by 'a sense of community based on history and culture'.[12] And it is to the study of such *ethnie*—or 'peoples'—that historians are now increasingly turning as they struggle to establish 'what constitutes the identities of the different parts of the British Isles'.[13]

Were the Cornish, then, 'a people'? At first sight it would appear not. R.R. Davies, whose splendid series of articles on 'the peoples of Britain' has transformed our understanding of this subject, asserts that 'by 1400 . . . these islands could . . . be claimed to be the home of four major peoples': English, Irish, Scottish and Welsh. No mention is made of the Cornish. They are thus implicitly assigned to the ranks of the 'regional' sub-groups whom Davies is careful to distinguish from the peoples proper.[14] On the surface, then, Davies' work reinforces the view of the Cornish as 'honorary Englishmen'. Yet, at a deeper level, it helps to subvert it. As part of his argument, Davies rehearses the chief 'identifying characteristics' which were thought to distinguish a *gens*, or people, during the medieval period. To qualify for this title, a group ideally had to possess a tradition of descent from a 'founding patriarch'. Its members had to have their own 'language, law, life-style, dress . . . agricultural practices, [and] code of social values', together with their own naming forms, and cultural practices. Finally, they had to regard themselves—and be regarded by others—as distinct.[15] If these various criteria are applied to the Cornish, they emerge as a 'people' on every count.

To explore the question of descent first, it is instructive to turn to the 'Brutus myth', that ancient legend—reworked by Geoffrey of Monmouth in the twelfth century—which deals with the founding of Britain.[16] As students of British history are nowadays well aware, the legend tells how Albion was colonized by refugees from Troy under King Brutus, how Brutus renamed his new kingdom Britain, and how the island was subsequently divided up between his three sons—the eldest inheriting England, the other two Scotland and Wales. The tripartite nature of this division is often commented upon by scholars.[17] Yet what is usually forgotten is that, according to the legend, it was not just one group of Trojans who originally arrived in Britain but two. The smaller group was led by a warrior named Corineus, to whom Brutus granted extensive estates. And just as Brutus had 'called the island Britain . . . and his companions . . . Britons', so Corineus called 'the region of the Kingdom which had fallen to his share Cornwall, after the manner of his own name, and the people who lived there . . . Cornishmen'.[18]

No other region is picked out for such special treatment; it is clear that, as far as Geoffrey was concerned, Cornwall had possessed a separate identity even before the creation of Scotland and Wales had taken place. Significantly, this identity is not precisely defined in juridical terms. The legend states that the Cornish were set apart, and that they possessed their own leader, but it also states that they were subject to Brutus and inhabitants of his kingdom. The inference is plain: from the very beginnings of British history, Cornwall's political position had been anomalous, unclear, the region forming a semi-autonomous province, which was neither wholly part of what would later become England nor wholly separate from it.[19] This was a refrain which was to be frequently repeated over the succeeding centuries (most notably, perhaps, by the eighteenth-century writer who confessed, in some perplexity, that Cornwall 'seems to be another Kingdom').[20] Yet if the Brutus myth was somewhat vague about the status of Cornwall as a territorial entity, it was much clearer about the status of the Cornish themselves as a separate people, with Corineus as their 'founding patriarch'.

Cornishmen and women continued to regard themselves as the descendants of Corineus until well into the early modern period. They spoke of him with pride, alleging him to have been 'the firste that recyved the title and dignitye of Duke of Cornwall'.[21] And because they believed themselves to be sprung from his stock, rather than from that of Brutus, they naturally believed that their very blood was different from that of the English (another sure mark of a people). As late as the 1680s, a Cornish gentleman urged his fellow countrymen to eschew 'forreigne marriages' in England—a practice which, he hinted, had had enfeebling results—and to marry within their own 'race' instead, thus preserving their ancient 'Brittish Blood'.[22]

It is no coincidence that this plea for racial purity was made within the context of a work which sought to encourage the preservation of the 'primitive . . . speech of Cornwall'.[23] Language was considered to be one of the most important badges of a people, and the existence of the Cornish tongue—a Brythonic language, closely allied to Breton and Welsh—did more than anything else to set the Cornish apart.[24] Yet the territorial and social range of the Cornish language was constantly diminishing during the pre-modern period, a fact which is too rarely appreciated by scholars. Textbooks often suggest that, as late as 1530, the boundary between the Cornish and English-speaking areas of south-west Britain lay along the line of the Tamar.[25] But this had not been the case for many hundreds of years. From the eighth century onwards, English settlers had been steadily moving into East Cornwall, while the eventual Saxon conquest had seen an alien ruling class being imposed across the whole country. By 1086 the Celtic inhabitants of Cornwall were governed 'by an Anglo-Saxon minority, who lived chiefly at the eastern end of the county, but had settlements and extended their authority throughout'.[26]

Over the following centuries the English language gradually advanced from its original strongholds (see Map 2), until Cornwall had become divided into three linguistic blocs. In 1450 the situation was roughly as follows: West Cornwall was inhabited by a population of Celtic descent, which was mostly Cornish-speaking; the western part of East Cornwall was inhabited by a population of Celtic descent, which had largely abandoned the Cornish tongue in favour of English; and the eastern part of East Cornwall was inhabited by a population of Anglo-Saxon descent, which was entirely English-speaking.[27] To make matters more complicated still, these three regional sub-groups were overlaid by an elite class which was generally English-speaking, but which contained a certain number of individuals who could also speak Cornish.[28]

The members of these four groups had much in common. All Cornishmen and women were held to be descendants of Corineus, for example, and all were thought to share in the alleged national characteristics of 'valiancy' and 'stoutness'.[29] All were believed, by the English at least, to affect a ragged, bare-legged style of dress, and during the 1610s two stereotypical Cornishmen were twitted on the London stage as 'Redshanks' (a derisive term which, significantly, the English also applied to the peasantry of Ireland and Scotland).[30] The distinctive Cornish sports of wrestling and hurling were practised throughout the entire county.[31] So were a number of unusual agricultural practices,

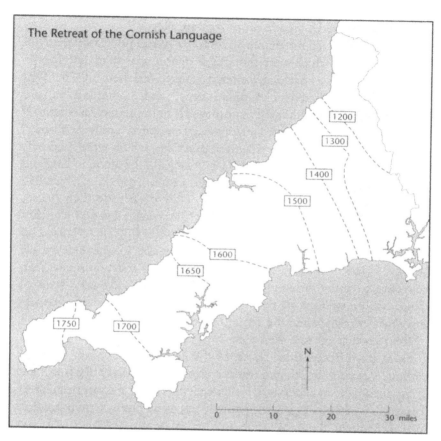

Map 2

including the use of the 'Cornish acre', a measurement which, as John Norden observed in the 1590s, was 'not [known] ellswher in Englande'.[32] In addition 'the whole county of Cornwall' fell under the jurisdiction of the Stannary courts (of which more below) and, as a result, local people enjoyed a unique set of legal privileges.[33]

Even the anglicized inhabitants of East Cornwall possessed many of the characteristics which were thought to denote a people, therefore—but only the Cornish-speaking westerners possessed them all. The West Cornish had distinctive naming-customs, and continued to use patronymics in the Welsh fashion until well into the sixteenth century.[34] They appear to have preserved an unusually extended family structure.[35] They possessed their own agricultural practices, which were markedly different from those employed in East Cornwall—let alone in England proper.[36] They continued to use an archaic weapon, the sling, which had long been abandoned by the English.[37] They even rode their horses differently: Richard Carew remarked that 'the meaner country wenches of the western parts do yet ride astride, as all other English folk used [to do] before Richard the Second's wife brought in the side-saddle fashion'.[38] (It is intriguing to note in the light of this comment, that, according to the fourteenth-century Statutes of Kilkenny, 'style of riding' was considered to be one of the main distinguishing features between the English and the Irish peoples.[39])

Nor does this exhaust the list of ways in which the cultural practices of the West differed from those of the East. The Cornish sport of 'hurling', a game in which two teams competed for a silver ball (see Plate 3), has already been alluded to. Fuller described it as 'a sport peculiar to Cornwall', while Norden made broadly the same point, remarking that Cornishmen had 'the peculiaritie [in hurling] because elswhere it is not in manner used'.[40] Hurling was played in two ways: 'to goals' in East Cornwall and 'to the country' in West Cornwall.[41] The distinctiveness of the West Cornish style of play was reinforced by the fact that local people embellished their hurling balls with mottoes in Cornish (a practice which suggests that language, hurling and Cornishness were all regarded as inextricably linked in this region).[42] Yet the clearest sign of West Cornwall's cultural distinctiveness was the fact that plays in the Cornish language were regularly performed here. Known as 'gwaryes', these productions were staged in 'Plen-an-gwarrys' or 'rounds': earthen amphitheatres of a type which are not to be found anywhere else in the British Isles.[43]

In terms of blood and descent, then, of language, life-style, dress and cultural practices, the West Cornish truly deserved the name of 'a people'—and all the evidence suggests that this was how others perceived them. As we have seen, the English generally regarded the inhabitants of Cornwall with amused disdain. When it came to the West Cornish, however, disdain could sometimes transform itself into open dislike. Such hostility was particularly evident amongst the English-speaking gentry of Cornwall itself. As early as the 1540s, a group of gentlemen who had gathered at Penryn, in the heart of the Cornish-speaking West, reported that 'the people hereabouts be very ignoraunte'.[44] Fifty years later, the English-speaking gentleman Richard Carew made a series of veiled criticisms of the West Cornish in his *Survey of Cornwall* (written, be it noted, at Carew's mansion house in the extreme south-east of the county).[45] Another English-speaking East Cornishman went much further in 1648, roundly condemning West Cornwall as 'those westerne heathen partes'.[46] And when the English puritan preacher Roger Williams complained in 1652 that 'we have Indians . . . in Cornwall, Indians in Wales, Indians in Ireland', there can be little doubt which specific inhabitants of Cornwall he was referring to.[47]

'Indians' and 'heathens': both these terms were routinely applied by the inhabitants of Stuart England to groups which they felt to be quintessentially 'un-English'. That such epithets, redolent as they were of 'paganism' and 'barbarism',[48] should have been applied to the West Cornish is clear evidence that they were considered by the English to be a separate and inferior people. The point is underlined by Williams' bracketing of the Cornish with the Irish and the Welsh: groups which were invariably recognized as distinct.[49] To clinch the case for the contemporary perception of the West Cornish as a distinct *gens*, one need only add that this was how they saw themselves. They spoke of Cornwall not as a county, but as a country ('Kernow'), they spoke of their language not as a dialect, but as a separate tongue ('Kernowok'), and they spoke of the English not in any affectionate way, but as Saxons ('Sawson').[50] Like the Welsh, moreover, they clung fiercely to their own language as a mark of their separate identity.

As late as the 1590s, Richard Carew noted with evident irritation that although many of the West Cornish by now understood English: 'yet some so affect their own, as to a stranger they will not speak it, for if meeting them by chance, you enquire the way or any such matter, your answer shall be "Meea Navidna Cowzasawzneck": "I can speak no

17

Saxonage'".[51] Significantly, Carew's translation is not quite accurate: the phrase is better rendered 'I *will* speak no Saxonage', and therefore provides still clearer evidence of the West Cornish determination to resist cultural assimilation with England.[52]

Measured against all contemporary yardsticks, then, the West Cornish were indeed a people. They were a small people, admittedly (recent estimates suggest that the Cornish-speaking population stood at around 33,000 in 1450),[53] but a distinct one nevertheless. It is therefore possible to argue that Cornish history is worthy of consideration in a British, as well as in a merely English, context. Indeed, J.G.A. Pocock—the 'true begetter' of the new British historiography—has recently indicated his tentative support for just such a view. 'One did not have to be a kingdom in order to have a history', Pocock writes, and 'we must avoid . . . distinguishing between peoples that have histories and peoples that have none.'[54] Among the 'many histories' of these islands which deserve to be written, Pocock goes on to suggest, 'Cornish history' might conceivably be one.[55] The second half of this chapter will argue that Pocock's suggestion deserves to be followed up; that Cornish history did indeed form part of a wider 'British' history during the early modern period; and that the turbulence which beset the extreme south-western corner of the Atlantic Archipelago between 1450 and 1650 was, at least in part, the product of a collision between two different peoples and two different histories.

II

Inevitably, the chief physical locus of this cultural clash was West Cornwall, where a largely Cornish-speaking peasantry lived cheek by jowl with an anglicized elite.[56] When social inequalities are mirrored by linguistic divisions in this way, tension is almost bound to arise—and the situation was exacerbated by the fact that many of the West Cornish felt themselves to be the descendants of a conquered people.

'One point of their former roughness . . . these western people do yet retain', wrote Richard Carew in the 1590s:

and therethrough . . . verify that testimony which Matthew of Westminster giveth of them together with the Welsh, their ancient countrymen, namely, how fostering a fresh memory of their expulsion long ago by the English, they second the same with a bitter repining at their fellowship; and this the worst sort express in combining against and working them all the shrewd turns which . . . they can devise.[57]

Carew's reference to the Welsh is significant, for, in many ways, West Cornish society during the pre-modern era was a miniature version of that contemporaneous Welsh society whose complexities have been so superbly evoked by R.R. Davies in his study of Owain Glyn Dwr. In Celtic West Cornwall, just as in Davies' Wales, 'two worlds, two peoples and two sets of aspirations' were locked together 'within one small community'; in West Cornwall, just as in Wales, 'ethnic suspicion and contempt were never far below the surface'; and in West Cornwall, just as in Wales, a conquered Celtic people, deprived of a 'practical and present-oriented political culture' looked for their deliverance instead to a 'mythological and prophetic ideology' associated with the past.[58]

Like the Welsh, the Cornish had never fully reconciled themselves to Saxon dominance. Instead, they continued to cling to the belief that the legendary British hero, King Arthur, would one day return from the magical realm in which he slept, and lead his people to victory against the Saxon usurpers. During the twelfth century a near-riot occurred in Bodmin when a party of visiting Frenchmen had the temerity to question this myth.[59] And three hundred years later an anonymous English writer observed: '[the] Cornysch sayeth thus, that [Arthur] levyth yet . . . and schalle come and be a kyng [again]'.[60] Such prophecies betrayed a hidden longing to humble the Saxons and to resurrect the imagined glories of Cornwall's independent past.

The combination of this subversive vaticinatory lore with Cornwall's deep-seated ethnic divisions was a potentially explosive one, and the rulers of medieval England did their best to placate the Cornish. In 1337 Cornwall was made a royal Duchy, and the title 'Duke of Cornwall' was henceforth conferred on the heir to the English throne.[61] The notion that the Crown looked on the Cornish with special favour was strengthened by the existence of the Stannaries: royal institutions which regulated the local tin-mining industry and conferred many privileges on Cornish miners.[62] As Philip Payton has observed, the Duchy and Stannary organizations provided Cornwall with an 'aura . . . of territorial semi-independence', and this doubtless helped to reconcile the Cornish to English rule.[63] Yet the granting of 'quasi-national institutions' was not enough in itself to guarantee the continued existence of the Cornish as a people. And while official attitudes towards the Cornish remained benign throughout the medieval period, more insidious processes were at work beneath the surface, processes which put the very survival of 'Cornishness' in doubt.

By the mid-fourteenth century, the 'people characteristics' which served to define the Cornish as a separate *gens* were coming under increasing threat. This can be clearly demonstrated in the case of the Cornish language, which was steadily eroded between 1350 and 1450. From a language still spoken by most of the inhabitants of Cornwall, it gradually fell away to the west until the balance between Cornish and English-speakers was almost equal.[64] Intriguingly, it was during this same period that plays in the Cornish language began to appear: between 1350 and 1375 a complete cycle of miracle plays was written at the collegiate church of Glasney, near Penryn.[65] Later evidence shows that some local people believed that Cornish identity was dependent on the survival of the language,[66] so it seems at least possible that the plays were partially intended to bolster the ancient tongue.[67] And by the late 1400s, attempts to resist the encroaching tide of Englishness had begun to manifest themselves in the political sphere as well.

During the 1480s Cornwall provided support for Henry Tudor in his attempts to seize the English throne. Henry, a Welshman by birth, claimed to be descended from King Arthur, and his supporters averred that the return of 'Arthur's line' would bring about the Celtic resurgence of ancient prophecy.[68] Such promises did not go entirely unfulfilled; after Henry's triumph at Bosworth many Cornish (and Welsh) gentlemen were richly rewarded.[69] Yet the favours lavished on the Cornish gentry did nothing to stem the erosion of traditional Cornish identity. Rather, they accelerated that process, drawing the local gentry into a still closer alliance with the central government, and prompting them to jettison their native customs. As a result the split which already existed between rulers and ruled in West Cornwall grew wider. Towards the end of the fifteenth century, moreover, English replaced Cornish as the majority language in Cornwall.[70]

These developments made it possible for the attitude of communal cultural defensiveness which A.D. Smith has labelled 'ethnicism' to emerge.[71] And although the unprecedented series of risings and near-risings which gripped the West Country between 1497 and 1549 had a multiplicity of causes—including economic distress, religious discontent and governmental weakness[72]—the disturbances cannot be fully understood unless the determination of ordinary Cornish people to preserve their own distinctive identity is also taken into account. Throughout these turbulent years, it was Celtic West Cornwall which was the storm-centre of popular protest.

In 1497 the first and greatest of the Cornish risings broke out at St Keverne, in the Lizard pensinsula. Henry's demand for a subsidy was the immediate cause of the rising.[73] Yet the King's decision to suspend the Cornish Stannary privileges—privileges which not only protected the miners' livelihoods, but also helped to symbolize royal recognition of Cornwall's quasi-autonomous status—may well have been a contributory factor, stirring up cultural anxieties and adding to the impression that Cornishness itself was under attack.[74] The Cornish rebels (together with the motley collection of English malcontents who joined them) were defeated at Blackheath in June. But four months later West Cornwall exploded into rebellion once more, when the Yorkist pretender Perkin Warbeck landed at Penzance and attracted 3,000 men to his cause.[75] Beyond the fact that the rebels supported Warbeck's claim to the throne, there is little evidence as to their motivation. Of those who are known to have assisted Warbeck, however, over a third came from the Cornish-speaking hundreds of Kerrier and Penwith (for the hundreds of Cornwall, see Map 3).[76]

Warbeck was quickly defeated and his adherents punished; for the next forty years Cornwall remained quiet. Yet during the 1530s and 1540s government attacks on the Catholic Church—a Church which had always proved itself extremely accommodating of Cornish language and culture—reawakened the spirit of defiance in West Cornwall. In 1536 rumours of impending trouble sent one of Cromwell's agents hurrying down to Penryn, and a year later the local gentry were thoroughly alarmed by a supposed plot to raise a new rebellion in St Keverne.[77] In 1547 Penryn was the scene of an angry demonstration against religious innovations.[78] And in 1548 the reformist Archdeacon William Body was stabbed to death in the West Cornish town of Helston by a mob which included many St Keverne men. Body's murderers declared that anyone else who embraced 'new fashions' would perish in the same way[79]—and they may have been alluding to cultural/linguistic fashions here, as well as religious ones. Some 3,000 West Cornishmen were soon up in arms, and the local gentry were forced to call for outside help before they could restore order.[80]

The disturbances of 1497–1548 were all primarily West Cornish

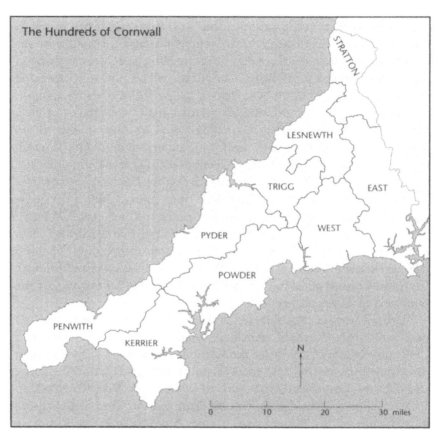

Map 3

affairs, in their initial stages at least. But how does the so-called 'Prayer Book Rebellion' of 1549 fit into this pattern? Ever since the 1590s, the 1548 rising has been viewed as the precursor of the 1549 revolt.[81] Helen Speight has recently challenged this view in her valuable study of local gentry government. Speight, who sees the 1548 rising as 'no more than a serious . . . village riot', can find 'no substantial thread to connect the two uprisings'. The scale was different, she observes, the two revolts had different leaders, and, most importantly of all, 'the venue was different', for 'the riot of 1548 began in West Cornwall, and was apparently confined [there] . . . while the 1549 rising began in . . . [Mid] Cornwall and moved rapidly eastwards'.[82] Speight's argument obviously tends to contradict the thesis of the present chapter—that the two revolts formed part of an ongoing tradition. How convincing are her claims?

The first point to make is that the dismissal of the Western Commotion of 1548 as 'a village riot' will not do: a rising of 3,000 armed men was a serious disturbance by any standards. That the 1548 rebels spoke out against the Edwardian religious reforms, moreover, just as the 1549 rebels were later to do, provides good evidence of a common ideological 'thread' between the two rebellions. And that the first rising was led by commoners while the second possessed some gentry support is not, in itself, very significant; the 1548 rising was crushed so quickly that the rebels had no time to coerce members of the local elite into joining them. On the question of geography, however, Speight appears to have an important point. According to the official indictment (almost our only source for the early stages of the 1549 rising), the rebels first assembled at Bodmin in Mid-Cornwall, while of the twenty individual Cornishmen who can be identified as participants, twelve came from Mid-Cornwall and only five from the West.[83] These pieces of evidence would appear to confirm that West Cornish involvement in the 1549 rising was peripheral. Matters are not as clear-cut as they first appear, however.

The events of June 1549 remain shrouded in mystery and, on current evidence, there is no way of knowing whether Bodmin was the initial focus of the disturbances, or whether the rebels had simply made their way there from somewhere else. Bodmin was one of Cornwall's chief administrative centres, and the traditional venue for 'assemblyes for the publique service of the whole Dukedom'. It was the very first place, in other words, for which any determined group of rebels would have headed.[84] Obvious parallels could be drawn here with the behaviour of

Kett's men in East Anglia during the same year, and we should also note the precedent set by Warbeck's supporters in 1497, who had first gathered in West Cornwall, but had then marched to Bodmin to summon support.[85] Even if the 1549 rebellion did begin in Bodmin, moreover, it is clear that many West Cornishmen quickly became involved. Re-examination of the government's unpublished draft 'Answer' to the rebels has led Joyce Youings to suspect that the insurgents may have initially 'aspired to a liturgy in their own tongue'.[86] And although the rebel leaders were later to settle for the retention of Latin instead, the way in which they chose to phrase this request—'we wyll have oure olde service . . . in Latten as it was before. And so we the Cornyshe men (wherof certen of us understande no Englysh) utterly refuse thys newe Englysh' (see Plate 2)—makes it clear that a determination to resist what they saw as English cultural aggression continued to motivate many of the insurgents.[87]

The 1549 rebellion clearly drew on West Cornish grievances, then, and was supported by many West Cornish people. Like the earlier protests, it was, at least in part, an attempt to protect Cornish identity and like those earlier protests it failed. During the summer of 1549 the rebels were cut to ribbons by government forces. For those who sought to resist assimilation, this defeat had calamitous implications. Now there could be no hope of returning to the old, accommodating Catholic faith, no hope of resisting the English liturgy. By forcing Protestantism on the Cornish, it seemed, the government would force Englishness upon them too. Yet many Cornish people contrived to resist this process. They did so, not by refusing to become Protestants, but by becoming Protestants of a very traditional kind, largely untinged by the puritanism which suffused the reformed faith throughout much of England.[88] By 1600 or thereabouts the Cornish had thus managed to reinvent a distinctive religious identity for themselves. And the language, too, continued to cling on: as late as 1644, Cornish was still widely spoken in the area west of Truro.[89]

In October 1642 the inhabitants of this last bastion of Cornishness took part in yet another revolt. As England broke down into Civil War, thousands of Cornishmen rose up against the supporters of Parliament and ejected them from their county. This demonstration of support for the King was partly founded on a deep distaste for the intolerant, zealously Protestant form of Englishness which seemed to be the mark of the Parliamentarians.[90] The 1642 rising drew on the same cultural anxieties as the Tudor revolts which had preceded it, in other words, and, like them, it was most strongly supported in the Celtic West.[91] Roundhead propagandists drew the appropriate parallels, specifically likening the 1642 rising to that of 1549, and denouncing the King's Cornish adherents as 'rebels'.[92] For the next three years Cornwall remained firmly in Royalist hands. Cornwall's continued support for Charles I partly reflected the skill with which the King harnessed the Cornish sense of difference to his own ends: Charles permitted the formation of exclusively Cornish regiments, for example (see Appendix 4), and placed Cornwall off-limits to other Royalist units.[93] Such concessions to local feeling encouraged the Cornish to fight stoutly in the King's cause. But, once again, they had backed the losing side. In 1646 the King was defeated and Cornwall occupied by Roundhead troops.

Over the following years traditional Cornish identity came under sustained (though largely accidental) assault, as Parliament's national drive to extirpate religious and cultural conservatism began to be implemented locally. Between 1646 and 1649 the Parliamentarians did all they could to topple the pillars of Cornish Anglicanism; many local clerics were ousted and their cures handed over to 'foreign' intruders.[94] Nor was this all. Parliamentary soldiers demolished a number of the chapels and monumental stones which formed part of the very landscape, while even local sports came under attack.[95] Naturally enough, this cultural offensive sparked off peculiar outrage in the far west of Cornwall, where the Cornish language continued to cling on in some twenty to thirty parishes.[96] In May 1648 violence erupted.

The trouble began in the Land's End peninsula, still almost entirely Cornish-speaking at this time, where a force of 300–500 men rose up in the name of the King and occupied Penzance. From here the rebels bade defiance to the forces of the Parliament and attempted to gain support from the surrounding countryside. Their calls for assistance did not go unheeded in the other Cornish-speaking communities of the far West. There were mutterings of support in St Ives and Helston, for example, and both towns might have gone over to the rebels had it not been for prompt action on the part of Parliamentarian officials and soldiers. But the chief hope of the insurgents rested on the Lizard peninsula, the traditional home of Cornish rebellion, and by now the only substantial area of Cornwall—apart from the area around Land's End itself—in which Cornish speakers remained in the majority.[97]

The rebels' hopes of assistance from this quarter were well-founded. An emissary sent to the Lizard met with a warm reception, and quickly managed to raise 120 men. Intriguingly, the members of this emergent rebel band at once made their way to St Keverne. It is hard to resist the conclusion that the Cornish rebels of 1648 (like other groups of insurgents before them) were hoping to draw on a pre-existent 'tradition of riot' in order to generate support for their cause.[98] Certainly, their numbers quickly began to swell once they had arrived in St Keverne. Some 350 men were soon in arms and, as this force set off to assist the Penzance rebels, many may have hoped that the triumphs of 1497 were about to be repeated.[99]

It was not to be. The rebels at Penzance had already been crushed, while elsewhere popular support for the rising had failed to spread beyond the Cornish-speaking districts. As a result the Roundheads were able to deploy all their strength against the forces marching up from the Lizard. The rout at 'the Gear', alluded to at the beginning of this chapter, was the inevitable consequence. And as the beaten rebels fled south (their route, ironically enough, taking them through St Keverne)[100] they can hardly have failed to recognize that this defeat marked the end of the line for the Cornish as a puissant 'people': a group able to defend their own culture, their own traditions, and—in the last resort—their own identity, by force of arms. The subsequent, near-suicidal decision of some of the defeated insurgents to hurl themselves into the western sea must surely have been influenced by this bleak realization.

The victors, too, appreciated the definitive nature of the defeat. Soon afterwards, Parliamentary soldiers led a captive group of rebels in a triumphal march around Penryn, humiliating them in front of the townsfolk. It is of crucial significance that the Roundhead soldiers who led this tragi-comic parade brandished, upon the points of their swords, 'three silver balls used in hurling'.[101] The public violation of these key symbols of Cornish identity bore witness to the soldiers' conviction that they had administered the *coup de grâce* to traditional Cornishness. Their vaunting was justified, for the twelve years of uninterrupted Parliamentary rule which followed saw English ways and customs intruding themselves into every aspect of West Cornish life, and by 1660 the Cornish language was fading fast. As it did so, the visceral sense of difference which had helped to fuel the risings of 1497–1648 likewise melted away. By 1750 the last monoglot Cornish-speaker was dead, and the spark of Cornish ethnicity practically extinguished.[102]

26

III

Between 1450 and 1650 six major revolts against the central government had broken out in Cornwall. All but one had involved over 3,000 men, all but one had begun in the Cornish-speaking far west and most had displayed a quite unusual degree of geographical mobility. This was a record of repeated, deep-rooted and purposeful rebellion which few, if any, English counties could match. Yorkshire had been the seat of almost as many insurrections over the same period, but these protests had been distributed across all three Ridings and had tended (like most English rebellions) to be physically static.[103] Yorkshire was, in any case, so much larger and so much more populous than Cornwall that its record of insurrection appears, if anything, rather unimpressive by comparison. The one county which had evinced a genuinely similar pattern of rebelliousness was Kent. Not only had six serious revolts broken out here—in 1450, 1549, 1554, 1643, 1645 and 1648—but most of them had been centred upon the same district (the area within a fifteen-mile radius of 'busy Maidstone'), while the Kentish rebels had several times displayed the same capacity for urgent movement as their Cornish counterparts.[104]

Intriguingly, Kent was, after Cornwall, perhaps the most culturally distinctive shire in England: a county whose inhabitants held themselves to be descended from the Jutes, and believed (like the Cornish) that 'their country was never conquered'.[105] It seems reasonable to suggest that it was a determination to preserve this 'unconquered', or quasi-autonomous, status which helped to make the inhabitants of both provinces unusually sensitive to threats of encroachment from the centre, and thus unusually prone to rebel. Certainly, if any two counties may be said to have been regarded by their inhabitants as 'countries' in something approaching the modern sense of the word during the early modern period, then those two counties were Kent—and to a far greater degree—Cornwall.[106]

If Cornish rebellions were more frequent, and in some respects more vigorous, than those which took place in other English counties, how did they compare with those which occurred elsewhere in mainland Britain? Wales saw few major insurrections between 1485 and 1650: partly because—in this inaccessible country, where the native language and culture continued to thrive, despite English political dominance—fears over identity were much less acute than in beleaguered Cornwall.

27

However, the two great revolts against the centre which did occur in Wales (in 1642 and 1648) closely resembled the simultaneous popular movements in Cornwall.[107] And clear parallels can also be drawn between the behaviour of the West Cornish and the Scottish Highlanders, another British people whose concern to preserve their traditional identity led them into frequent rebellion during the early modern period and later.[108]

The Cornish paid a terrible price for their rebelliousness. Many hundred Cornishmen were killed at Blackheath in 1497; 300–400 more died in Warbeck's assaults on Exeter later that year; an unknown number were executed after the 1497 risings; seven were hanged in 1548; 2,000 were slaughtered in 1549; perhaps as many more died fighting against Parliament in 1642–6, and around seventy were slain in 1648.[109] These figures may not sound very large, but then neither was the total population of Cornwall.[110] And if, as seems probable, a disproportionate number of the casualties came from West Cornwall, then the effect of these periodic blood-lettings on the Cornish-speaking population must have been little short of catastrophic. It is small wonder that traditional Cornish culture eventually collapsed beneath the impact of these successive blows.

The wonder, rather, is that the Cornish managed to resist English cultural hegemony for so long, and with such striking (if ephemeral) military success. Vast disparities of size and wealth meant that, in any conflict with Cornwall, England was bound to emerge as the victor. Nevertheless, in 1497, in 1549, and again in 1642–6, the Cornish presented a serious challenge to their English neighbours, while of all the desperate armies which rose up on the 'Celtic fringe' between 1400 and 1750, it was the Cornish rebels of 1497 who came closest to the heart of English power. Such incursions may have been relatively infrequent and short-lived, but they left long memories behind them. The smallest of the Celtic peoples had managed to mount a series of challenges to the central government which were out of all proportion to their numerical strength, and which had briefly threatened the stability of the English state. For the sheer tenacity with which they raged against the dying of their own particular light, the Cornish surely merit an honorable place in the pantheon of 'British history'.

2

'Knowest Thou My Brood?'

Locating the Cornish in Tudor and Stuart England

'The folk of these parts are quite extraordinary, being of a rebellious temper and obdurate in the face of attempts to teach and correct'.[1] The despairing words of Adam de Carleton, written in a letter of 1342 in which he resigned from his position as Archdeacon of Cornwall, may be regarded as one of the earliest surviving—and most pithy—attempts by an outsider to define the Cornish 'national character'. It is clear that, as far as de Carleton was concerned, the Cornish were not only different—'extraordinary'—they were also potentially disobedient and so stubbornly attached to their accustomed way of doing things as to appear virtually dim-witted. Such views were deeply entrenched in England during the late medieval and early modern periods. Indeed, the stereotypical view of the Cornish enunciated by de Carleton was still firmly embedded in the English psyche a century and a half later—but with one very important modification. When de Carleton had referred to the Cornish as 'being of a rebellious temper' ['*rebellis*'] it seems probable that he had merely intended to imply that they possessed a generalized spirit of truculence: that they were habitually 'agin authority' of all sorts. In the aftermath of the 1497 risings, an altogether novel form of rebelliousness began to be associated with the Cornish: that of outright sedition and armed resistance to the authority of the English state. The consequences of this most sinister shoot being grafted on to the established stock of Cornish 'national reputation' were to be profound.

In the previous chapter, attention was focused on Cornish self-perceptions during the early modern period, although it was noted, in passing, that the English had been both keenly aware of Cornish difference and openly contemptuous of Cornish manners and *mores*. Over the following pages, English attitudes towards the Cornish during the 150 years which preceded the Civil War will be examined in more depth. The chapter will begin with a discussion of the extent to which Cornwall continued to be regarded by the English (and, indeed, by foreign observers) as a distinct territorial entity—and of the extent to which the Cornish themselves continued to be regarded as a separate 'people'. Next a brief pen portrait of the Cornish as they appeared to their English neighbours—or, at least, as their English neighbours preferred to represent them—will be essayed. Attention will then turn to the way in which the great Cornish rebellions of 1497 and 1548–9 altered, forever, the established reputation of the peninsula's inhabitants. Finally, an attempt will be made to ascertain precisely what the long-term effects of this shift in reputation may have been: not only for the Cornish gentry class, but for ordinary Cornish people and for Cornish culture and society in general.

I

If one had inquired of a group of late fifteenth-century Londoners whether Cornwall was an integral part of England, or merely an awkward appendage to it, it is doubtful that one would have received a unanimous answer. At first sight, matters seemed clear enough. Technically, Cornwall was an English county. It was divided up into parishes and hundreds for administrative purposes, just as other English counties were, and it sent its representatives to the English Parliament, just as other English counties did. It was a district which, as Adrian Hastings has recently affirmed, had 'participated in the institutional development of England at every point'.[2] Yet, as we have seen, it was also a district which possessed unique administrative institutions of its own, in the shape of the Duchy and Stannary organizations, and which was physically so far cut off from the rest of England as to appear a virtual island. There can be no doubt that, prompted by considerations such as these, many outside observers continued to regard Cornwall as wholly distinct from England proper until well into the sixteenth century.

That this view was commonplace during the medieval period is made clear by the matter-of-fact references to '*Anglia et Cornubia*'—England

and Cornwall—which appear in contemporary documents, and by the use of phraseology such as that which was employed in a letter sent to the Sheriff of Cornwall in 1351, in which he was ordered to ascertain which of the lands under, his jurisdiction were 'held by the men of Cornewaille *and* England'.[3] A comment made by an English traveller in 1478, that the river Tamar marked the boundary 'of the County *and Province* of Cornwall', neatly encapsulates the way in which Cornwall tended to be thought of by outsiders throughout the Middle Ages: as an English shire, certainly, but at one and the same time as a semi-detached 'province' with a character all of its own.[4] This view continued to flourish at the beginning of the sixteenth century and was never more trenchantly expressed than in Polydore Vergil's famous history of England, the *Anglica Historia*, first published in 1535.

In the introduction to this work, Vergil—an Italian collector of papal taxes who had been resident in England for almost 30 years—wrote that: 'the whole Countrie of Britain . . . is divided into iiii partes; whereof the one is inhabited of Englishmen, the other of Scottes, the third of Wallshemen, [and] the fowerthe of Cornishe people, which all differ emonge them selves, either in tongue, either in manners, or ells in lawes and ordinaunces'. That the author of the *Anglica Historia* regarded England, Cornwall and Wales as three quite separate territorial units is incontrovertible. A little later on in his text, Vergil remarked that 'Englonde, being the chiefest parte of Britaine . . . is limited . . . on the Weste parte with the boundes of Cornewall and Wall[e]s', while a few pages later still he repeated his initial observation that Wales was 'the third parte' of Britain, and Cornwall 'the fourthe'.[5]

It could be argued that Vergil's view was a deeply idiosyncratic one— and the view of a foreigner at that. Vergil's statements must surely have reflected what he had been told by his English friends and acquaintances, however—and there is good evidence to suggest that his conception of the kingdom of England as an essentially tripartite structure was widely shared during the first half of the sixteenth century. In 1515, for example, an English official seeking to further the colonization of Ireland urged that 'one man [should] be sent from every parish of England, Cornwall and Wales to inhabit Ulster', while in 1548 the London chronicler Edward Hall described Cornwall as 'the least part of the realm': a choice of words which hints that he, too, subscribed to the view of Cornwall as the smallest of the three distinctive 'provinces' which made up the kingdom of England.[6] It was a conceptual

31

framework which was to endure until well into the seventeenth century. Writing in 1616, Arthur Hopton stated that 'England is . . . divided into 3 great Provinces, or Countries . . . every of them speaking a several and different Language, as English, Welsh and Cornish'—and statements betraying a similar perception continued to be made as late as the 1640s.[7]

If it is clear that the English regarded Cornwall as, in many respects, a separate country during the late medieval and early modern periods, then it is equally clear that they regarded the Cornish themselves as a separate ethnic group or 'race'. Once again, this was a conviction which frequently communicated itself to foreign visitors. In 1506 the Venetian diplomat Vincenzo Quirini—fretting aboard ship in the Carrick Roads, near present-day Falmouth, after his voyage to London had been delayed by contrary winds—informed the Signory that he was 'in a very wild place which no human being ever visits, in the midst of a most barbarous race, so different in language and customs from the Londoners and the rest of England that they are as unintelligible to these last as to the Venetians'.[8] Twenty-five years later, another Italian visitor to England, Lodovico Falier, made it very plain that he, too, viewed the Cornish as a separate people. 'The language of the English, Welsh and Cornish men is so different that they do not understand each other', wrote Falier in a dispatch to the Venetian Senate in 1531—adding that 'the Welshman is sturdy, poor, adapted to war and sociable; the Cornishman is poor, rough and boorish; and the Englishman mercantile, rich, affable and generous'.[9] These remarks can only have reflected the opinions of Falier's metropolitan English hosts.

Further evidence for the contemporary perception of Cornwall as a distinctive 'country' and the Cornish as a distinctive 'race' can be produced from throughout the sixteenth century. It is noteworthy, for example, that when Andrew Boorde wrote his *Fyrst Boke of the Introduction of Knowledge* in c.1542—a work which might fairly be described as one of the earliest tourist guides for the English traveller abroad—he commenced his discussion of foreign parts with a section devoted to 'Cornewall and Cornyshe men'. The list of everyday Cornish expressions which Boorde helpfully provided for his readers still further underlines the perceived 'foreignness' of the Cornish at this time.[10] Hans Holbein's decision to subscribe his drawing of one of the two Reskymer brothers, both of whom were active at the Court of Henry VIII during the 1530s and 1540s, as 'Reskemeer: a Cornish Gent' (see Plate 1) also appears significant, for the painter did not bother to identify the counties from which his other, English, sitters came.[11] Revealing, too, is an aside made by John Florio in his late sixteenth-century English translation of Montaigne. When speaking of animals, Florio remarked in passing to his English readers that 'it is no great marvell if we understand them not: no more doe we the Cornish, the Welch, or Irish'.[12] His comment implies that he scarcely felt the Cornish to belong to the same species as the English, let alone to the same ethnic group.

Still more interesting evidence comes from a letter which the Venetian ambassador in London wrote to his political masters in April 1603 to inform them of the death of Queen Elizabeth I. The late Queen had been a most accomplished ruler, the ambassador observed, and had been renowned for her intellectual abilities. Particularly worthy of note, he went on to remark, was the fact that Elizabeth had 'possessed nine languages so thoroughly that each appeared to be her native tongue; [and that] five of these were the languages of peoples governed by her: English, Welsh, *Cornish*, Scottish . . . and Irish'.[13] Almost certainly, the ambassador exaggerated, swept up as he was in the eulogistic mood of the moment. That Elizabeth had been fluent in all four of the non-English tongues then spoken in the British Isles seems hard to credit. That she had possessed a smattering of each of these languages, on the other hand—that she had known just enough of them to have been able to greet visitors from the non-Anglophone parts of her kingdoms with graceful salutations in their own tongue—seems eminently plausible.[14] And that Cornish was one of the languages which the Queen was believed, whether rightly or wrongly, to have taken the trouble to master is a point of some significance. The ambassador's words reinforce the point that, as late as 1603, the inhabitants of Cornwall were still widely regarded as a separate ethnic group: as one of the five distinctive 'peoples' over whom the monarchs of England ruled, and who were held to be distinguished from each other as much by language as by anything else.

II

Language apart, what did the English consider the chief distinguishing marks, or qualities, of their Cornish neighbours to be? A good deal of evidence on this point has already emerged. In the previous chapter, it was shown that, while early modern English observers had generally acknowledged the Cornish to be a stout and valiant race, they had also tended to view them as ragged, ignorant and uncivilized. The present discussion has furnished examples of the Cornish being described as 'obdurate' and 'barbarous'—and further testimony could be adduced to show that, in late medieval England, the Cornish were criticized as being both innately untrustworthy and unusually violent.[15] It seems fair to suggest, however, that it was Falier's characterization of the Cornish as 'poor, rough, and boorish' which best summed up contemporary English attitudes towards the 'West Britons'. A 'boor' is defined by the *OED* as 'a peasant; a coarse, rustic clown'—and, from the medieval period right down to the present day, it is as archetypal boors or rustics that the Cornish have most commonly been seen in England. As early as the 1100s, Richard of Devizes instructed a young man who was about to travel to Britain that, for the qualities of ignorance and boorishness, he should 'always look on Cornish men as we in France consider our Flemings', while, during the following century, a versifier at the Court of Henry II derided Cornwall as 'the fagg end [i.e. backside] of the world': an insult which prompted one Michael of Cornwall to write a series of verses in defence of his homeland.[16] This literary riposte had no discernible effect on English attitudes, and had 'Merry Michael', as the poet was later known,[17] been able to foresee that, over 700 years later, a correspondent would be writing to a London-based magazine from Penzance to complain that a recent article had depicted the Cornish as 'a primitive bunch of . . . peasants', and that this was indicative of the way in which the county's inhabitants were usually portrayed in the English press, he would doubtless have thrown down his quill in despair.[18]

Contempt for the Cornish as rustics was frequently expressed during the early modern period. In 1497 no less a figure than King Henry VII himself had publicly exhibited his contempt for the military prowess— and thus, by extension, the social status—of the Cornish in the aftermath of the rebel defeat at Blackheath. Returning to London in triumph, Henry had refused to permit any elaborate celebrations to be staged, 'saying that he had not gained a worthy victory, having been against such a base crew as those Cornish men'.[19] Nine years later, Vincenzo Quirini had described West Cornwall as 'a wild spot where no. . . [one] ever comes, save the few boors who inhabit it'.[20] The picture which Andrew Boorde painted of the Cornish in 1542 was even more redolent of primitivism and rusticity. Boorde's supposedly 'representative' inhabitant of Cornwall introduces himself thus:

Iche cham a Cornyshe man, al[e] che can brew;
It wyll make one to kacke, also to spew;
It is [th]ycke and smoky, and also it is [th]yn;
It is lyke wash, as pygges had wrestled [the]ryn.[21]

One would hardly have expected Boorde to have portrayed the Cornish as urban sophisticates of course, but—even by his own frankly crude and rumbustious standards—this was taking matters to the opposite extreme. Intriguingly, one of the most blistering attacks on Cornish 'clownishness' was launched by Sir John Eliot, MP, scourge of the Crown during the early Parliaments of Charles I and himself a native-born Cornishman. Writing to Sir Robert Cotton in July 1628 from St Germans, in the far south-east of Cornwall, Elliot fulminated against 'the ignorance of these Cornish parts, almost as much divided from reason and intelligence as their island [is] from the world' and then went on to bemoan the 'dullness and insensibility' of the local people. 'This is a bad character, I confess, which I give you of my country', Eliot observed in closing, 'but such as it deserves.'[22] Eliot's disdainful words—betraying, as they do, their writer's underlying anxiety to disassociate himself from his fellow countrymen and to assert his primary identity instead as being that of an English gentleman—hint that the English view of the Cornish as a race of boors was by this time so all-pervasive that it had begun to be subscribed to even by some of the Cornish themselves.

It was not a view which went entirely uncontested in early modern England, however. Indeed, there is evidence—albeit fragmentary—to suggest that this view may have been implicitly condemned by none other than Queen Elizabeth I herself. As we have seen, Elizabeth was reputed to have learned the Cornish tongue and this fact implied, in itself, that she was thought to believe that Cornish culture had some intrinsic worth: that it was not irredeemably 'base'. Fascinating, too, is the remark which the Queen is alleged to have made that 'Cornish gentlemen were all born courtiers, with a becoming confidence': a comment which could well be interpreted as a deliberate attempt to subvert the traditional reputation of the Cornish as boors, and to turn it upon its head.[23]

Nor was Elizabeth I the only influential figure to defend the Cornish against their traducers during the late sixteenth century, for it is also possible to argue that they had William Shakespeare on their side. In his play *Henry V*, first performed in 1599, Shakespeare presented his audience with a caricature of an extreme English nationalist in the shape of Ensign Pistol: a posturing braggart who exhibits a scornful contempt for the Welsh. In a violent exchange towards the end of the play, Pistol derides the upstanding Welsh soldier, Captain Fluellen, as a 'base Trojan [i.e. a Briton]' who 'smell[s] of leek', only to be soundly cudgelled by the object of his derision. Fluellen then humiliates Pistol still further by compelling him to swallow a portion of leek (then, as now, a symbol of Welsh pride) and the virtuous English Captain Gower appears on the scene to point up the moral. 'You thought, because he [Fluellen] could not speak English in the native garb, he could not therefore handle an English cudgel', Gower tells Pistol. 'Now', he adds, 'you find it otherwise; and henceforth let a Welsh correction teach you a good English condition.'[24] In Shakespeare's view, 'a good English condition' was clearly an attitude of mind which embraced the Welsh as equals, rather than rejecting them as 'base' inferiors.

But where do the Cornish come into all this? The answer is in Act 4, scene 1, where Pistol—standing guard on the night before Agincourt—is approached by King Henry V in disguise, demands to be told the stranger's name, and is given the answer 'Harry Le Roy'. To this, Pistol makes the—somewhat unexpected—response: 'Le Roy! A Cornish name: art thou of Cornish crew?'[25] These words clearly require an explanation, and a recent article by Alan Kent has attempted to provide just that; by arguing, first, that Pistol's reply may be regarded as a perfectly credible sixteenth-century English response to any name that was recognized to be 'foreign', or 'outlandish'; second, that one of the chief functions of Pistol's speech is to underline the contemporary perception of the Cornish as 'different'; and third that Shakespeare included this brief reference to the Cornish in *Henry V*—a play which much concerns itself with the subject of British identities—in order to convey a specific message to his audience about the place which Cornwall occupied in the wider English state.[26]

With all three of these suggestions one can happily concur, but what exactly was the message which Shakespeare was trying to get across? Kent asserts that, by referring to the Cornish as a 'crew', Pistol was demonstrating his 'fondness, familiarity and respect' for them, and thus, by implication, conveying the impression that he regarded the position of the Cornish within the English nation as being one of 'proud inclusion'. Yet in fact precisely the opposite was the case! The word 'crew' was generally employed in a contemptuous sense during the early modern period to signify a low-born mob or rabble[27]—in exactly the same sense as Henry VII had used it to describe the Blackheath rebels, in other words—so, by applying this particular epithet to the Cornish, Pistol revealed that he saw them in just the same way as he saw the Welsh: as 'base' and inferior, as well as essentially 'foreign'. Once this point has been appreciated, Shakespeare's true purpose in making Pistol allude to the Cornish becomes clear. By indicating that the Cornish and the Welsh are both targets of the ultra-nationalist Englishman's disdain, the playwright establishes that Pistol is a contemner of the British nation as a whole, and thus makes it possible for the Cornish, as well as the Welsh, to share in his eventual discomfiture. Seen in this light, Gower's final speech—in which we surely hear Shakespeare's own voice—becomes a reproof to those who would mock either group for their lack of facility in the English tongue, and an assertion that it is part of 'a good English condition' to respect both the Welsh and the Cornish.

This was doubtless a point of view which Elizabeth I—and, indeed, anyone else in England who had given careful thought to the best way of ensuring the continued stability of the realm—would have shared, but the attitudes of the vast majority of contemporary English men and women probably approximated more closely to those of Pistol than they did to those of Gower. Nowhere are these attitudes better represented than in Thomas Middleton and William Rowley's play *A Fair Quarrel*, first performed on the London stage in 1617, which features among its central characters 'Chough, a Cornish gentleman' and 'Trimtram', his man.[28] The names accorded to these two figures are richly symbolic. The appellation 'Chough' would have been recognized, first of all, as a reference to the red-legged crow: a bird which haunted the coastline and clifftops of Cornwall and was commonly known as 'the Cornish chough' (pronounced 'chuff').[29] During the medieval period, a number of Cornish gentry families had incorporated the symbol of the chough into their coats of arms: clearly, at this time the bird's associations had been positive ones.[30] By the end of the sixteenth century, however, if not long before, the term 'Cornish Choughs' had come to be adopted by the English as a derogatory nickname for the Cornish people themselves. So, at one level, the playwrights' decision to style their chief Cornish protagonist 'Chough' was simply a means of underlining the fact that he *was* Cornish.

Yet there was another significance to this particular epithet too. In late medieval English idiom, the word 'chuff' was used to denote a rustic, a clown or a boor[31]—and this almost certainly helps to explain why the term 'Cornish Choughs' had attached itself so tenaciously to the Cornish in the first place. Every time that an Englishman referred to the Cornish as 'choughs', he simultaneously reminded his listeners of the alleged Cornish 'national characteristic' of boorishness. Thus, by naming their Cornish 'gentleman' Chough, Middleton and Rowley fatally undermined the character's pretensions to gentility even before he set foot on the stage. The choice of the name 'Trimtram' for Chough's servant is also intriguing. On the one hand, it seems intended to awaken echoes of Sir Tristram, the mythical Cornish knight who was reputed to have been one of the chief followers of King Arthur[32] (also, be it noted, a legendary Cornishman, and one who was believed to have been transformed into a chough after his death![33]). On the other hand, it is clearly designed to convey the sense of foolishness, absurdity and, above all, apishness which was usually associated with this word during the early modern period, and thus to heap yet more scorn on the Cornish.[34]

The expectations aroused by these two ridiculous names are fully met in the play. Chough is depicted throughout as an ignorant country bumpkin, devoid of good manners and completely at sea amid the sophistication of the capital. Having travelled up to London from St Michael's Mount in the far west of Cornwall, Chough first sets out to woo a young gentlewoman, but his clumsy advances leave her cold and she dismisses him as 'an odious fool'. Chough then enrols himself at a 'roaring school', where a group of conmen—taking advantage of Chough's rather basic command of English—teach him a set of nonsensical words which they claim are all the rage among the fashionable young blades of London. A dispute then takes place between Chough and Trimtram (who behaves at all times as the equal, rather than as the inferior of his master—another sure sign of Chough's boorishness). 'I know thee, and thy brood', the servant scornfully expostulates at one point in this debate. 'Know'st thou my Brood?', Chough splutters angrily in return, 'I know thy brood too, thou art a rook [i.e. a cheat, but also a species of crow].' 'The nearer akin to the Choughs!', retorts Trimtram triumphantly, thus implying that master and man are related, and thereby puncturing Chough's claims to gentility once again.[35]

Amity eventually restored, Chough and Trimtram return to the pursuit of the reluctant gentlewoman; are told, falsely, that she is a whore; and then—in what the authors clearly regarded as one of the comic highlights of the play—attempt to make use of their newly learnt 'roaring' vocabulary in order to inform the girl's father of their suspicions. 'I'll tell thee plainly [Sir], thy daughter is a bronstrops', declaims Chough; 'Nay. . . she is a fucus, a minotaur, and a tweak,' affirms Trimtram, eager, as ever, to outdo his master. 'Good Sir[s], speak English to me!', wails the bewildered man, unable to make head or tail of this stream of gibberish. 'All this is Cornish to thee', Chough triumphantly replies, making it crystal clear to anyone in the audience who had somehow missed the point that the nonsense which he and Trimtram are spouting is intended to be a side-splitting parody of the Cornish language.[36]

Boors speaking nonsense: this was the essential view of the Cornish peddled by Middleton and Rowley, and a precisely similar portrait emerges from Richard Brome's rather later play, *The Northern Lasse* (1632), in which the mock-Cornish character is actually called 'Nonsense'. Nonsense is, in effect, a rather pallid, one-dimensional version of Chough: indeed it is hard not to suspect that he was modelled on him. Like Chough, Nonsense is a gauche, unpolished Cornish gentlemen in London; like him, he seeks—in vain—the hand of a scornful English gentlewoman; and, like him, he has a penchant for gibberish: he speaks, we are told at one point, 'most perfect nonsense', and this is no more than the literal truth.[37] There are other similarities too. Like Chough, Nonsense is depicted as boorish—when told that there is a 'feast' is in the offing, the height of his expectation is that the meal may include 'whitepots' (a kind of milk pudding then much favoured in Cornwall)—and like Chough he is depicted as bilingual: both men deliver themselves of genuine Cornish phrases at various points in the plays.[38]

The fact that both Chough and Nonsense, these two archetypal Cornish clowns, are represented as being able to speak Cornish is of crucial significance, for it tends to suggest that, by the beginning of the seventeenth century, the 'boorishness' which had traditionally been associated with all Cornish people had become particularly identified with the Cornish-speaking westerners. Quite when this identification had first begun to be made is hard to say, but it is interesting to note that, as early as the 1550s, William Humberstone had described the people of the eastern part of Cornwall as 'more civil' than those of the West, indicating that the perception of the East Cornish as more 'refined' and 'polite' than their western brethren was already well-established.[39] If the speaking of Cornish had, indeed, come to encapsulate the condition of boorishness in the English popular imagination, then it is hardly surprising that so many of the hedge gentry and middling sort of West Cornwall began to abandon their ancient tongue during the century before the Civil War. Stage caricatures like Middleton and Rowley's 'Chough' not only lampooned traditional Cornish identity, in other words, they also helped to hasten its decline.

Yet even as late as the mid-seventeenth century, there were still educated Cornish speakers who were prepared to reject—in private, at least—the negative stereotype which had been imposed upon them and their culture. In a children's story entitled 'The Dutchesse of Cornwall's Progresse', written in Cornish some time after 1657, Mr Nicholas Boson of Newlyn wove an elaborate fantasy about a visit made to the Land's End district by a great noble woman and her entourage at some unspecified point in the distant past. 'The common people flock'd about her', Boson assured his children:

> some of which underst[ood] little other than the Cornish Language, yet such was their Ayre & meene that some of the courtiers who had been travellers assured her Highness that amongst all the vulgar people of all parts they had ever travell'd, they never observed any that had naturally so little of boorishness and peasantry as they observ'd in these vulgar Cornish.[40]

In this strangely moving passage, we surely hear both an echo of Queen Elizabeth's compliment to the Cornish gentry (though here, be it noted, applied to the common people instead) and Boson's own determination to ensure that his children would grow up to be proud, rather than ashamed, of their much-traduced West Cornish identity.

III

The imputation of boorishness was something which the Cornish people had had to live with for centuries, but the two great rebellions which shook the far South-west of Britain during the thirteenth year of Henry VII's reign added an unwonted—and, as far as most Cornish folk were concerned, unwanted—air of menace to their traditional reputation. In his *Survey of Cornwall*, first published in 1603, the Cornish antiquarian Richard Carew referred to 1497 as the 'fatal year of revolts'.[41] His comment hints at the intense regret with which he and his gentry contemporaries still looked back on the popular rebellions which had occurred in Cornwall during the early Tudor period. In their eyes, those revolts had been 'fatal', not only in terms of the lives which had been lost but also in terms of the damage which had been done to the reputation of Cornwall in general—and of the Cornish gentry class in particular. Throughout his text Carew was careful to refer to the rebels in the most disparaging terms, as 'rakehells' and 'rascals', and to make it clear that the Cornish gentry elite had actively opposed them.[42]

The sense of shame and embarrassment which memory of the risings long continued to invoke among the West Country gentry emerges more clearly still from the work of the Devonshire antiquary Thomas Westcote, whose survey of Devon was written during the 1620s. Westcote compared the rebellion of 1549 to a scar disfiguring the otherwise unblemished face of Devon's history. He acknowledged that many of his readers would have preferred him not to have alluded to the rising at all, but stressed that a concern for strict historical accuracy had compelled him to do so. Still, he maintained, Devonians had comparatively little with which to reproach themselves. Few Devon gentry had taken part in the rebellion, indeed, they had played an important part in helping to contain it. And, most importantly of all, the rising had not begun in Devon. Instead, as Westcote pointedly reminded his readers, 'that viper . . . [of rebellion] was . . . hatched . . . in Cornwall'.[43] It was a vivid image—and it should not be thought that Westcote was unusual among early modern Englishmen in instinctively associating Cornwall and its people with the slithering serpent of rebelliousness. On the contrary, an impressive amount of evidence survives to suggest that, in the wake of the 1497 risings and the Edwardian revolts which followed them, the view of the Cornish as a people teetering perpetually on the brink of sedition had become commonplace.

During the reign of Henry VIII a whole series of alarms took place concerning supposed manifestations of unrest in Cornwall. In July 1531, for example, it was reported that the Marquis of Exeter had 'been charged with assembling the people of Cornwall and the neighbourhood', while in 1537—as Henry's religious innovations began to stir up increasing resentment on the ground—there were whispers of a fresh rising at St Keverne.[44] Around the same time, it was reported from Exeter that the citizens were 'halfe afeard of a prevy insureccyon of Cornyssmen', and in August the Dean of Exeter, Simon Heynes, wrote to the Lord Privy Seal, Thomas Cromwell, warning him that 'this is a perilous Country, for God's love let the King's grace look to it in time'.[45] Henry VIII himself seems to have been sufficiently alarmed about the situation in Cornwall to have 'written to Sir Thomas Arundel [a local JP] about it, demanding more effective action'.[46] On this particular occasion, no revolts materialized, but the King almost certainly kept a watchful eye on the Cornish thereafter. Indeed, when Henry set up the short-lived Council of the West in 1539 and briefly toyed with the idea of establishing a Cornish see in the same year, one of the chief roles which he envisaged for these two institutions may well have been that of providing a more effective curb on the Cornish propensity to revolt.[47]

Cornish gentlemen several times felt it necessary to assure the King and his ministers that Cornwall was in 'a good order of justice' during the mid-to-late 1530s, and thus implicitly to deny any imputation of rebelliousness. In 1536, for example, Dr John Tregonwell affirmed that 'the country is as quiet and true to the King as any shire in the realm'.[48] Informed opinion in the capital almost certainly took such protestations with a pinch of salt, however, and a letter sent from London by Gaspard de Coligny Chatillon, the French ambassador at the Court of Henry VIII, hints that contemporary English attitudes towards the Cornish were by now very suspicious indeed. The kingdom in which he found himself was by no means an entirely homogeneous one, Chatillon informed a French correspondent in December 1538, for it also 'contains Wales and Cornwall, natural enemies of the rest of England, and speaking a [different] language'.[49] That Chatillon should have referred to the Cornish as 'natural enemies' of the English is deeply revealing, for it suggests that, as a result of the 1497 risings—and perhaps in part too as a result of the opposition which the Cornish had recently voiced to Henry VIII's religious policies—the county's inhabitants had come to be seen as intrinsically hostile, even dangerous, to the English in a way that they had not been for many centuries. That a concealed sense of hostility to the English did indeed exist in early modern Cornwall is not in doubt: the evidence of the previous chapter amply confirms this, as does the comment of the seventeenth-century Cornish antiquarian William Scawen that, during the Tudor period, 'the Cornish people had wont to call any stranger whom they liked not *Size* (i.e. *Sax* or Saxon, whom they had no cause to love)'.[50] For Cornish hostility to the English to be openly discussed in diplomatic correspondence was almost unprecedented, however—and Chatillon's comment provides an excellent illustration of the new and altogether more menacing aspect which the Cornish had by now come to assume in the eyes of the wider world.

Suspicions of the Cornish as an innately rebellious people were confirmed in spades by the major revolts which broke out in the county during 1548–9 in reaction to the Edwardian religious reforms. The welter of orders and proclamations which Edward VI's government issued against the western insurrectionaries—including one which specifically condemned the King's 'Commons . . . in . . . Cornwall . . . now [in] open rebellion against his most Royal Majesty'—and the virulent popular ballads which were circulated against them on the streets of London can only have strengthened the link between Cornishness and rebelliousness which had already become established in many English minds.[51] The accession of the Catholic Queen Mary in 1553, with whose religious policies the great bulk of the Cornish people almost certainly sympathized, briefly created a politico-religious atmosphere in which this stereotype could begin to be reversed: in 1554 it was noted by Cardinal Pole that, during the accession crisis of the previous summer, the people of Cornwall had proved themselves among 'the most faithful and well-affected' of the new Queen's subjects.[52] Mary's replacement by her sister Elizabeth in 1558, however, and the resumption of a broadly Protestant religious policy, ensured that the image of the Cornish as potential rebels would quickly reassert itself.

Throughout Elizabeth's reign, Spanish agents looked eagerly to Cornwall for signs of renewed insurrection, though their hopes seem to have faded with time.[53] The Queen's servants, too, kept a weather eye on Cornwall; described by the Privy Council in 1589 as 'that disordered countie'.[54] In 1577 Bishop William Alley of Exeter was greatly alarmed to hear that radical religious opinions had been expressed in Liskeard, 'which doctrine, being straunge, offended the ears of the sympell Cornishe men', and—'fearinge of some daunger that might arise therbye'—he at once rode to the town himself in order to put a stop to the controversy.[55] Nagging fears that the Cornish might one day rebel again persisted throughout the late sixteenth century—and indeed such fears may well help to explain the particular care which Elizabeth took to flatter the county's inhabitants.

43

As John Chynoweth has remarked, 'the sensitivity of the government to the threat of trouble from the Cornish' is clearly revealed in Richard Carew's account of the dispute which arose as a result of the Queen's 'attempt . . . to abrogate the rights of the Duchy's conventionary tenants' in 1594.[56] Shortly after news of this scheme got out, a group of Cornish gentlemen wrote a letter of protest to the Privy Council, affirming that the Queen's 10,000 Cornish tenants:

> weare soe much agreved [by the project] as they purposed by multitudes to have fled to her Majesty. . . for succour. And to what dangerous consequence it may growe in time . . . wee have great cause to feare. Wherefore . . . wee have . . . stopped that course of theirs by presuming to become humble peticioners to your Lordships in their behalfes.[57]

As Chynoweth rightly observes, 'this was a thinly-veiled threat that unless the . . . [gentry petitioners] received satisfaction . . . large numbers of angry tenants would descend on the capital'. More striking still is the fact that the petitioners 'had originally intended to remind the Queen that the rebellions of 1497 and 1549 had not caused her predecessors to reduce the tenants' rights', until they were dissuaded from this course by friends in London, who considered that subject too 'dangerous to be mentioned'.[58] Almost half a century after the Western Rising, fear of Cornish rebellion was still very much a live issue in English politics.

With the passing away of Queen Elizabeth, the last of the Tudor monarchs, in 1603 and the establishment of a new Scottish dynasty— in whose collective memory Cornish rebellions can scarcely have bulked very large—the perception of Cornwall as a district in which armed insurrection might, at any moment, break forth once again almost certainly began to fade at Whitehall. Yet a keen awareness of Cornwall's past propensity for rebellion remained firmly embedded in the English popular imagination; an awareness which was sustained, at one level, by handed-down memories and, at another, by a whole series of influential publications which looked back to the events of 1497 and 1548–9 in order to tell a stirring tale or to point up a moral lesson. Chronicle histories like those of Holinshed and Stow introduced new generations of educated men and women to the great Cornish rebellions of the Tudor period, as did the much reprinted *Mirrour for Magistrates* (1563) and Francis Bacon's *History of Henry VII* (1621).[59] Stage plays, too, helped to keep the image of the rebellious Cornishman current in the early seventeenth century. 'What news?', asks King Henry VII of one of his courtiers at the beginning of John Ford's historical drama *Perkin Warbeck* (1634): '10,000 Cornish, grudging to pay your subsidies, have gathered a head' comes the grim reply.[60] It is clear that by this time, if not long before, the image of thousands of Cornishmen surging across the Tamar had become an established literary trope.[61]

IV

To be saddled with a reputation for rebelliousness was, in the early modern English state, to be placed in a political position which was both acutely uncomfortable and potentially very vulnerable—and the fact that the gentry governors of Cornwall found the county for which they were responsible effectively 'locked into' this position throughout the period 1497 to 1642 undoubtedly influenced both their outlook and their behaviour. The sense of shame which the Cornish gentry felt about their failure to prevent the revolts from catching fire in the first place has already been alluded to—and it does not seem too far-fetched to suggest that the unstinting devotion which so many Cornish gentry families later displayed to the Royalist cause during the Civil War was, at least in part, the product of a determination to redeem themselves from the imputation of rebelliousness and recover their reputation for fidelity to the Crown.[62] More far-reaching still in its consequences, however, may well have been the effect which the local gentlemen's desperate anxiety to rid themselves of the taint of disloyalty had upon the continued survival of the Cornish language.

That the Reformation sounded the death-knell for the Cornish tongue is an historical truism.[63] In the words of Adrian Hastings, the fate of Cornish:

> was . . . finally decided by the Reformation. While Latin was the language of the liturgy, Cornish had remained that of the community, and, doubtless, also that of many sermons. With the Reformation, Latin was replaced by English . . . No attempt was made to provide a book of Common Prayer in Cornish. The effect was a very rapid decline in the use of Cornish, and, in consequence, of the singularity of the Cornish ethnic identity within England.[64]

45

In essence, Hastings's analysis is undoubtedly correct. That the Welsh secured a translation of the Book of Common Prayer into their own tongue (in 1567) while the Cornish did not, surely does more than anything else to explain why one Brythonic language survived, while the other, eventually, died.

Yet why was no Cornish liturgy ever produced? It was by no means inevitable that the Protestant Reformation would prove a disaster for the Cornish tongue. To suggest that its English-speaking architects were inherently hostile to the Cornish language would almost certainly be unfair. Addressing himself to the Cornish-speaking rebels in 1549, the protestant writer Phillip Nicols remonstrated with them for their 'presumption' in summarily rejecting the new English prayer book. 'If ye had understood no English, and for that consideration had by the way of petition made humble request to the King's Majesty . . . [that the new liturgy should be translated] . . . into our Cornish speech', Nichols averred, 'I doubt not but the King . . . would have . . . provided for the accomplishment of your desires.'[65] Clear evidence that the advanced Protestant party in England was not opposed, in principle, to the use of the Cornish language for religious instruction emerges from a puritan petition of c.1560 which requested that 'it may be lawful for such . . . Cornish children as can speake no English to learn the Praemises in the . . . Cornish language'.[66] And that the Church of England—whose Supreme Governor, after all, appears to have spoken some Cornish herself—was prepared to adopt a similarly pluralist stance is demonstrated by the fact that the Cornish tongue continued to be used in prayers and church sermons long after 1559.[67]

Neither the Queen, the ecclesiastical authorities nor the more zealous sort of Protestants appear to have felt any great animosity towards the Cornish language. The question therefore reasserts itself, why was no attempt made to produce a Cornish liturgy? And to this insistent question—among the most important in the entire history of the Cornish ethnic identity—only one, tantalizingly brief, reply appears to exist. In his *Antiquities Cornu-Brittanic*, written between 1678 and 1689, the Cornish antiquary William Scawen observed that the 'Service Book' had not been translated into Cornish, as it had been into Welsh, because:

> our people, as I have heard in Q: Elizabeths time, desired that the common Liturgy should be in the English Tounge to which they were then for novelties sake affected.[68]

46

Scawen's suggestion that it was the Cornish themselves who had rejected the idea of a Cornish liturgy—that the fate of the language had been sealed by a more or less deliberate act of self-inflicted 'glotticide'— has been diversely received by later generations of Cornish historians. On the one hand, there have been those who have simply accepted Scawen's statement at face value.[69] On the other, there have been those—chiefly of the nationalist school—who have either ignored it, or have angrily refused to believe that there is any truth in it at all.[70] What no one has done before is to analyse Scawen's words in depth.[71]

Four salient points emerge from this crucial, twenty-nine word statement. The first is that Scawen was writing over a century after the alleged request for an English liturgy may be presumed to have been taken place (i.e. at some time between 1559 and 1563, when the decision to sanction a Welsh prayer book was finally made).[72] His informants can hardly have possessed a perfect recollection of events, therefore—but this does not mean that their evidence should be ignored. The second point to make is that a specific request for the liturgy in English would hardly have been made unless the possibility of providing a liturgy in Cornish had been seriously raised first: something which, in turn, implies a degree of support for the latter proposition. Scawen's evidence points to a divided response to the prospect of a Cornish liturgy, then, rather than to the entirely negative one which a casual reading of his text might at first suggest. Third, Scawen's assertion that the underlying rationale for the request was the fact that English was a tongue to which the Cornish were, 'for novelties sake affected' seems inherently implausible. As we have seen, English had been spoken throughout the whole of East Cornwall for centuries before this, and was common among the gentry and the clergy in the West, too: it is simply inconceivable that the language would have been regarded as in any way new or unusual during the 1560s. Fourth, and most important of all, Scawen's statement that 'our people' had 'desir'd' the Queen for an English liturgy is deeply ambiguous. Who, exactly, were these 'people'? And how, exactly, had they made their 'desire' known?

Should we take these words to imply, as many previous historians have done, that the entire local community had expressed itself in favour of the English prayer book? As soon as one stops to consider the mechanisms by which such sentiments might have been first voiced, and then communicated to the centre, doubt begins to creep in. The only conceivable way of representing Cornish popular opinion to the Queen would have been by means of a petition, for which not a shred of evidence survives. And even if one were to postulate the existence of a 'lost' petition, such a document would surely have been far more representative of the desires of the literate, English-speaking gentry and middling sort than of the Cornish-speaking westerners. It seems altogether more probable that the request for an English liturgy was made directly to the Queen and her ministers by the gentry governors of Cornwall: the individuals who would have had by far the best opportunity to press such a suit, whether through letters, through speeches in Parliament or through informal approaches at Court. Scawen's reference to 'our people', in other words, is much more likely to have been an allusion to a small group of Cornish gentlemen—or, at most, to a group of commoners sponsored and encouraged by such men—than to the Cornish population as a whole.

Yet why should anyone have wished to oppose a Cornish liturgy during the 1560s, at a time when many thousands of Cornish people still spoke the language? The previous discussion of English attitudes towards the Cornish surely holds the key. Not only was the Cornish tongue intimately associated to the east of the Tamar with 'foreignness' and 'boorishness'—both wholly negative attributes which ambitious Cornish gentlemen would have been anxious to shake off—but, after 1549, it was inextricably associated with rebelliousness as well. By demanding that they should be provided with a liturgy in their own tongue—or, at the very least, by causing the government to believe that this is what they had demanded[73]—the prayer-book rebels had turned the question of linguistic diversity in Cornwall—hitherto largely ignored in the rest of England—into a contested issue, and had inadvertently ensured that the Cornish language would be tainted thereafter, in the eyes of the ruling classes, with the stain of sedition. To an English-speaking gentry elite, desperate to play down Cornwall's reputation for rebelliousness in the aftermath of the risings of 1497 and 1548–9, the Cornish language had thus become even more of an embarrassment than it had been before—and something from which it was imperative that they distance themselves. What better way of doing so, and at the same time of striking at the very roots of the language itself, than by opposing renewed calls for a Cornish liturgy?

If the interpretation of events outlined above is correct, we must conclude that it was not the Reformation *per se*, but Cornish attempts to resist that Reformation, which eventually sealed the fate of the Cornish language. Not only did the rebellions of 1548–9 result in large numbers of Cornish-speaking West Cornishmen being killed, they also ensured that the rebellious Cornish would be denied the liturgy in their own tongue which had been vouchsafed to the quiescent Welsh. That liturgy was not denied to the Cornish as a result of the deliberately racist policies of a 'tyrannous' English government, however. Rather, it was denied at the specific request of an unknown number of—probably well-connected, probably English-speaking—Cornishmen, who, for a variety of reasons, had come to find the Cornish language an embarrassment. The English did not strike the fatal blow which led to the death of Cornish, in other words. Yet it could very well be argued that—by so thoroughly deriding Cornish ethnicity over the preceding centuries that it had been transformed into a 'stigmatised identity' which the local elite felt compelled to disown[74]—English popular prejudice had helped to create the atmosphere in which the dark deed could be done.

3

'England No England, but Babel'

English 'Nationalism', Welsh and Cornish Particularism and the English Civil War

As the entrenched assumption that 'nationalism' was a product of the modern age begins to break down, so whole new vistas of historical enquiry are opening up before us.[1] The prospect is especially dazzling, perhaps, for historians of England, who are beginning to accustom themselves to the notion that England may have been not only the archetypal nation-state, but the very cradle of 'nationalism' since as early as the tenth century. This view, brilliantly advanced in a number of recent studies,[2] has the potential to transform our understanding both of narrowly English and of wider British history—and, indeed, of the interlocking series of national and quasi-national histories which lie in the interstices between them. By studying the ways in which the English viewed themselves during the pre-modern period, we may come to a better understanding of the ways in which they reacted to others—and of the ways in which others reacted to them. This chapter suggests that such an approach may profitably be applied to the events of the 1640s—and that anxieties about 'nationhood' were central to the English Civil War.

For over 350 years the Civil War has held a peculiar fascination for the English. The search for its causes has preoccupied generations of scholars and the perspectives which have been gained as a result of this long-running game of historical hunt-the-thimble are incalculable. Yet so overwhelming has been the concern to elucidate the causes of the Civil War, that the conflict itself has often been somewhat cursorily treated[3]—and recent shifts in historical fashion have had the effect of pushing the events of 1642–6 still further from the historiographical limelight. As English scholars—keen to build on the work of historians of Ireland and Scotland and to refute charges of Anglocentrism—have rushed to embrace a 'British' perspective of the mid-seventeenth-century crisis, so the English Civil War has been increasingly relegated in status.[4] In many ways this shift in emphasis has been immensely valuable and productive. Yet it would be a mistake to conclude that there is nothing left to say about the Civil War in England—or, for that matter, that the general approach adopted by the new breed of British historians cannot be improved upon and refined. Much of their work so far has been 'top-down', rather than 'bottom-up' in its approach: it has been concerned to elucidate the inter-relationships which existed between the 'great men' of England, Scotland and Ireland, rather than those which existed between the ordinary inhabitants of those countries.[5] In addition, British historians have tended to concentrate on Irish and Scottish reactions to the English rather than exploring English reactions to perceived threats from the so-called 'Celtic periphery'.[6] Finally, they have tended to articulate their arguments in terms of kingdoms rather than peoples, thus privileging certain ethnic groups at the expense of others.[7] This chapter sets out to restore the balance by exploring how popular fears about group identity were aroused in the Kingdom of England during the Civil War: not only among the English but among their Welsh and Cornish neighbours too.[8]

I

Throughout the early modern period the pride and self confidence of the English nation was proverbial. Girdled by the seas which protected it from foreign invasion, England formed a precociously homogeneous whole, both in administrative and in ethnic-linguistic terms, while its rulers exercised an increasingly firm dominion over the 'Celtic' peoples who inhabited the regions to the North and West. Cornwall, once an independent British polity, had been incorporated into the English state as far back as the tenth century; Wales, effectively subordinated during the Middle Ages, had been formally assimilated in 1536–43; Ireland had been ruled by England's monarchs as a separate kingdom since 1541.[9] With the uniting of the two Crowns of Scotland and England in the person of James I in 1603, English power in the Atlantic Archipelago appeared to have reached its apogee. Yet less than forty years later, that power collapsed to its lowest point for centuries.[10] Rebellion in Scotland in 1637–9 was followed by English military defeat in the North in 1640 and rebellion in Ireland in 1641. By January 1642 Charles I had lost control of two of the three kingdoms which his father had bequeathed him, and both the Scots and the Irish had succeeded in carving out a *de facto* independence for themselves.

English pride was thoroughly humbled by these events—and national fears and insecurities thoroughly aroused. Having been ejected from the territories which they had long regarded as their own back yard—and having been made all too painfully aware of the inadequacies of English military power—thousands of Englishmen and women succumbed to an almost hysterical fear of foreign invasion during 1641–2.[11] As historians have frequently observed, the violence of their reaction was in part a reflection of the strength of anti-Catholicism in English society.[12] Even before Charles I's accession many godly Protestants had suspected the existence of a deep-laid 'Popish plot', designed to subvert England's liberties and deliver the country into the hands of foreign Catholic powers. Such fears were exacerbated by the events of the Personal Rule, exploited by the Crown's political opponents during the early 1640s and brought to fever pitch in the aftermath of the Irish Rebellion.[13] Yet the fear of foreign assault which permeated the country at this time did not involve Catholic foreigners alone. Supporters of the Crown had long been stoking up fear of the Calvinist Scots, and throughout 1642 rumours continued to circulate that armies of Protestant Danes, as well as Catholic Spaniards and Frenchmen, were preparing to descend on England.[14]

By the time that Charles I established himself at York in March 1642, many English people had come to believe that hordes of foreign enemies were poised to invade.[15] And as the country fell apart into two armed camps during the following months, some, at least, made their choice of political allegiance primarily according to their perception of which side would best protect the national interest. Richard Baxter concluded that 'if both their causes had been bad as . . . each other, yet that the subjects should adhere to that party which most secured the welfare of the Nation'.[16] And that Baxter himself, together with hundreds of thousands of other Englishmen and women, eventually decided that it was Parliament's party, rather than the King's, which was the most likely guarantor of the nation's welfare is hardly surprising. As Gardiner observed long ago, Charles I—'born of a Scottish father and a Danish mother, with a grandmother who was half-French ... with a French wife, with German nephews and a Dutch son in law'—was hardly a figure around whom English patriotic sentiment could easily rally.[17]

Parliament, on the other hand, was a potent symbol of nationhood. As the body which was held to articulate the wishes of the entire realm—a body which was physically composed, moreover, of men drawn from every part of England—it had long been identified, in an almost mystical sense, with the nation itself.[18] Parliament's traditional roles as the guardian of English 'liberties' and the upholder of the Protestant religion made its intimate connection with Englishness clearer still.[19] So did the fact that most MPs came from the south and east of the Kingdom, the districts in which English national consciousness was most deeply rooted and unambiguous. Since the reign of King James, if not before, those who were most firmly opposed to 'new courses' in government and to 'innovations' in religion, those who were most deeply outraged by any slight to the institution of Parliament, had styled themselves—and been styled by others—as 'patriots'.[20] The Parliamentarian party of the 1640s grew out of this patriotic political tradition, and during the Civil War the two concepts of 'patriotism' and 'Parliamentarianism' became ever more closely intertwined.[21]

Despite Parliament's initial closeness to the Scots, many individual Parliamentarians clearly believed their party to be the party of Englishness. Thus Edmund Ludlow explained that he joined the Roundhead army in 1642 because 'I thought it my duty ... as an Englishman ... to enter into the service of my country', while a group of Suffolk countrymen averred in 1643 that 'so longe as they remember themselves to be English-men, they will not forgett to love and defend an English Parliament'.[22] Such comments were legion during the 1640s and the perception of the Parliamentarians as patriots proved a remarkably enduring one thereafter. Sympathetic historians continued to refer to the Parliamentarians as 'the patriotic party' until well into the past century,[23] and it was only with the rise of explanations of the Civil War centring on 'class'[24] that the identification of the Parliamentary cause with that of England itself began to be abandoned by historians. Today that association is too often overlooked. Yet all the evidence suggests that the perceived conjunction between Parliamentarianism and Englishness was of immense importance in shaping popular attitudes at the time—not only in England, but in the neighbouring dominion of Wales too.

II

Wales's role in the Civil War has been unaccountably neglected.[25] Until very recently, most general studies of the period paid little or no attention to the experiences of the Welsh, and even now historians continue to assert that there was no uniquely Welsh dimension to the Civil War, and that the Welsh behaved very much as their English neighbours did between 1642 and 1646.[26] Bearing the previous history of Wales in mind, such an assumption seems inherently unlikely. Although Wales and England had been formally united since 1536, and although the Welsh gentry class became increasingly anglicized thereafter,[27] the common people of the two countries remained strikingly different. On the eve of the Civil War, 'the vast majority' of Wales's *c.*400,000 inhabitants still spoke Welsh.[28] They continued to live in isolated rural communities, quite unlike the towns and villages of southern England; they continued to preserve their distinctive traditions; and they continued to nurse a concealed resentment against their '*Saison*' (Saxon) neighbours who, after centuries of conflict, had not only defeated them and incorporated them into the English state, but who also, all too frequently, looked down upon them as boors and half-wits.[29]

Amicable co-existence between the Welsh and the English was by no means pre-ordained then, and that the two peoples got along together as well as they did during the 150 years which preceded the Civil War in large part reflected the political dexterity of the reigning monarchs. Henry VII himself was of partially Welsh parentage, and he and his successors had striven to improve Anglo-Welsh relations. At the same time, they had taken care to flatter Welsh self-esteem and to ensure that Wales was provided with sufficient 'constitutional accommodation' to mask the true extent of English dominance. Much stress was laid on the uniquely close links which existed between Wales and the Crown: on the Welsh ancestry of the royal house, for example, on Wales's status as a royal Principality and on the fact that the monarch's eldest son was its Prince.[30] Wales also remained under the special jurisdiction of the Council in the Marches, again emphasizing the extent to which it was regarded as distinct from England proper.[31] There were other ways, too, in which the Tudor monarchs encouraged the Welsh to view themselves as honoured partners of the English rather than as despised vassals. Thus the term which had long been used to denote the Welsh— 'Britons'—was appropriated to refer to all the subjects of the Crown, while 'home rule' was effectively conferred on the Welsh gentry.[32]

More important than any other factor in reconciling the Welsh to English rule, however, may well have been official recognition of the myth of the 'British origins' of the English Church. During the early years of the Reformation the Welsh had clung tenaciously to the old Catholic faith (at least in part, perhaps, because they disliked what were felt to be 'English' innovations).[33] Determined to remedy this situation, the Elizabethan regime had ordered the translation of the scriptures into Welsh. Crucially, the Welsh clerics charged with this task had prefaced their completed translations with quasi-historical introductions, which repeated and elaborated the old tradition that 'the true faith of the Reformation was a restoration of that which had flourished in the early Celtic church'.[34] The public promulgation of this thesis was of immense importance because it enabled the Welsh to see Protestantism not as an alien faith which had been imposed upon them by the English, but rather as their own traditional faith reborn in the Church of England.[35] Thanks in part to this radically altered perspective, Wales gradually embraced Protestantism over the next forty years: albeit Protestantism of a very conservative, traditional kind, almost devoid of the puritan zeal which was so commonplace among members of the reformed faith in England.[36]

By the end of the sixteenth century it seemed that, thanks to a mixture of good luck and judicious royal policy, Wales had been firmly 'jointed in' to the English state. The rule of the first two Stuart Kings, which was generally beneficent as far as Wales was concerned, did nothing to alter this happy situation.[37] It was only as the authority of the Caroline regime began to crumble during the early 1640s that the essential fragility of the partnership between England and Wales was exposed, and the dark forces of ethnic hatred re-emerged. The process seems to have begun in England, where the view of the Welsh as 'outlanders'—ridiculous and uncivilized at best, treacherous and semi-barbarous at worst—had never been wholly abandoned.[38] During the early 1640s, as fears of some sort of foreign attack or domestic insurrection grew, increasing numbers of Englishmen began to turn a suspicious eye towards Wales. Those who were most suspicious of the Welsh tended to be critics of royal policy, perhaps because such individuals—coming as they did from a puritan, 'patriotic' tradition—were peculiarly sensitive to real or imagined threats to English nationhood, perhaps because they had long regarded religiously-conservative Wales as a citadel of popery.[39]

In 1640 and 1641 rumours circulated in England that 'Popish armies' were being assembled in Wales.[40] Following the Irish rebellion such whispers became louder and more persistent and in late 1641 a full-scale panic was caused in London by reports of a papist plot centring on the Catholic Earl of Worcester's castle in Monmouthshire.[41] These scares fanned the flames of anti-Welsh feeling in England—and reinforced the suspicions of the nascent Parliamentarian party that the Welsh were disaffected to their cause. Such suspicions were in great measure justified. As we have seen, the Welsh had every reason to venerate the Crown. It was the Tudors who had granted them their special privileges, and Charles I and his eldest son who symbolized, in their very persons, the constitutional accommodation which had been granted to Wales. Parliament, on the other hand—which included only a handful of Welsh MPs—had a much weaker claim on Welsh affections.[42] And during late 1641, as 'oppositionist' MPs in the Long Parliament launched determined attacks on royal authority, meddled with the jurisdiction of the Council in the Marches[43] and, worst of all, challenged the doctrines of the established Church, unease at the drift of events at Westminster began to spread throughout the Principality.

In England itself, meanwhile, the growing conviction that the Welsh were unwilling to espouse the cause of further reformation had exacerbated anti-Welsh feeling among supporters of the Parliament. Clear evidence that this was so—and that the swelling tide of English criticism was causing great alarm in Wales—appeared in early 1642 when a petition was presented to the Commons in the name of 'many hundred thousands, inhabiting within the thirteene shires of Wales'. This hitherto unnoticed document encapsulates the sense of puzzled hurt which pervaded the Principality on the eve of the Civil War. Having stressed Wales's loyalty to both King and Parliament, the petitioners complained that 'notwithstanding, we are disrespected, and shamefully derided with ludibrious contempt, more than any other Countrey what so ever, wherefore we beseech you that the authors, urgers or suggesters of the same may be found out ... and suffer exemplary ... punishment for their reproaching us'. If steps were not taken to end 'this Epidemicall derision of us', the petitioners went on, 'it ... will become a great discouragement to all our Countreymen'.[44] There was a clear warning to Parliament here—but it was a warning that was ignored.

During the first half of 1642 a stream of violently anti-Welsh pamphlets poured off the London presses: pamphlets which not only ridiculed the country's inhabitants, but also sought to reawaken old English fears about Welsh political aspirations—by claiming, for example, that there were plans afoot to call a 'Welsh Parliament'.[45] As the accusations levelled against the Welsh in the capital grew ever more defamatory, so the inhabitants of the Principality aligned themselves ever more closely with the King. Only a political victory for Charles I, it seemed, could protect the Welsh from the virulent new strain of English xenophobia which was so evident in his opponents' camp, and as a result the King increasingly came to be regarded as a national—as well as a politico-religious—champion in Wales.[46] It is this which chiefly explains why, when Civil War eventually broke out, almost all Wales declared for the Crown. The Welsh were not just demonstrating an abstract loyalty to Charles I, they were signalling their determination to protect Wales's position within the Stuart state—and, indeed, the very identity of Wales itself—from what they perceived to be a resurgent English threat.

To many English Parliamentarians, the Principality's declaration for Charles I in 1642 represented Welsh rebellion on a grand scale: even more threatening, in its way, than the revolt of Owain Glyn Dŵr over two centuries before. Anger and fear proliferated throughout the whole of southern England and during the first two years of the war Parliamentary pamphleteers did everything they could to exacerbate English dislike of the Welsh.[47] Soon animosity between the two peoples was spiralling out of control, as the English were encouraged to believe that the King's Welsh soldiers were 'enemies to the English nation', greedy for 'fertile ... English soyle', while the Welsh were assured by the Royalists that a Roundhead victory would lead to the wholesale slaughter of Welsh men, women and children.[48] For English Parliamentarians the Civil War had by now become, at least in part, a struggle to reassert England's dominance over Wales: while for Welsh Royalists it had more than ever assumed the aspect of a struggle for national survival.

III

If the tensions which existed between the English and the Welsh have been neglected by previous historians, those which existed between the English and the Cornish have been virtually ignored. Standard accounts of the Civil War continue to treat Cornwall as if it were just another

English county. Yet this is to miss the significance of Cornwall's unique cultural heritage. The Cornish, like their Welsh cousins, were descended from British stock. For centuries they had defended their homeland—a bleak, jagged peninsula in the extreme south-west of Britain—from Anglo-Saxon incursions. And even after Cornwall had finally been conquered and absorbed within the English state, the Cornish had retained many of the marks of a separate 'people'.[49] Throughout the medieval and early modern periods the Cornish, like the Welsh, were treated with lofty disdain by their English neighbours, who mocked them as uncivilized peasants.[50] Many Cornish people, for their part, nursed a bitter sense of grievance against the 'Saxon' invaders who had subjugated their forefathers—and in 1497 and 1548–9 these simmering ethnic tensions had helped to fuel several violent rebellions in the county.[51]

Cornwall, like Wales, presented special problems of governance, then, and in Cornwall, as in Wales, the English Crown had long sought to mollify its Celtic subjects by providing them with special marks of royal favour and at least an illusion of residual autonomy. As Wales had been made a royal Principality, so Cornwall had been made a royal Duchy; as the English Kings' eldest sons had been created Princes of Wales, so they had also been created Dukes of Cornwall; and as Wales had been placed under the special jurisdiction of the Council of the Marches, so Cornwall had been placed under the special jurisdiction of the Stannaries—royal institutions which oversaw the local tin-mining industry, and which bestowed remarkable privileges on many thousands of Cornishmen.[52] In one respect, indeed, Cornwall enjoyed an even greater degree of constitutional accommodation than Wales, for the Tudors—perhaps wishing for more political antennae in this notoriously rebellious county—had created many new Parliamentary seats there. As a result Cornwall, which had only around 90,000 inhabitants in 1640, boasted no fewer than 44 MPs: more than any other county (though by no means all of those elected were native Cornishmen).[53]

Cornwall's generous Parliamentary representation, combined with the fact that it had been far more thoroughly 'anglicized' than Wales, might lead one to suspect that the Cornish would have been less alarmed that their Welsh cousins by the emergence of the Parliamentarian party in England during 1641–2. Yet in fact this was not the case. By threatening the established Church—a Church held to be built on Celtic Christian foundations—and by attacking the authority of the Crown—

that same authority which underpinned the Duchy and Stannary organizations on which Cornwall's unique constitutional status depended—'opposition' MPs in London offered, albeit unintentionally, as grave an affront to Cornish 'national pride' as to its Welsh equivalent.[54] By countenancing, if not positively encouraging, the spread of a xenophobic, 'English nationalist' form of political rhetoric, moreover, they added insult to injury. Under these circumstances, resistance to Parliament's policies was almost bound to develop in Cornwall. A Cornish petition in defence of the established Church appeared as early as February 1642, and over the following months Cornish public opinion moved ever more firmly behind the King.[55] By April it was being whispered that 30,000 men stood ready to resist the Parliament in Cornwall, and soon Roundhead sympathisers were alluding to the possibility of a Cornish military incursion into England itself.[56]

Unlike most of the Welsh counties, Cornwall contained a vigorous and well-organized Parliamentarian faction.[57] Parliament's Cornish supporters were mainly gentlemen and clerics, however, and their influence was largely confined to the far east of the county, where Cornish cultural distinctiveness had been most heavily eroded. Everywhere else—and especially in the Cornish-speaking West—it was the King's partisans who were most numerous, and in September Parliament's Cornish adherents were forced to call for outside assistance. News that 'foreign', English, forces were preparing to intervene in Cornwall caused general panic, and in October some 10,000 Cornishmen rose up in arms under the command of the local Royalist gentry and chased the pro-Parliamentarian 'traitors' out of the county. Within days all Cornwall was held for the King, and within weeks a Cornish Royalist army had been raised.[58]

As one might expect, Cornwall's 'rebellion' sparked off intense hostility in the Parliamentary press. The poisonous effusions of the London pamphleteers, combined with the sense of betrayal which many Parliamentarians felt at Cornwall's decision to side with the Crown, reawakened the old English suspicion of the Cornish, and the string of victories which the Cornish Army won during 1643 did nothing to soothe Parliamentarian feelings.[59] Anglo-Cornish relations were further exacerbated by the Lostwithiel campaign of 1644. In this, the greatest Royalist victory of the war, Essex's Parliamentary army was trapped in Cornwall by the King's forces and smashed to pieces. No one contributed more to Charles' victory than the Cornish, who had been driven to fury by this new 'foreign invasion' of their county, and who fought the Roundheads tooth and nail. For English Parliamentarians, the defeat of their main south-eastern field force—Essex's 'prodigious ... [army] of Cocknies' as it was termed by one Irish Royalist[60]—at the hands of the despised Cornish was little short of a national humiliation. Gripped by an intense desire for revenge, they began to disparage the Cornish in the same terms as the Welsh and Irish—as 'inhumane, barbarous commoners'—and to swear they would give them no quarter.[61] The Cornish themselves came to believe that none would be spared if the Parliamentarians ever re-crossed the Tamar.[62] Thus, in Cornwall, as in Wales, the Civil War increasingly took on the aspect of an ethnic conflict.

IV

The enthusiasm which Wales and Cornwall exhibited for the Royalist cause did nothing to strengthen Charles I's fragile credibility as an English national leader. On the other hand, it did less than one might imagine to weaken that credibility still further. This was chiefly because, over the preceding centuries many, quite possibly the majority of, Englishmen and women had come to accept the Cornish as honorary English and the Welsh as—if not quite this—then at least as 'the closest ... of foreigners'.[63] It was the existence of such attitudes which enabled many English Royalists to fight alongside their Welsh and Cornish allies—albeit somewhat sniffily—even as they were being denounced in the Roundhead camp as 'barbarians' and 'heathens'. Parliamentarian claims that the Welsh and Cornish were 'foreigners' initially failed to convince a large proportion of the King's English subjects then, and so did Parliamentarian claims that they, rather than their opponents, represented the true party of Englishness. This wider failure must partly have reflected the fact that, during the first year of the Civil War, Parliament had been as guilty as the King of calling in foreign assistance.

Scottish professional soldiers were the first arrivals: many joined the Parliamentary army in 1642–3.[64] There were Scottish volunteers on the King's side too, of course,[65] but they were less numerous and less visible than their Parliamentarian compatriots, many of whom bore exalted military rank: in summer 1643 Scottish professional soldiers commanded no fewer than five of the eleven regiments of Sir William Waller's army.[66] The high profile of the Scottish volunteers caused growing resentment in the Parliamentary ranks, even prompting a violent affray between English and Scottish officers at Westminster Hall in March 1643.[67] And to the uncommitted and the straightforwardly Royalist, the ubiquity of Scots professionals in the Roundhead armies was a constant reminder of Parliament's close links with England's traditional northern enemy. Equally damaging to Parliament's public image was its use of military professionals imported from abroad. The role which European mercenaries played in the Civil War has never been properly explored. A good deal of attention has been paid to the foreign soldiers of the King, most notably his German nephew Prince Rupert.[68] Yet it is too often forgotten that, during the initial stages of the conflict, soldiers from the Continent were highly visible in the Parliamentarian ranks too.[69] Several Dutch and French officers served in the original Roundhead army of 1642,[70] while Hans Behre, soon to become one of Essex's most trusted cavalry commanders, was a German, who led a troop composed entirely of 'strangers'.[71] Foreign professionals like these did much to enhance the military effectiveness of Parliament's forces. Yet by taking the decision to employ such men, Parliament—like the King—ran the risk of alienating ordinary English people, who took it for granted that Continental mercenaries were, by their very nature brutal, untrustworthy and, above all, addicted to plunder and rapine.[72]

As armed 'strangers' flooded into the land during 1642–3, English people of all political persuasions grew increasingly frightened and angry, and the pamphleteer who predicted that, until the war was brought to an end, 'England will not be England, but ... Babel perpetually' would have found many to concur in his opinion.[73] Popular conviction that England was being overrun by foreigners was greatly strengthened by the arrival of 8–9,000 troops from Ireland to serve the King during winter 1643–4. Howls of outrage against this influx of 'Irish rebels' were at once raised in the London press—and to this day the King's 'Irish' soldiers remain among the best-known 'foreign' participants in the Civil War.[74] This being the case, it is somewhat ironic that the vast majority of these troops were not native Irishmen at all, but Englishmen who had previously been shipped over to Ireland in order to fight the insurrectionists there.[75] Charles I's apologists were quite unable to convince public opinion that this was so, however, and throughout the rest of the war many continued to believe that the King's armies were full of Irish soldiers.[76]

The horrified public reaction to the arrival of the English-Irish forces made it harder than ever for Charles to convince his English subjects that he had their interests primarily at heart. Yet the intervention of Scotland on Parliament's side in 1644 presented him with a chance to turn the tables on his opponents. Despite, or perhaps in part because of, the union of the two Crowns, English distrust of the Scots remained extremely strong during the early seventeenth century.[77] The events of 1637–40 had turned this distrust to extreme dislike among the supporters of the King, while even among his opponents many had grown increasingly suspicious of the Scots' intentions.[78] The withdrawal of the Scottish army from England in 1641 had briefly stilled English fears but, as we have seen, the influx of Scottish fighting men during 1642–3 revived them. When it became clear that a fresh Scottish army was preparing to march into the North in late 1643—this time at Parliament's express invitation—the Royalists saw their chance to exploit the growing popular antipathy towards the Scots while at the same time challenging their opponents' English nationalist credentials.

The King's subsequent decision to summon a Royalist Parliament to Oxford to consider the Scots' 'invasion' was clearly intended not only to undercut the authority of the Westminster Parliament, but to convey the impression that Charles, as England's ruler, was co-ordinating a national response to a national emergency. A proclamation issued at the time made the Royalists' desire to appeal to English nationalist sentiment very plain. Having asserted that the Scots were bent on nothing less than 'a designe of Conquest', it went on to urge 'a Union of English hearts, to prevent the lasting miseries which this Forreign Invasion must bring upon this Kingdome'.[79] Over the following months the need to eject the 'northern invaders' from English soil became a constant refrain of Royalist propagandists[80]—and there can be no doubt that it struck a chord with many thousands of English people. Popular antipathy towards the Scots was expressed on numerous occasions during the Civil War, most notably in the West Midlands, where the arrival of a Scottish army in 1645 aroused violent local hostility.[81] According to later oral tradition, one straggling Scottish soldier was baited to death with dogs after he had been captured by the infuriated country folk.[82]

The anti-Scottish card was, potentially at least, one of the strongest in the Royalist hand. Yet it was also a card which Charles I—thanks to his own Scottish background, his special fondness for the Scottish people and even, perhaps, his innate humanity—was incapable of playing with any genuine conviction.[83] Throughout much of 1644–5 the King attempted to square this circle by adopting the characteristic Caroline device of saying one thing while doing another. Fiery anti-Scottish rhetoric was thus produced for public consumption, while at the same time Charles continued, in private, to surround himself with Scottish courtiers,[84] to appoint Scottish officers to his armies[85], and to angle for an alliance with the Scots against the Parliament.[86] Quite how long it took for the contradictions between the King's public and private stances to become common knowledge is hard to judge. Yet by mid-1645, at the latest, Charles I's never terribly convincing claim to be England's national champion against the Scots had acquired a sadly hollow ring. A door of opportunity now stood open to his domestic enemies—and it was a door through which they were already poised to step.

As we have seen, there had always been those in the Parliamentary camp who disliked fighting alongside the Scots and other foreign 'soldiers of fortune'. Many English Roundheads had felt deeply ambiguous about the decision to call in the Scots in 1643, and when the Scottish army occupied the North of England during 1644 but made no move to march south against the King, suspicions began to fester among the Parliamentarians that their allies had no intention of seeking con-clusions with the Royalists, but were simply out to grab what they could for themselves.[87] As the conviction that 'strangers', on both sides, were prolonging the war in order to profit from England's misery grew, so disputes between English Parliamentary officers and their foreign allies multiplied.[88] And by no means the least of the motives which prompted Cromwell and others to push for a reorganization of Parliament's military forces in late 1644 was their desire to create an army that was more entirely English than any which had gone before: a force which those with 'true English hearts, and zealous affections towards the weal of our Mother Country' might be proud to acknowledge their own.[89]

Very few of the Scottish and European officers who had served Parliament with such distinction during 1642–4 were appointed to the New Model Army.[90] And from the moment that army strode forth onto the public stage, its public spokesmen and image-makers seized every chance to stress its intensely English character.[91] Even the care which was taken to prevent its troops from plundering may have been intended to convey the message that this was an English army, which respected the rights and property of English civilians, as the polyglot forces of the

King did not. Following Parliament's victory at Naseby in June 1645—
a victory which not only shattered Charles I's main army, but also laid
bare his negotiations for military assistance from abroad—the
perception of the New Model Army as the army of England itself quickly
took root. By July, Parliamentary pamphleteers were terming it 'a great
blessing . . . that in all our battailes and armies formerly, there hath been
a mixture with some of other Nations; but in this Armie . . . there was
not one man but of our owne Nation'.[92]

That ordinary people all over southern England began to flock into
the New Model Army during summer and autumn 1645 may well have
owed as much to their conviction that this force would finally liberate
them from 'outlandish' military rule as anything else. And, as tension
between Parliament and the Scots mounted[93] and Charles continued to
make overtures to his northern subjects,[94] the final piece of the jigsaw
was about to fall into place. The King, it seemed, his party in England
in tatters and his military forces increasingly confined to the Celtic
periphery of the kingdom, was seeking to put himself at the head of an
unholy alliance of Scots, Irish, Cornish, Welsh and other 'outlanders' in
order to bring his recalcitrant English subjects to heel. Faced with this
appalling prospect, public opinion across England swung ever more
firmly behind the Parliament and all but the most die-hard English
Royalists began to abandon their allegiance. By the end of 1645 the Civil
War in England was effectively won, thanks in large part to Parliament's
success in securing a near-monopoly on English nationalist sentiment.
Yet where did this leave the Welsh and Cornish?

It left them, as usual, hopelessly outnumbered and exposed. If England's
initial collapse into chaos during 1641–2 had permitted the semi-
independent Welsh and Cornish polities of the past to flicker back into
a sort of spectral half-life—and if, under the subsequent extraordinary
pressures of war, these geo-political revenants had briefly moved still
further from shadow towards substance[95]—Parliament's forcible
reunification of England in 1645 heralded the imminent exorcism of
their troubled spirits from the body-politic. Parliament now had ample
military means at its disposal to restore Cornwall and Wales to the
English fold, and all that remained to be seen was the degree of
ruthlessness it would employ in doing so. Herein lay perhaps the most
dangerous challenge that the Parliamentary leaders had to face in their
struggle to re-knit the kingdom. Had they heeded the urgings of their
more rabidly nationalist supporters and permitted English soldiers to

overrun Wales and Cornwall with fire and sword, the reverberations would have rung down through the succeeding centuries. Fortunately, wiser and more humane counsel prevailed. Thanks in part to the endeavours of Welsh MPs in London,[96] Parliament's official attitude towards the two Celtic regions had long been growing more conciliatory and during 1645–6 great efforts were made to rein back vengeful Roundhead soldiers on the one hand, and to soothe the fears of the King's Celtic followers on the other.[97] These tactics, which had they been employed in 1641–2 might well have prevented Charles I from gathering a substantial army in the first place, succeeded—when combined with overwhelming military force—in detaching from him his last remaining allies in the kingdom during 1645–6. By August 1646 both Cornwall and Wales had finally been reduced by Parliament—and the English reconquest of Britain had begun.

4

'Pagans or Paragons?'

Images of the Cornish during the English Civil War

In August 1635 a traveller from East Anglia set off on a sight-seeing tour of the western counties. Over the next few weeks he passed through Somerset, Dorset and East Devon, remarking upon each district with evident interest and approval. On reaching Exeter, however, the traveller decided that he had gone far enough. Next day he turned back towards the east, observing in his journal that he had 'no desire [to pass] over Tamar [into Cornwall], to [visit] ye horned-nockhole Land's-end, nor . . . the rough, hard-bred and brawny strong-limbed wrastling inhabitants thereof'.[1] This early Stuart tourist's contemptuous comments perfectly illustrate how most contemporary Englishmen and women thought of Cornwall (if, indeed, they thought of it at all). England's westernmost county was regarded as a craggy, pitted Ultima Thule, its inhabitants as uncivilized roughnecks. Few educated people had any wish to visit Cornwall, and owing partly to this lack of interest, partly to the county's sheer remoteness, historians possess only limited information about English perceptions of their Cornish neighbours during the early modern period.

The events of 1642–6 provide a precious window through this wall of indifference. During the Great Civil War Cornwall impinged directly and dramatically upon the national consciousness, in a way that it had not done for almost a hundred years. In late 1642 Cornwall became the one county in southern England to declare itself unequivocally for Charles I. Thereafter, the county's inhabitants supported the King with quite exceptional vigour, providing thousands of men for the Royal armies. The Cornishmen's behaviour bewildered and enraged the Parliamentarians and, as the war dragged on, Roundhead resentment grew. This chapter charts the development of anti-Cornish feeling among Parliament's English supporters, and shows how Roundhead propagandists drew upon old prejudices and stereotypes in order to demonize the King's Cornish followers. It shows too how the events of the Civil War itself led to new, and even more negative, images of the Cornish people being formed in many Parliamentarian minds, while, at the same time, a rival myth of the Cornish as supremely loyal subjects was being fostered in the Royalist camp. Finally, the chapter explores the Cornish people's self-image during this troubled period—and asks what it was that they felt themselves to be fighting for.

Set on a jagged peninsula thrusting deep into the Atlantic Ocean, Cornwall is the most physically isolated of all the English counties. 'Nature hath shouldered out Cornwall into the farthest part of the realm', wrote the Cornish antiquary Richard Carew in 1603, 'and so besieged it with the ocean that [it is] as a demi-island in an island.' The length of this 'demi-island' Carew estimated at 'about seventy miles', while its breadth, he observed, was 'almost nowhere equal, so in the largest place it passeth not thirty [miles], in the middle twenty, and in the narrowest of the west part three'.[2] Some 90,000 people dwelt within this narrow, tapering tract of land during the early seventeenth century, the vast majority scratching out their livings from occupations connected with agriculture, tin-mining and the sea.[3]

The extent to which Cornwall was set apart from the rest of England by considerations other than those of mere distance has long been a subject of scholarly debate. In many ways, as writers from the medieval period until the present day have been keen to point out, Cornwall was very similar to other English counties.[4] 'Cornewayle is in Engelonde', the *émigré* Cornish scholar John Trevisa stated flatly in the 1300s 'and is departed in hundredes, and is i-ruled by the lawe of Engelonde, and holdeth schire and schire dayes as othere schires doeth.' Anyone disputing this simple fact, Trevisa added testily, 'wot nought what he maffleth'.[5] Yet Trevisa protested too much, and as he himself must have known very well, there were many respects in which Cornwall differed greatly from its eastern neighbours.

Perhaps most important of all was the fact that Cornwall possessed a distinctive history. Cornwall had remained a Celtic kingdom under its own rulers long after the rest of Britain had been conquered by the Saxons. It was not until the tenth century that it came completely under English rule and even after that date the process of Saxon colonization remained very slow. In 1200 Cornwall remained an overwhelmingly Celtic society; one in which there were no major towns, in which the pattern of settlement was very dispersed and in which the vast majority of the population still spoke Cornish. Admittedly, the Cornish language slowly retreated towards the west over the next 500 years, pushed back by the encroaching tide of Englishness. English continued to be a minority language in Cornwall until well into the fifteenth century, however, and as late as the 1640s the district to the west of Truro was still largely Cornish-speaking.[6]

The linguistic division of early modern Cornwall into a Celtic west and a more 'English' east was reflected variously. The surnames of 'the western Cornish', for example, were often very different from those of their eastern cousins, for—as Richard Carew observed—the former group made use of lengthy patronymics '[in which] they partake in some sort with their kinsmen the Welsh'.[7] Similarly, the characteristically Cornish sport of 'hurling' (a boisterous variant of football, which involved two teams competing for a silver ball) was played in a quite different style in the two different regions of the county.[8] Weights and measures were also very different, and a survey of the 1550s found that 'the manorial customs and methods of husbandry in the manors of east Cornwall had more in common with those of Devon than with those of West Cornwall'.[9] Yet despite these divisions—and many others like them—the ordinary inhabitants of the English-speaking districts of Cornwall clearly felt a greater identification with their western brethren than with the English proper.

In part, Cornish clannishness was founded on that sense of loyalty to one's own county which was common to all English people during the early modern period, but other factors served to strengthen the bond still further. First there was the fact that many thousands of Cornishmen were employed in an industry which was unique to their own county (and to certain parts of Devon): that of tin-mining. Tin-miners were generally very poor, their job was acknowledged to be an exceptionally hard one, and the manner in which they lived and worked set them apart from society at large. Special royal institutions known as Stannaries had been set up to govern the tin-mining areas during the medieval period, and the miners fell under the jurisdiction of these bodies, rather than of the ordinary law courts. Tin-mining was probably the single biggest occupation in seventeenth-century Cornwall (even those who usually farmed or fished would dabble in tinning when times were hard) and there can be little doubt that mass participation in this distinctive industry served to bind the county's inhabitants more tightly together and to differentiate them more sharply from those who lived elsewhere in England.[10]

The Cornish sense of identity was further strengthened by an exceptionally high degree of intermarriage. Geographically isolated as they were, most Cornishmen and women had little choice but to find a marriage partner from within the same county, and it was commonly said that 'all Cornish gentlemen are cousins'.[11] The truth of this proverb is borne out by the fact that, between 1509 and 1640, some 70–80 per cent of marriages among the lesser Cornish gentry were to Cornish brides.[12] Among the common people, rates of intermarriage were almost certainly higher still. A recent study of the Penwith peninsula, in the far west of Cornwall, found that parishes there experienced immigration on an exceptionally local scale during the early seventeenth century, leading the author to conclude that the communities of this region had been of an almost entirely 'closed' nature.[13] Endogamous marriages were probably a little less common in the east of the county, of course, but even so Cornwall was clearly one of the most interbred counties in England.

The situation at the very top of Cornish society was rather different. The greater gentry of Cornwall—those who actually ruled the county by serving as Sheriffs, Deputy Lieutenants and Justices of the Peace— were far more likely to marry a 'foreigner' than were their social inferiors.[14] And their willingness to look beyond the Tamar for a wife was just one of the ways in which they differed from their fellow countrymen. The greater gentry were much richer than their neighbours, they were much better educated, and they were much more concerned with national affairs.[15] Needless to say, they were all English-speakers: indeed it is clear that many of the greater gentry of eastern Cornwall felt positively contemptuous towards the Cornish language.[16] That this should have been so is hardly surprising, for the puritan gentry families of this district were probably the most 'anglicized' group of people in seventeenth-century Cornwall: the location of their estates, their social status and their membership of a much wider godly network all serving to direct their attentions far beyond the county boundaries.[17]

During the summer of 1642 Cornwall's peace was shattered by rumours of Civil War; rumours which prompted the formation of two rival factions in the county. Under the influence of their puritan religious beliefs, many of the East Cornish gentlemen came out for the Parliament, and by late September they had gathered a small force together at Bodmin, under the command of Sir Richard Buller.[18] Buller's position was a precarious one, however. Parliament's Cornish supporters were gentlemen rather than commoners, and their influence was largely restricted to the most easterly—and most anglicized—part of the county. Everywhere else, popular opinion was firmly on the King's side, and in the Celtic far west support for the King was almost unanimous. This was made abundantly clear on 4 October 1642 when Sir Ralph Hopton and other leading Royalists summoned the *posse comitatus* (or county gathering) to appear at Moilesbarrow Down. The response was overwhelming. Local Parliamentarians stated that 'all the west part' of Cornwall had come out for the King, 'in so much as it was a rare thing to see a man about Trurow, or in any of the westerne parts'.[19] One anonymous Roundhead claimed that 'fifteene or sixteen thousand men' had appeared at the meeting, while other correspondents spoke of 25,000 or even 30,000 men having turned out.[20] These rumours were clearly exaggerated, but more credence should be given to the account of Richard Arundell—an experienced soldier whose father was 'one of the chiefe meanes of raising the *posse*'.[21] According to Arundell, the meeting had attracted '10,000 men at least reddye to serve his Majestye, whereof 4,000 immediately marched in armes'.[22]

The Royalist force thus massively outnumbered its Parliamentarian counterpart, and Buller, who possessed just 6–700 men, can hardly be blamed for abandoning Cornwall and fleeing precipitately across the Tamar.[23] October 1642 did not see a contest between two well-matched groups, but the rout of a small body of Roundhead gentlemen and their retainers by a vast, and somewhat unruly, Royalist mob. This point is important, because it helps to explain why the initial Parliamentarian reaction to the events of 1–4 October was to claim that a popular uprising—a 'hurly-burly', 'insurrection', or 'rebellion'—had taken place in Cornwall.[24] Supporters of the King were often described as 'rebels' by Parliamentary propagandists, of course, but this term took on a particular significance when applied to Cornishmen. As English people knew only too well, Cornwall possessed a long tradition of rebelliousness, from the risings of 1497 to the 'Prayer Book Rebellion' of 1549; an episode which West-country folk termed 'the Commotion'.[25] By rising tumultuously in support of King Charles in October 1642— this at a time when the rest of southern England seemed solidly behind the Parliament—the Cornishmen had confirmed the view that they were an innately rebellious people. That the comparison between 1549 and 1642 was specifically drawn at the time is shown by the bitter reference of one local Parliamentarian to 'Cornwall's second commotion'.[26]

News of the dramatic developments in Cornwall alarmed Parliament's supporters in the neighbouring county of Devon. Letters from Plymouth dated 13 October admitted that many of the townsfolk were 'afraid of Cavaliers in Cornwall', and a week later it was reported from Barnstaple that 'the Cornish Cavaliers put us here in no small fright . . . some say they are 12,000 strong, others 8,000, but 5,000 is the least we heare of'.[27] This letter was subsequently republished in a London news pamphlet, marking the first known appearance of the sobriquet 'Cornish Cavaliers'. The nickname was to remain a staple of Roundhead propagandists for the next twelve months, and only fell out of general use in late 1643—by which time everyone was presumably felt to have been apprised of the fact that Cornishmen were, by definition, supporters of the King.[28] The fears of the Devon Roundheads were well founded. By late October Cornwall had been 'brought back to complete loyalty to his Majesty' and a formidable Royalist army was preparing to take to the field.[29] In November Hopton advanced into Devon with 2–3,000 Cornishmen and over the next four months bitter fighting raged back and forth across the river Tamar. Despite the best efforts of the rival commanders, however, neither side was able to prevail, and in March the two warring parties agreed to a temporary truce, or cessation, one which eventually lasted throughout most of April 1643. For the moment, at least, the war in the South-west had come to a halt.[30]

Hostile stereotypes of the Cornish were well established by this time, for Roundhead propagandists had drawn on pre-existent prejudices, together with the new grievances aroused by the fighting, in order to project a negative picture of Cornwall across the country as a whole. The gibes which appeared against Cornish 'rebels' have already been noted. The charge most commonly levelled against the Cornish people during the first six months of the war, however, was that they were poor and rapacious. This accusation did have some basis in fact. Cornwall was much less fertile than its eastern neighbours and found it hard to support its growing population during the early modern period. Richard Carew, himself a Cornishman, admitted in 1603 that 'few shires can show more . . . [poor people] than Cornwall'.[31] Every year, hundreds, possibly thousands, of poor Cornish folk, took to the roads of lowland England looking for work.[32] This regular influx of vagrants aroused antagonism in the richer counties to the east, and resulted in Cornish people becoming associated with poverty and shiftlessness. Perhaps it is no coincidence that a popular ballad of the time, dealing with a deceitful beggar, was entitled 'The Stout Cripple of Cornwall'.[33]

Roundhead propagandists seized on this well-established theme during 1642–3, stressing Cornwall's poverty in order to denigrate the county's inhabitants and excite fears of plunder in the hearts of prosperous Englishmen. Cornwall itself was described in the bleakest possible terms: as '[a] barren country', 'a mountainous country', and a 'countrey [not] of itself . . . very fertile'.[34] Cornish soldiers were depicted in a similarly negative way. In November 1642 it was remarked that Hopton's soldiers are 'poore Cornish men most of them', while a few months later his forces were described as '4,000 almost starved pore Cornish'.[35] When Hopton's 'ragged regiments of foot' occupied Crediton, Devon, in early 1643 the Parliamentarians reported that the town had been 'miserably pillaged' by the 'beggarly Cavaliers'.[36] The link between Cornishmen and beggars was specifically made here. The comment of another Roundhead correspondent—that the Cornish prisoners taken at Modbury were 'such ragged lowsie varlets that we esteeme them not'—also hints at a mental association between Cornishmen and vagrancy.[37] It was important for the pamphleteers to reinforce the view of the Cornish as a race of beggars, because this allowed them to imply that Cornishmen were serving the King simply out of a desire for plunder. It could then be argued that, by resisting the 'Cornish Cavaliers', ordinary English people were protecting their own property.

Allegations of poverty and rapaciousness dominated Parliamentary accounts of the Cornish during the opening stages of the war, but the county's inhabitants were portrayed in other ways too. Some pamphleteers pushed the view of the Cornish as dupes; ignorant rustics who had been 'seduced into the quarrell against the Parliament' by Royalist agitators.[38] Others depicted them as quasi-Catholics; religious conservatives who were hostile to the radical Protestantism associated with the Parliamentary cause. This point was touched on in January 1643, when a commentator noted that the King '[finds] his partie is most . . . [in Cornwall] it being a place full of . . . popishly affected persons'.[39] The links between the Cornish tin-mining industry and Royalism were also quickly identified, one pamphleteer commenting that Hopton's 'footmen of Cornwall [are] most miners, being very good pioners and better indeed with the spade and shovell then with the pike and musket'.[40] By early 1643 an alarming composite picture of the Cornish had already been established in many English minds: they figured as a race of poverty-stricken, popish ignorants, who periodically issued forth from their 'lurking holes' in the tin-mines in order to pillage and plunder.[41]

Roundhead attitudes towards the Cornish were to become yet more negative following the collapse of the South-western peace talks in April 1643. Predictably enough, the Parliamentarians blamed their opponents for the failure of the cessation, claiming (somewhat hypocritically) that the Cornish had never intended to make peace in the first place, but had simply entered into negotiations in order to gain themselves time to reorganize and regroup. Accordingly, the word 'traitor' was added to the growing lexicon of anti-Cornish abuse. A Parliamentarian declaration of 12 April described Hopton's adherents as 'rebels, traitours, Cornishmen and others' (a phraseology which implied that simply being a Cornishman was disreputable in itself), while further references to 'the treacherous Cornish' appeared in subsequent Roundhead newsletters.[42]

The end of the truce and the renewal of the fighting led to disaster for the Parliamentarians. On 16 May Parliament's western army was decisively defeated at the battle of Stratton, in Cornwall, and the Royalists then went on to win a whole string of victories in Somerset, Wiltshire, Dorset and Devon. By late 1643 the Cornishmen had captured almost all of South-west England for the King. These developments put the Roundhead pamphleteers in a somewhat uncomfortable position, for they made it clear that, however 'poor', 'ignorant' and 'treacherous' the Cornishmen might be, they were also doughty fighters. This discovery should have come as little surprise, for the county's inhabitants had long possessed a supremely martial reputation. During the 1590s Burghley had been informed that the miners of the Western Stannaries were 'twelve thousand of the roughest, most mutinous men in England', and forty years later, Cornwall was still reputed to be 'prolific in the most warlike men of the Kingdom'.[43] During the initial stages of the Civil War, Parliamentary pamphleteers tried to play down this unhelpful aspect of the Cornishmen's pre-war reputation. Some reports accused the Cornish soldiers of cowardice, and one pamphleteer even went so far as to claim that Hopton's troops '[are] poore Cornish men most of them, that are . . . easily vanquish'd'.[44] Such statements carried little conviction, however, and when an Exeter shop-keeper heard that two local men were setting out to fight the Royalists in November 1642, he advised them 'to go home againe to their wives for the Cornish would sett wyldfire in their tayles'.[45] Throughout the rest of the war, observers continued to express the greatest admiration for the Cornishmen's fighting abilities.

When the Royalist Captain Richard Atkyns encountered the Cornish army at Chard in 1643, he declared that they 'were the best foot that ever I saw, for marching and fighting'.[46] A month later the Roundhead General William Waller was forced to acknowledge that, although his troops had initially occupied a very advantageous position at the battle of Lansdown, the 'Cornish hedgers' had eventually beaten them from it.[47] (The term 'hedgers' was probably used here first to allude to the Royalists having beaten their enemies from hedge to hedge, and second to imply contempt for the 'beggarly' Cornish—hedges being almost invariably associated at this time with those who slept under them.[48]) The storming of Bristol boosted the Cornishmen's military reputation still further, and during the siege of Lyme it was reported that the Cornish were 'more terrible to [the Parliamentary defenders] than any other of the King's forces'.[49] By mid-1643 Roundhead propagandists had effectively given up trying to pretend that Cornishmen were cowards. Henceforth, little more was to be said on the subject in the Parliamentary press, though from time to time comments did appear hinting at an exaggerated respect for the Cornishmen's fighting abilities. Significantly, when 100 Royalist soldiers were captured near Plymouth in 1645, a pamphleteer specifically underlined the fact that three of the captives had been 'Cornishmen'.[50]

By 1644 a combination of propaganda, pre-existent prejudice and their own military success had established the Cornish as Parliamentarian *bêtes noires*. The depth of hatred which was now beginning to be felt for them was made clear in April 1644, when Prince Maurice arrived before the Dorset port of Lyme with a Royalist army. Almost the first action of the Roundhead garrison was to send out a message declaring 'that they would give no quarter to any Irish or Cornish'.[51] It is unclear whether these bloodthirsty words were ever translated into actions, at least as far as the Cornishmen were concerned, but the fact that the Cornish could now be mentioned in the same breath as the hated Irish shows just how much Roundhead attitudes towards the county's inhabitants had hardened. And it was against this background of growing hatred and intolerance that a new Parliamentarian invasion of Cornwall took place. In July 1644 the Earl of Essex, fresh from raising the siege of Lyme, led a large Roundhead army over the Tamar—and immediately ran into trouble. The entire adult male population took to their heels, causing Essex to note with bewilderment and growing alarm that 'through many townes and villages where my army passes, there is none but women and children left'.[52] Infuriated by this reception—and no doubt keen to settle old scores as well—Essex's soldiers embarked on an orgy of rapine, 'vaunt[ing] over the poore inhabitants of Cornwall as if they had bin invincible'.[53] Meanwhile Royalist forces under the King and Sir Richard Grenville were massing in Devon and West Cornwall, and in August they began to close in on Essex's army.

The ensuing weeks were nightmarish for the Parliamentarians, who found themselves trapped in a hostile countryside. On 2 August Essex complained of 'the country rising unanimously against us' and two weeks later he was in despair, crying out that 'intelligence we have none, the country people being violent against us; if any of our scouts or soldiers fall into their hands, they are more bloody than the enemy'.[54] Another Roundhead lamented that 'the [people here] are so base . . . that if any of our soldiers chance to stragle abroad . . . a great number of the countrey meete with them [and] . . . cut their throats'.[55] Royalist sources told the same story, observing that 'the country people were so incensed against [the Roundheads] . . . that they could not straggle out of their quarters but they were presently slain or taken'.[56] The Cornish also held back food from the invaders. It was reported in London that 'the Cornish men will not bring victuals . . . [to Essex's army] but hide it'.[57] Local sources confirm this claim, a Roundhead minister observing in his diary that provisions had had to be shipped into Cornwall from Plymouth 'since all that countrye is so rotten, and would bring in noe provisions to our Army'.[58] It is clear that the Cornish people—already deeply hostile to the Parliamentary cause—had now been driven to fury by the excesses of the Roundhead soldiers.

Late in August Essex came to realize that his position was hopeless. Hemmed in by the King's forces and the enraged local population, he no longer had any hope of leading his army out of 'the Cornish mousetrap'.[59] On 30 August he ordered his horse to break through to the east. Next day Essex himself, accompanied by most of his senior officers, embarked for Plymouth in a fishing boat. There was to be no escape for the Roundhead foot soldiers, however, who were left behind to make the best terms they could with the advancing Royalists. What was left of Essex's army surrendered to the King at Fowey on 2 September. The terms were relatively favourable; all able-bodied men were to be allowed to march back to the east under the protection of a Royalist convoy, while the sick and wounded were to be transported by sea to Plymouth.[60] Unfortunately, neither the Royalist soldiers nor the Cornish people were prepared to let their enemies get away so lightly. No sooner had the disarmed Parliamentarian soldiers set off on their march than the King's troops began to rob and abuse them. Worse was to come, for when the dejected Roundheads reached the town of Lostwithiel they were set upon and mobbed by 'the inhabitants and the country people'.[61] A crowd of 'Cornish dames' attacked the Parliamentarian camp followers, stripping them of their clothes.[62] Similar scenes were enacted 'in other towns' on the Roundhead line of retreat, the Cornish women again proving especially violent.[63] Terrified, the Parliamentary soldiers fled for the Tamar, 'never thinking themselves secure till they were got out of this county of Cornwall'.[64] These accounts all emanate from Royalist sources, and make it impossible to doubt that the defeated Roundheads were treated with quite exceptional severity by the Cornish. The campaign as a whole took a terrible toll of Essex's men. Of the 6–7,000 foot soldiers who originally marched into Cornwall, only 1,000 made it back to the east.[65]

The events of summer 1644 outraged the Parliamentarians and 'in the immediate aftermath of Essex's defeat' denunciations of the Cornish in the London press became almost hysterical. The county's inhabitants were reviled in the most bitter terms—as 'cruel Cornish', 'perfidious Cornish' and 'cursed Cornish'—while their mistreatment of the Parliamentary soldiers was described in vivid detail.[66] One newsbook described how Essex's soldiers had been stripped to the skin by the 'heathenish Cornish, who pillaged our foot, yea and commanders too . . . and stript many to their shirts, and pulled off their boots, shoos and stockings . . . and made them go barefoot'. The writer went on to complain about the treatment accorded to 'the sick and maimed souldiers that were left behind', alleging that 'the Cornish women came and stript their shirts off their backs and took away many of their clothes, and left them so lying, naked on straw . . . under hedges'. Finally, he noted the Cornish people's continued refusal to supply Essex's men with food, observing that 'the country would not bring in any provisions at all, so they were forced to march 30 miles without a bit of bread'.[67]

Further accounts in a similar vein soon followed, most notably *A True Relation of the Sad Passages Between the Two Armies in the West*, (first published in London on 2 October). This pamphlet, which gives a vivid, blow-by-blow account of events in Cornwall, and contains many impassioned attacks upon the local populace, is worth quoting from at length. 'When we came from the King's Army to Listithiel', its author begins, 'the poore souldiers were assaulted with . . . [great] crueltie by the townsmen and women . . . who stripped many men stark naked . . . I saw them strip a [newly delivered] woman of our partie to her smock', he adds, 'they tooke her by the haire of her head, and threw her into the river, and there . . . almost drowned her; the woman dyed within twelve houres after.' The writer is at pains to stress that this incident had not been an isolated one and that 'divers other men and women were served in the like nature', indeed he claims that 'it is not five sheets of paper will contain the . . . tragedies of this kind. They so coursed and harried our soldiers that many fell down under their merciless hands.'[68] Those in the Parliamentary quarters who read this account can have been left in little doubt that the Cornish were a bloody, barbarous people. Indeed, the *True Relation* closely resembles the lurid pamphlets which appeared in the wake of the Irish Rebellion of 1641 (even including the same vivid motif of Protestant women being thrown off bridges by inhuman Celts) and, like them, was clearly calculated to arouse popular hatred against an 'alien' people.[69] This underlying motive is made clear by the *True Relation*'s ominous concluding words: 'as they have done to others, so shall it be done to them'.[70] By late 1644 the Parliamentarian desire for revenge against the Cornish was overpowering.[71]

On 8 October it was reported that Essex's soldiers at Portsmouth 'Cry "Revenge, Revenge" for the perfidious dealings of the enemy'.[72] A week later letters from Plymouth averred that the defenders 'hope to be revenged of the Cruell Cornish'.[73] Shortly afterwards it was claimed that the Parliamentarian soldiers who had been almost starved in Cornwall 'mean either to give the Cornish a dieting in requitall here, or send them to Break-fast in another world'.[74] Such reports were not simply propagandist inventions. Colonel Martin Pindar wrote to Speaker Lenthall from Reading on 24 October, informing him that the Parliamentary forces were moving to intercept the King's army as it returned from the West: 'nothing more [animating the soldiers and] overcomming the difficultyes of the march than hopes to fight with their

Cornish enemyes, whose barbarisme will never be pardoned untill some proporcionable requitall [has been obtained].'[75]

The Roundhead soldiers finally got their chance on 27 October, when the King's army—now stiffened by a number of Cornish regiments— clashed with the forces of Essex and Waller at Newbury. The engagement proved indecisive, but the fighting was bloody and vindictive. One Parliamentary writer crowed that 'ours gave no quarter to any whom they knew to bee of the Cornish', and another source confirmed this, boasting that 'very few of that country had quarter afforded'.[76] A group of wounded Royalists found sheltering in a nearby manor house after the battle were slaughtered out of hand by the Parliamentarians. Royalist propagandists later reproached the Roundheads for their inhuman conduct but such protests fell on deaf ears.[77] Even two weeks after Newbury, by which time one might have expected the Roundhead blood-lust to be sated, Essex's soldiers were still 'exclaim[ing] against Cornwall'.[78] All things considered, it was probably as well for the Cornish who had marched east with the King that they were ordered back to the west again in November 1644.

During 1644–5 Parliamentarian resentment against the Cornish reached its peak. At the same time Roundhead propagandists became both more vindictive and more imaginative in their treatment of the county's inhabitants; resurrecting ancient slurs and gibes against the Cornish, while simultaneously pressing new ones into service. As a result the collection of negative stereotypes already associated with the Cornish people was developed and expanded, leading to the formation —or perhaps one should simply say the enunciation—of an intriguing complex of interconnected images.

By 1644 the view of the Cornish plunderer, so heavily pushed during 1642–3, had become an established national stereotype. A pamphleteer sneered that the King's commanders 'have French to ravish, Welsh to thieve [and] Cornish to . . . plunder'.[79] Even so, specific references to the Cornish propensity for plunder became much less frequent after 1643. Why was this? It was partly because the pamphleteers now had much more heinous crimes of which to accuse the Cornish. Yet it was also because they had rediscovered a time-hallowed nickname which made the link between Cornishmen and plundering implicit. Throughout the early modern period the cliffs of western Britain were frequented by the red-legged crow (*Pyrrhocorax pyrrhocorax*), then known as the 'Cornish chough'. This bird appeared in the Cornish coat-of-arms and, as we have seen, its close association with the county eventually led to the nickname 'choughs' being jeeringly applied to Cornish people. Writing in 1603 Carew observed that the chough was 'the . . . slander of our county'. He went on to give a description of the bird, a description which concluded—most significantly—with the comment that the chough's 'condition . . . is ungracious, in filching and hiding of money and such short ends'.[80] The kleptomaniac reputation of the Cornish chough was a gift to the Roundhead pamphleteers. Just as the nickname 'Cornish Cavaliers' had been used to suggest that all Cornish people were Royalists, so the nickname 'Cornish Choughs' could be used to imply that all Cornish people were plunderers.

The London pamphleteers took some time to recognize the potential of the sobriquet, but scathing references to Cornish soldiers as 'chaftes' became increasingly common during 1644 and by the end of that year the term had passed into general use.[81] Once the link between Cornishmen and crows had been firmly established, the way was open for the propagandists to make many new sneers and sallies. Remarking on Cornish desertion from the Royalist armies in late 1644, one writer remarked that 'the Cornish Choughs have taken their flight home again', while, after a group of Cornish soldiers had allegedly fled from battle, the same author crowed 'now I see the Choughs are but a craven brood'.[82] By referring to the Cornishmen as crows, the pamphleteers were essentially dehumanizing them, suggesting to their readers that Cornish people were scarcely people at all. And this same motive clearly underlay the production of a whole series of similar images during 1643–5, all of which equated the Cornish with birds and animals. One variant of 'Cornish Choughs' was the nickname 'Cornish Cormorants'.[83] Cormorants, like choughs, were closely associated with Cornwall at this time and, like them, possessed a bad reputation, their voracious eating habits having made them a byword for greed.[84] Once again, the pamphleteers had found an image which could be used to mock the Cornish while at the same time denouncing them as plunderers.

Another well-known creature of the South-western shoreline offered itself up for this sport: the crab. In the wake of the Royalist defeat at Cheriton, it was sneered that 'the Western Choughs . . . [had] turn'd into Crabs, and crawl'd backwards'.[85] Almost certainly, this image of the Cornish as crabs was a pun upon the contemporary perception of Cornwall as a 'crabbed [i.e. cross-grained] peninsula'.[86] Cornishmen were also compared with moles, and once again this allegory worked at several levels.[87] The mole's subterranean lifestyle resembled that of the tin-miners, of course. Yet the mole was also notoriously short-sighted, and therefore served as fitting emblem for 'the blinded and seduced Cornish', who had, according to the pamphleteers, been so completely taken in by Royalist agents.[88] Yet another animal nickname appeared in 1645, when a writer, describing the bloody repulse of a Royalist attack on Plymouth, gloated that 'the Cornish blood-hounds have had their bellies full'.[89] It is not clear if the term 'bloodhound' possessed any specific associations with Cornwall, but the comparison of Cornish soldiers with bloodthirsty dogs was certainly a vivid and insulting one.

Newsbooks occasionally alluded to the sports which were associated with Cornwall as well. Only one reference to 'hurling' has so far been encountered in the pamphlet literature of the Civil War: a comment of 1643 that Hopton's soldiers had managed to escape over the fields after the battle of Modbury because 'many of them . . . [were] Cornish Hullers [*sic*], who were nimble of foot'.[90] Much more frequently referred to (probably because it was more widely known) was the Cornish sport of wrestling. Prior to 1642 Cornishmen had been renowned as the greatest wrestlers in the kingdom, and as the war dragged on, propagandists on both sides made increasing use of wrestling imagery when referring to Cornwall and its inhabitants.[91] This trend may have been initiated by the Royalist journal *Mercurius Aulicus*, which noted in 1643 that Waller's forces had 'lately received a Cornish hugge' at the hands of Hopton's men.[92] A Cornish hug was a type of wrestling throw—described by Fuller as 'a cunning close with . . . [a] fellow combatant, the fruits whereof is his . . . fall'—and from 1643 onwards the term was used by Royalist writers to allude to defeats inflicted on the Roundheads by Cornish soldiers.[93] Thus when Sir Thomas Fairfax, commander of Parliament's New Model Army, was advancing on Cornwall in 1645, a Royalist pamphlet expressed the hope that 'his Excellency of 1645 [i.e. Fairfax]' will find 'that there is as much danger in a Cornish hugg, as was to his Excellency in 1644 [i.e. Essex]'.[94]

Parliamentarian writers, understandably, turned this wrestling imagery on its head. In the Roundhead newsbooks, a Cornish hug (or 'hop') became a defeat inflicted *on* the Cornish, rather than a victory obtained by them. One account of the battle of Newbury describes how the Parliamentary soldiers, having attacked the King's forces and captured their cannon, 'were no sooner possest of the ordnance (which were a part of those which were lost in Cornwall) but our western sparks, with exceeding great joy, hug'd and kist them and cryed out "Now will wee shew them a Cornish hop!"'.[95] The fact that, in the subsequent battle, the King's Cornish soldiers received no quarter is significant. It suggests that, in Parliamentarian hands, the term 'Cornish hug' had become invested with a new and much more sinister meaning: now implying nothing less than the administration of the *coup de grâce* to an individual Cornishman. Such suspicions are confirmed by a report from Plymouth, dated 1645, which nonchalantly describes how a raiding party 'went [out] to . . . [the Royalist quarters] and gave eight or ten of them the Cornish hug'.[96]

That the killing of these men should have been regarded as a fit subject for humour is one more indication of the sheer depth of hatred which the Parliamentarians had now come to feel for the Cornish—and a further cluster of propagandist images helps to explain how this pitiless attitude had come about. It has already been noted that, from the very beginning of the war, occasional references to the religious conservatism of the Cornish people had appeared in the London press, but from 1643 onwards these references were increasingly accompanied by accusations which placed the Cornish still further beyond the religious pale. In March 1643 a report appeared alleging that Cornish soldiers had profaned a church in Devon by using it as 'a jakes', or latrine.[97] There-after, references to the irreligious and 'prophane Cornish Cavaliers' became commonplace. In March 1644 one pamphleteer lamented 'that the men of Cornwall are very heathens, a corner of ignorants and atheists, drained from the mines'.[98] This reference to the tin-mines shows how Cornishness, irreligion and tin-mining were all inextricably linked together in Parliamentarian minds.

The events of summer 1644 confirmed the Roundhead opinion of Cornwall as a 'heathen' county, and when *Mercurius Aulicus* (correctly) reported that Essex's men had damaged a church there, one Roundhead propagandist affected not to believe it. 'I . . . question whether there were any church in that Pagan Principality, or not', blustered the editor of *Mercurius Britanicus*, 'it may very well be questioned, whether they ever had any church or gospell there; if you knew but the carriage and demeanour of that wretched blinde generation [you would doubt it]'.[99] He went on to refer to the Cornish as the King's 'westerne pagans', a term which was now coming into general use.[100] Letters from Plymouth, written at about the same time, spat venom at the 'cursed Cornish' and went on to aver that 'they are as very heathens as the ignorant Welch that know no religion, nor God'.[101] Several other writers suggested that it was monarchy, rather than divinity, which was worshipped in Cornwall and that 'the Cornishmen . . . know no other God but a King'.[102]

From seeing Cornwall as an intrinsically irreligious place it was only a small step to seeing it as an intrinsically evil one. Cornwall began to be associated with malignant spirits (references to 'Cornish elfe[s]' reminding us of the present-day obsession with 'Cornish piskies'), and even with hell itself; witness the reference of the Roundhead propagandist John Vicars to 'heathenish, I had almost said Hellish, Cornwall'.[103] The composite picture of Cornwall which the pamphleteers had built up by 1644 was a hellish one indeed; and the constant emphasis which they laid on the tin-miners' Royalism was surely no coincidence.[104] In the 'Cornish mettal-men'—'those subterraneous spirits of darknesse' who had been 'raysed' (note the significance of this word) from the fiery pits and shafts of the Western Stannaries in order to fight against Parliament's armies—the pamphleteers had found a race of men who could be credibly presented as living demons.[105]

So far, this chapter has concentrated on Parliamentarian images of the Cornish. But there was an alternative, Royalist, viewpoint as well, and needless to say it was an extremely favourable one: Charles I's supporters repeatedly commented on the remarkable enthusiasm with which the Cornish people had embraced his cause. Such comments became particularly frequent during mid-1644, when the King's army was campaigning in Cornwall. Even before crossing the Tamar in pursuit of Essex, the Royalist soldiers had been told that 'they were now entering a country exceedingly affectionate to his Majesty'.[106] They were not to be disappointed. As soon as the King marched into Cornwall the able-bodied men who had hidden themselves from Essex came flocking to join him.[107] Clarendon speaks of 'the general conflux and concurrence of the whole people of Cornwall' to the King.[108] Edward Walker, the King's secretary, was equally impressed. Indeed he saw the strength of popular support for the King in Cornwall as unique, commenting that 'not till now were we sensible of the great and extraordinary advantage the rebels have over his Majestie's armies throughout the kingdom by intelligence . . . which by the loyalty of the [Cornish] people, the rebels here were utterly deprived of, no country in his Majestie's dominions being so universally affected to his Majesty'.[109] Richard Symonds, an officer in the King's lifeguard, confirmed Walker's statement, noting that 'divers of the country people came to the King with much joy to tell him of his enemyes, where they lay, and please his worship'.[110]

Reports like these led Royalist propagandists to paint the Cornish people in the most glowing colours. Two themes in particular—the military prowess of the Cornishmen and their affection for the Crown—were constantly stressed by the King's apologists. *Mercurius Aulicus* frequently praised the fighting qualities of the Cornish, variously describing them as 'brave', 'stout', 'valiant', 'gallant' and 'resolute'.[111] '[He] is no Cornishman', *Aulicus* once sniffed disdainfully, after a Royalist officer had behaved in an unsoldierly way.[112] The theme of loyalty was pushed more strongly still. *Aulicus* extolled the county's inhabitants as 'the most loyall Cornish', while the King himself sent an open letter to the people of Cornwall in 1643, specifically thanking them for their loyalty (see frontispiece).[113] Sir John Berkenhead, editor of *Mercurius Aulicus*, never tired of repeating that it was loyalty to the monarchy which had spurred the Cornish on. In July 1644 he declared that '[the] gallant Cornish . . . are all resolved to spend their lives for his Sacred Majestie', and a month later he noted that 'tis impossible to express that heartinesse and welcome which his Majestie's Armie finds in this county of Cornwall'.[114] Such comments reached their apogee with Berkenhead's claim that 'no Prince in Christendom hath better subjects [than the Cornish]', to which he added the dramatic aside that 'they still value their honour and their consciences above their blood'.[115] Whether Berkenhead may have overstated the extent to which an abstract loyalty to the Crown was the chief motivating force behind Cornish Royalism is a subject which will be returned to below. What is certain is that, by praising the Cornish people to the skies, Berkenhead goaded the London pamphleteers into excoriating them still further. It is no coincidence that, of all the Roundhead journals, it was *Mercurius Britanicus*—a publication entirely devoted to rebutting *Aulicus*—which was most virulent in its attacks on the Cornish.

The violent hatreds engendered during the first two years of the war helped to ensure that, despite growing unrest in those parts of Cornwall where Parliamentary sentiment had always been strong (St Ives, for example, and the area around Stratton), most of the county's inhabitants remained solidly behind the King—or at least solidly against the Parliament—during 1645.[116] This was in marked contrast to the situation elsewhere in England, where war-weariness and the undisciplined behaviour of the King's troops had steadily reduced the commitment of many naturally Royalist communities.[117] As late as September 1645 Cornish 'country people' were still prepared to rise up against the Roundhead raiding parties which descended on their coasts. In one such skirmish the Roundhead sailors killed three Cornish women.[118] Continued outrages like these doubtless help to explain why, in December 1645, with the King's cause faltering almost everywhere else, the Royalists were still able to count on the support of 2,400 men of the Cornish trained bands as well as 2–3,000 regular Cornish soldiers.[119] These men were not just unwilling conscripts. In January 1646 a Royalist officer assured a friend that 'at the rendezvous this afternoon the Cornish were very cheerful and expressed much forwardness to fight'.[120] One may doubt that the Cornish soldiers were 'cheerful' (in the modern sense of the word, at least), but one need not doubt that they were committed. As the King's territory shrank, and as the New Model Army moved inexorably closer to the Tamar, Cornishmen must have been steeling themselves to protect their homes and families from the long-predicted Roundhead revenge.

That Cornwall was eventually subdued without a bloodbath was chiefly thanks to the foresight shown by the Parliamentary leaders. Confident of military victory, their thoughts had by now turned to the need to secure a stable peace. It was clear that this would be impossible to achieve without the grudging consent of the King's Celtic supporters, and Roundhead commanders on the ground were therefore encouraged to adopt a more conciliatory manner. Efforts had already been made to woo the Welsh with kindness during 1644–5, and at the very end of the war this same strategy was applied in the South-west.[121] As Fairfax's army advanced across Devon during 1646 great care was taken to conciliate the Cornish. Following the capture of Dartmouth each of the Cornish soldiers who had been taken prisoner there was released and given 2s for his journey home. Cornish prisoners taken at the battle of Torrington received similarly favourable treatment.[122] Meanwhile Fairfax was making careful arrangements to facilitate the regular payment of his troops when they finally entered Cornwall. This, he hoped, would prevent them from plundering the populace 'whereby the opposition that people might make would, in all likelihood, be taken off'.[123] Fairfax also ordered his troops to eschew all thoughts of revenge against the Cornish. He was anxious that they might disobey this command, however, and noted in a letter 'truly, I doubt the souldiers (especially those that were formerly strip't) will hardly overcome a passionate remembrance of the same'.[124]

The Parliamentarian advance into Cornwall finally began in February, the victory at Torrington having cleared the way. Even now, and despite Fairfax's best efforts, Cornish people clearly remained terrified of the invaders and, just as in 1644, a panic-stricken flight of the civilian population took place. The Roundhead chaplain Joshua Sprigge reported that, during the first stage of their march, the Parliamentarians 'had much cause to observe the people's frights, [they] quitting their habitations in fear of the army, the enemy [having made them believe] that no Cornish was to have quarter at our hands'.[125] The same line was taken by John Vicars, who claimed that the Cornish 'were made believe by the enemy that the Army would give no quarter to any Cornish man or woman, which they did for the most part believe'.[126] All the blame for the atmosphere of terror was laid at the door of the Royalists. One would never guess from these accounts that Cornish fears of vengeance had initially been aroused by the bloody threats, and actions, of the Parliamentarians themselves.

Once his forces were firmly established in Cornwall, Fairfax set about allaying the people's fears. Cornish soldiers captured at Launceston were released and sent home, just as their comrades at Dartmouth had been. Parliamentary sources noted that 'the townspeople of Launceston were much affected with such merciful usage', and it is clear that, as the peaceable demeanour of Fairfax's troops became obvious, local fears subsided.[127] By 5 March relieved Parliamentary writers were able to report that 'the Cornishmen . . . generally relinquish the busines, will fight noe longer, begin to confess how they have bin deluded'.[128] Ten days later the King's forces in Cornwall surrendered, effectively bringing the war in the South-west to an end. Throughout this period Cornish people continued to assert that they had been 'misled'. The Roundhead preacher Hugh Peters—who was himself a Cornishman and conducted several open-air meetings at this time in order to convince his fellow-countrymen of the error of their ways—noted that 'many of them confessed that they were deceived by ill reports brought of the Parliament and the crueltyes of this army'.[129] There was doubtless some truth in this claim, but it also served as a convenient excuse.

Cornish Royalism was not founded on deception and delusion alone, and many other factors had contributed to the strength of Royalist feeling in the county. Crucially important had been religious conservatism. Joseph Jane—a local gentleman, who later wrote a brief account of the county's history during the Civil War—considered that it was 'zele for the establisht liturgie', which had chiefly 'stirred upp' the Cornish people in support of the King.[130] Hugh Peters agreed, laying great stress on the contribution of 'their lude and ungodly ministers [who] . . . councelled and exampled them to the greatest part of their misery'.[131] The activities of local Royalist gentlemen had also been important, although their influence upon the common people should not be exaggerated.[132] In addition the Cornish had been greatly flattered 'by the King's and Prince's personall appearance among them; and by their promises . . . honouring them', while—in contrast to the Roundheads—the King's forces had generally treated Cornish civilians well.[133] Religion, deference, propaganda, experience: these are all common explanations for popular allegiance during the Civil War, but important as they undoubtedly were, they are not enough in themselves to explain the unique intensity of popular hostility towards the Parliament in Cornwall. To understand fully this hostility, we must conclude by examining the Cornish self-image.

The aim of this chapter has been to show that the Cornish were regarded as different at the time of the Civil War. What has not yet been made sufficiently clear, perhaps, is that this difference was still perceived in specifically national, even racial, terms. The English still saw the Cornish as foreigners during the 1640s: witness the words of a Devon Royalist who was later alleged to have been 'an incorriger of the King's partie comming out of Cornwall, saying that, though God had brought his people low, yet . . . rather than his people should fall he would bringe forraigne Nacions for their ayde'.[134] It is probably no coincidence that the early campaigns between the Parliamentarians in Devon and the Royalists in Cornwall were described, to a much greater degree than those fought elsewhere in England, in terms of 'invasions' and 'frontiers'.[135] Parliamentary appeals to the inhabitants of one English county (Devon) to oppose those of another (Cornwall) in February 1643 were unusual and again hint at the conceptual framework of a war waged between two nations.[136] The fact that thousands of irregular Devon 'Clubmen' did eventually turn out against the Royalists suggests that this perception of the Cornish as foreigners was shared at the popular level and was not just a propagandist invention. (For many years before 1642, Englishmen had been specifically enjoined to rise with clubs in the event of foreign invasion, an interesting point in view of the fact that so many of the Clubman risings of the Civil War were sparked off by the depredations of foreign troops.[137]) Further evidence of the extent to which the Cornish were regarded as foreigners is provided by the frequency with which pamphleteers spoke of them in the same breath as the French, the Irish and the Welsh—and by the fact that Cornish prisoners, like other 'alien' captives, were sometimes slain out of hand.[138]

If the English still saw the Cornish as foreigners, is it not likely that the Cornish still reciprocated this feeling? The county's inhabitants certainly continued to possess a strong sense of identity at this time. Throughout the Civil War, Cornish soldiers constantly feuded with Royalist units drawn from other parts of the country. Hopton's Cornish infantry 'many times let fly' at Prince Maurice's cavalry in 1643, while disputes with the King's foreign troops were even more common.[139] According to Parliamentary sources, the Cornish were unwilling to allow the 'beastly, buggering' Frenchmen of the Queen's Guard to enter their county in mid-1644, and earlier that same year the Dorset town of Beaminster was burnt to the ground 'by reason of a falling out between the French and the Cornish'.[140] The Cornish reserved a particular hatred for the Irish, and in 1643 a Parliamentary newsbook reported 'great contention' between the Cornish and Irish regiments in Hopton's Army; 'the English-Irish forces upbraiding the Cornish with the title of Cornish Choughes . . . the Cornish againe calling them Irish Kernes'. If this source is to be credited, the dispute eventually resulted in several deaths, prompting 500 of the Cornish to 'withdr[a]w themselves and . . . [return] to their native county'.[141]

Just how strong this Cornish sense of identity was is suggested by the fact that, unlike Royalist soldiers raised elsewhere in England, the King's Cornish soldiers tended to serve in exclusively Cornish regiments, under the command of their own officers (see Appendix 4).[142] The more one examines the evidence, in fact, the more forcefully one is struck by the impression that the Cornish were fighting as a people, rather than simply as supporters of Charles I. It is intriguing to note that—despite *Aulicus'* boasts about the supreme loyalty of the Cornish—hints occasionally appeared that the Royalists suspected them of possessing their own agenda. In November 1644, for example, Sir Samuel Luke informed the Earl of Essex that the Cavaliers at Oxford 'exclaim against Cornwall as much as your forces do, and it is believed that now the King has armed them they will suffer neither his Majesty's nor his Excellency's forces to come amongst them'.[143] This suspicion that the county's inhabitants meant to use their support for the King as a stepping-stone towards their own independence was aroused again in 1645, when the Cornish commander Richard Grenville proposed that the Prince of Wales, then titular commander of the King's forces in West Devon and Cornwall, should seek a separate peace with Parliament, effectively establishing Cornwall as a semi-autonomous state.[144]

Were the Cornishmen fighting chiefly in defence of their own country, and their own identity? Such a theory would certainly help to explain why Cornwall acted so completely differently from the rest of southern England in 1642, and why the county's inhabitants later showed such intense commitment to the Royalist cause. It would also help to explain why support for the posse in October 1642 was strongest in the far west of Cornwall. It was in this district that the old Cornish culture and language lingered on, and that a secret hostility against the English continued to fester. John Norden observed that the common people of Cornwall 'retayne a kinde of conceyled envye agaynste the Englishe, whome they yet affecte with a desire of revenge for their fathers sakes, by whom their fathers receyved the repulse'.[145] The 'insurrection' of October 1642 (and, indeed, the earlier Tudor rebellions of 1549 and 1497) were surely encouraged by this vague, inchoate, yet still very powerful, desire on the part of many ordinary Cornish people to 'revenge' themselves upon the English and strike a blow in defence of the old Cornish culture.[146]

Why should this ancient antagonism towards the English eventually have been converted into support for the King, rather than for Parliament? Religion was probably the vital factor here. In Scotland and Ireland attachment to non-Anglican faiths was, at least in part, an expression of national independence, of resistance to the military, political and cultural hegemony of England. When these faiths were perceived to be under serious threat, as in Scotland in 1637 and Ireland in 1641, religious and racial tensions combined together to form a molotov cocktail of hate. It seems probable that in Cornwall, too, a particular brand of religious faith—in this case conservative 'Anglicanism'—was seen as an integral part of national identity, and that, when this faith was threatened by Parliament, ethnic anxieties combined with religious ones to ensure that the bulk of the population fell in behind the King. Allied to this was the fact that the two secular institutions which most clearly served to set Cornwall apart from the rest of England—the Stannaries and the Duchy of Cornwall—were also inextricably linked to the Crown.[147] If, as seemed all too likely, Parliamentary attacks on the King led to the abolition of these institutions, then the Cornish people would lose two more of the planks on which their cherished sense of identity was built. (They would also, of course, lose the very considerable economic benefits which sprang from those institutions.[148]) More generally, it is easy to see why a people who felt that their ancient identity was under threat should have rallied to a monarchy which was closely associated with 'the old wayes'.[149]

It is tempting to conclude that particularist sentiment in Cornwall attached itself to the King, rather than to Parliament, because, while Charles I was seen as the King of Great Britain, the defender of the rights and privileges of all his subject peoples, the Parliamentarians were identified with a narrowly English interest.[150] Obviously, one should not take such conjecture too far, and hard evidence about the underlying motivation of the Cornish peasantry is almost impossible to find. Nevertheless Hugh Peter's comment that in 1646 there was 'a common muttering among [the Cornish] that their country was never conquered' is intriguing, and again suggests that many of the county's inhabitants saw the Civil War as a fight between England and Cornwall as much as a conflict between King and Parliament.[151]

There is, moreover, a postscript to this story. In May 1648, just two years after Cornwall had finally been subdued by the New Model Army, yet another 'insurrection' broke out in the county. Once again it took place in the far west of Cornwall, and once again it was in support of the King. On 25 May a Parliamentarian gentleman wrote to a friend from Launceston, telling him that he had lately been informed of 'some sturringes about Penzance and those westerne heathen partes' adding 'the spirit it seemes of malignancy is so prevalent with them, yt it will not suffer their disaffected spiritts to be at quiet, although their sturring is irrational and tend[s only] to their owne confusion'.[152] This sentence is fascinating, not only because it reiterates the view of West Cornwall as intrinsically 'heathen' and Royalist, but also because it shows that the precise motivation of those Cornish commoners who rose in support of the King continued to baffle their Parliamentary enemies long after the Civil War had come to an end. Were the 'irrational' motives of which this English-speaking gentleman so testily complained connected to the desire of Cornish-speaking commoners to defend what was left of their own culture?[153] And did this same desire contribute, not only to the county's original declaration for the King in 1642, but also to the frequency of rebellions in Cornwall throughout the early modern period?

The answer, in both cases, is surely yes. Many of the participants in the 1648 rising came from St Keverne in the extreme south-west of Cornwall, a parish which had a long history of rebelliousness. It was here that the insurrection of 1497 had broken out, here that attempts had been made to initiate another rising in 1537, and here that many of those who participated in the 'Cornish Commotion' of 1548 had lived.[154] The fact that St Keverne was also a stronghold of the Cornish language, and was, indeed, one of the last few parishes in which Cornish was spoken after 1700 seems unlikely to be mere coincidence.[155] If it was the presence of the tin-miners which provided the physical potential for rebellion in South-west England during the early modern period, it was surely the sense of a culture under threat, of embattled Cornishness, which provided the emotional charge. Like the Tudor rebels before them, Charles I's Cornish soldiers were fighting, at least in part, to defend the privileges and peculiarities which helped to set Cornwall apart from the rest of England: rather than pagans or paragons, they might better be described as patriots.

5

'The Last Refuge of a Scoundrel'

Sir Richard Grenville and Cornish Particularism,
1644–1646

Few Civil War commanders can have attracted as much opprobrium as Sir Richard Grenville (Plate 5). A deserter from the Parliamentary ranks, he was vilified by the London pamphleteers for his cruelty and inconstancy, while many on the King's side disliked him for his vindictiveness and his quarrelsome nature. If Grenville's contemporary reputation was a bad one, moreover, the image of him which was transmitted to future generations was positively malign. One of Grenville's most bitter enemies was Sir Edward Hyde, later Earl of Clarendon, who not only crossed swords with Grenville during the war, but later went on to draw an exceptionally hostile portrait of him in his *History of the Rebellion*.[1] As R. MacGillivray has observed, it was Grenville, rather than any of the Roundhead leaders, who was the true 'villain' of the *History*, and from Hyde's day until our own it is primarily as a villain that Sir Richard has continued to be seen.[2]

Admittedly, some attempts have been made to defend him. Grenville himself penned an exculpatory account of his wartime career in 1646.[3] During the 1730s a spirited vindication of Sir Richard was composed by one of his descendants.[4] And over the last century, scholars have come to agree that, in military affairs at least, he was possessed of far more merit than Hyde allows.[5] Yet if recent research into Grenville's wartime career has confirmed his strengths as a commander,[6] it has also uncovered new evidence about the barbarity of his methods and the cynical, self-interested nature of his approach. As the following pages will show, Grenville was not just an unusually tough Royalist officer.[7]

91

Rather, he was a brutal careerist, a man who starved prisoners of war to death and finally, when the chips were down, sought to bolster his own position through the exploitation of ethnic difference; truly, a villain for our own times. ,

Of Grenville's pre-war career, a subject which has been covered with admirable thoroughness by previous writers, little need be said here. Born at Stowe near Kilkhampton in 1600, he was the second son of Sir Bernard Grenville, a prominent Cornish gentleman. The Grenvilles were one of the most highly respected families in Cornwall, but Richard was to prove a sore trial to his relatives. Having fallen out with his brother, he made a disastrous marriage, was imprisoned twice for debt and spent much of the 1620s and 1630s serving as a professional soldier in Europe. In 1641 Grenville took service against the Catholic rebels in Ireland (where he soon acquired a taste for atrocities), and it was in this unhappy kingdom that he found himself when the English Civil War began.[8] Sir Richard had troubles enough of his own at this time. Even so, he must have taken a keen interest in what was going on 'across the water', especially as his brother, Sir Bevill (who had succeeded to the Grenville estates on his father's death), had emerged as one of the King's leading supporters.

It was a terrible blow for the Royalist cause when Bevill was killed, fighting at the head of his own Cornish troops, at Lansdown near Bath in July 1643—but for his penniless younger brother, watching and waiting in Ireland, the news of Bevill's death may well have suggested the possibility of future advancement.[9] Almost at once, Sir Richard resigned his command and took ship for England. In August he landed at Liverpool, then a Roundhead garrison. Arrested as a suspected Royalist he was sent down to London, where he quickly managed to persuade his captors that he was, in fact, a supporter of Parliament.[10] Grenville's protestations must have carried conviction; by the end of the year he had been appointed Lieutenant-General of Horse in Sir William Waller's Parliamentary army. Yet Grenville's true sympathies had always lain with the King and in March 1644 he defected. The Roundheads were shocked by Grenville's duplicity: Parliament condemned him to death *in absentia* and issued a proclamation denouncing him as a 'Skellum' (or 'scoundrel').[11] In Oxford, Grenville was welcomed with open arms. The Royalists hoped that he would be able to exert the same sort of influence over the Cornishmen as his brother had done—and these expectations were soon to be fulfilled.[12]

In mid-March Grenville joined the Royalist forces besieging the Roundhead garrison of Plymouth in Devon. He remained here for the next four months, but was unable to achieve very much, partly because of the town's intrinsic strength, partly because of a lack of men. The Cornish army which his brother had helped to raise in 1642 was elsewhere at this time, under the King's nephew Prince Maurice, so Grenville had to make do with scratch troops.[13] And in June all attempts to capture Plymouth had to be abandoned when the Parliamentary General Essex arrived in Devon with a powerful army. Heavily out-numbered, Grenville retreated across the Tamar and marched down the Cornish peninsula to Truro. Rallying his forces in the far west of the county, he then turned at bay and prepared to withstand Essex's army. Meanwhile, Charles I himself had arrived on the eastern borders of Cornwall with 10,000 veteran troops. Triumph now turned to disaster for the Roundheads. Trapped between two Royalist forces and harassed at every step by the enraged Cornish populace, they had no hope of escape. In September Essex's infantry surrendered to the King at Lostwithiel.[14] It was the most abject Parliamentary defeat of the war.

In the wake of this victory, the Royalists quickly regained control of Cornwall and most of Devon (although Plymouth continued to hold out). Grenville was handsomely rewarded for his services. Not only was he reappointed commander of the Royalist forces before Plymouth,[15] he was also made Sheriff of Devon and awarded extensive local estates to add to those which he had appropriated from his alienated ex-wife.[16] His rise to near-unfettered local power was to have grim results.

Historians have long been aware of the allegations, made by Hyde and various Parliamentarian writers, that Grenville treated Roundhead captives with quite exceptional severity while he was conducting the siege of Plymouth. Because these claims come from sources known to have been hostile to Grenville, there has been a tendency to treat them with a certain amount of suspicion.[17] Yet, as A.C. Miller points out, other Royalist commentators made very similar allegations.[18] Can the testimony of all these individuals be ignored? It would seem not, for recent research has uncovered a new and very sinister collection of evidence, all of it suggesting that Grenville's misdeeds before Plymouth were far more heinous than even Hyde ever acknowledged.

The most important pieces of evidence concern Grenville's treatment of prisoners. During early 1644 a gaol had been established in the town of Tavistock, some twenty miles to the north of Plymouth, in order to house captured Parliamentarians. Inevitably, some of these individuals died as a result of wounds, disease and neglect, and during the first half of 1644 the parish register noted the burial of nine 'prisoners'. Following Essex's defeat in Cornwall the gaol was re-established—but under a drastically different regime. Between 10 and 30 September the burial of no fewer than thirty-nine prisoners was recorded.[19] The death of these men was no accident. According to a local minister, they had been cast into the town hall and then 'starved' by the 'Cursed Cavaliers'.[20] The fact that the burial rate at Tavistock shot up at the very same time as Grenville reassumed command of the Royalist forces before Plymouth seems unlikely to be coincidence, for soon afterwards he is definitely known to have established a new, and even more fatal, place of confinement at Lydford Castle, a few miles away.

The very name of Lydford was enough to strike dread into West Country hearts at this time. A bleak, decaying hamlet, set on the edge of Dartmoor, Lydford was the seat of the notorious Stannary court, which dealt with cases involving the local tin-miners. 'Lydford law' was said to be particularly harsh and the Stannary judges were reputed to 'hang . . . [first] and sit in judgement after'.[21] Lydford was dominated by the squat, stone keep of the castle in which the Stannary prisoners were kept; a building described in the Henrician period as 'one of the most hainous, contagious and detestable [prisons] in the realm'.[22] Grenville's decision to turn this ill-famed place into a gaol for Roundhead prisoners may well reflect his malicious sense of humour.[23] Yet the main consideration which persuaded him to site a gaol here was undoubtedly the fact that the nature of the surrounding terrain would make it exceedingly difficult for prisoners to escape. It is hard not to suspect that Grenville may have had more sinister motives, too, for wishing his captives to be kept far from prying eyes. Immured in Lydford Castle, they could be starved and ill-treated with no one being any the wiser.

If Grenville hoped to conceal his crimes, he failed. By early 1645 horrifying descriptions of the prison at Lydford were appearing in the Parliamentary press, and during the post-war period a great deal of evidence came to light about Sir Richard's treatment of his unfortunate captives.[24] The minister who has already been quoted above recalled in the 1650s that the Royalists had 'starved' many prisoners at Lydford, just as they had done at Tavistock.[25] In addition, several former inmates of the castle survived to testify to what had been done there. One ex-Roundhead soldier deposed that he and several comrades had been thrown into Lydford Castle, where they endured 'unspeakable miseries, sixteen persons dying of famine in eight weeks'.[26]

The fate of some of the other victims was recalled by their surviving relatives. Particularly poignant was the petition of Widow Yolland of South Devon, which told how her husband, Walter, another Roundhead soldier, had been 'starved to death in the prison at Lydford by the inhumane dealing of the enemy'.[27] More damning still was the testimony of Roger Mallack, of Exeter, a former Royalist, who stated that his son-in-law, Simon Leach, had been 'taken upp by Sir Rich. Greenvill, and kept in prison in chaines, and so cruelly used that he died in 8 daies after I freed him'.[28] The accounts of the Parliamentary garrison of Plymouth contain several references to other prisoners of war who had died, like Leach, shortly after being ransomed from Lydford.[29] And Grenville's ultimate responsibility for these deaths is underlined by the statement of a local Royalist, who later deposed that he had been 'very industrious to convey reliefe to poore souldiers and others well affected to the parliament that lay in the Castle at Lytford by the commitment of Sir Richard Greenvile'.[30] Much more evidence in the same vein could be produced, from witnesses of every political persuasion; it is impossible to doubt that Grenville presided over one of the harshest and most loathsome of Civil War prisons.[31]

If Grenville's cruelties at Lydford have remained hidden until now, so has his role as a quasi-nationalist leader. All those who have written about Grenville have been aware that he was a Cornishman, of course, and that his local roots made him popular with the Cornish soldiers. Nevertheless, the precise role of 'Cornishness' in Sir Richard's wartime career has been neglected. Even the most perceptive of Grenville's biographers have only flitted around the edges of this subject. Mary Coate, herself a Cornishwoman, was the first to indicate that Grenville's nativity might have possessed a greater significance than had hitherto been accorded it. Writing in the 1930s she observed that one of his military schemes had been 'rooted in the particularism of a Cornishman'.[32] Thirty years later, M.D.G. Wanklyn took a similar line, claiming that Grenville had been a 'Cornish patriot'.[33] A.C. Miller, whose biography of Sir Richard appeared in 1979, was slightly more cautious, but acknowledged that some of Grenville's actions might be explicable in terms of 'local patriotism'.[34] All three historians assumed that Grenville himself had felt a genuine love for his native county then— and this may well have been so. Yet what really mattered was the use which he made of the local patriotism of others.

The strength of particularist sentiment in early modern Cornwall is too rarely appreciated. Unlike any other English county Cornwall was still a partially Celtic society on the eve of the Civil War. It had once been an independent state, it still possessed its own language and its inhabitants still retained a passionate sense of their own separate identity.[35] There was a long tradition of hostility between England and Cornwall. In 1497 and again in 1549, Cornish rebel armies had marched across the Tamar, motivated, at least in part, by a desire to resist the cultural and political hegemony of England.[36] And, as previous chapters have demonstrated, the decision of most Cornish people to back the King in 1642—this at a time when every other county in southern England had been secured for Parliament—should be viewed within the context of this ancient pattern of ethnic antagonism.[37]

From the moment that the Civil War began, the people of Cornwall behaved with a cohesiveness and an independence of purpose which was not to be found in any other English county. Having risen up *en masse* and ejected the few local supporters of Parliament from their county in 1642, they next raised a powerful army and used it to conquer most of South-west England for the King. It is important to recognize that this army was composed almost exclusively of Cornishmen and was frequently referred to, by observers on both sides, as 'the Cornish Army'.[38] That the Cornish soldiers were fiercely proud of this title, and wished to retain it even after their army had been merged with that of the Marquess of Hertford in June 1643 is revealed by the comment which an observer made about Hertford's formation later that year: 'this the Cornish would have styled "the Cornish Army"'.[39] As this remark suggests, the Cornishmen resented being lumped together with the King's English soldiers (not to mention his French and Irish mercenaries), and from mid-1643 onwards bitter disputes began to occur between the Cornish and non-Cornish units in the King's Western army. The Cornishmen, who were almost all foot soldiers, especially despised the Royalist cavalry, and fought them on several occasions.[40] Meanwhile, the heavy casualty rate suffered by Cornish soldiers during the first year of the war was causing disaffection to grow with the Royalist cause in Cornwall itself.[41]

This disaffection was contained, to a certain extent, by the praise which Charles I and his propagandists heaped upon 'the most loyal Cornish', and (perhaps more importantly) by a tacit agreement among the King's local commanders that 'foreign' Royalist troops should be kept out of the county.[42] The inhabitants of Cornwall did enjoy an unusual degree of autonomy during 1642–4, and to this extent they may well have felt that their support for Charles I had brought them tangible benefits. The alliance between the Cornish people and the King's military commanders was always an uneasy one, however, for, ultimately, the two groups had very different aims in view. True, the Cornish were fighting to defend the King and the established church, just as their English fellows were, but they were also fighting to defend the privileges, the institutions and the cultural traditions which made Cornwall unique.[43] Cornish royalism was a peculiar—and potentially very volatile—amalgam; and by autumn 1644 no one can have been more acutely aware of this fact than Sir Richard Grenville, who was not only a Cornishman himself, but had also travelled from one end of the county to the other during the previous summer.

Grenville had spent much of this time trying to drum up popular support, and he can scarcely have failed to listen to the views of ordinary people. It is tempting to suggest that it was in August 1644 that Grenville first came to appreciate the strength of Cornish particularist sentiment —and also came to see how he could use that sentiment to his own advantage. By putting himself at the head of the 'particularist' constituency, by portraying himself as a 'Cornish leader' with 'Cornish interests' at heart, he realized, he would be able to establish a formidable local power-base for himself, while at the same time working to maximize Cornish support of the King. It did not take Grenville long to put these ideas into effect, as a survey of his subsequent military career helps to show.

In September 1644 the victorious Royalist army began to return to the east. Grenville and his forces were in the advance guard, and the King ordered them to march into Devon with all speed. Yet Grenville chose to disobey this order. Instead, he marched to Saltash, the one town in Cornwall still held for Parliament, and ejected the Roundhead garrison there. This is significant, because it suggests that Sir Richard was already beginning to put Cornish interests above those of the Royalist war effort as a whole.[44] Twelve days later the King, apparently unperturbed by Grenville's disobedience, reappointed him as commander of the Royalist forces before Plymouth. The King and the bulk of his army then marched away to the east, leaving Grenville behind with just 800 men. At first it seemed that Grenville had been relegated to a relatively unimportant position—but within weeks of the King's departure the forces under Sir Richard's command began to grow at an exponential rate: by mid-November he was reported to have almost 4,000 Cornish soldiers under arms.[45] How had this phenomenal explosion in numbers occurred? To understand, we must again return to the question of Cornish particularism.

In September 1644 the confident expectation of the Royalist council of war had been that the Cornishmen who had flocked to the royal banner in such numbers during the summer would now march eastwards with the King's main army. But the Cornish themselves had other ideas. Rather than accompanying the King, most of them chose to remain behind and enlist themselves under Grenville instead. According to Hyde, Grenville actively encouraged the Cornishmen in their recalcitrance, advising them 'to stay for some time in Cornwall, and then to repair to him; as many of them did, for his forces suddenly increased; and the truth is, few of the Cornish marched outward'.[46] Naturally enough, the King's troops felt bitter about this desertion, and in November 1644 a Roundhead general was informed by one of his spies that the Cavaliers at Oxford 'exclaim against Cornwall as much as your forces do, and it is believed that now the King has armed them they will neither suffer his Majesty's nor . . . [Parliament's] forces to come amongst them'.[47] Rumours that the Cornish intended to hold themselves aloof from both sides were already beginning to circulate, therefore, and it is hard not to suspect that Grenville was capitalizing on (and possibly even exacerbating) this particularist mood.

Throughout the autumn of 1644 Grenville did everything he could to appeal to the ordinary inhabitants of Cornwall, ordering his officers to treat the common people with scrupulous fairness, while he himself extorted as much money as possible from the richer elements of local society in order to pay his troops. In this way he forged an alliance between himself and the ordinary people of Cornwall—those in whom the flame of 'Cornishness' burned most brightly—while at the same time treating many of the gentry and the middling sort—the most anglicized inhabitants of the county, in other words—with considerable harshness.[48] Grenville also took care to ensure that the army which he was raising to blockade Plymouth remained a predominantly 'Cornish' one. By December 1644 Grenville had recruited four new infantry regiments, each consisting of around 1,000 men (see Appendix 4 Nos 1, 2, 10, 14). Grouped together in a single brigade known as the 'New Cornish Tertia', these units were supported by auxiliary formations of Cornish horse.[49] Grenville could hardly have done more to emphasize the separate identity of the Cornish forces within the Royalist camp, and this surely contributed to the remarkable success of his recruitment. However the harsh exigencies of warfare were soon to threaten Sir Richard's achievement.

After some months spent in fruitless skirmishing before Plymouth, Grenville received orders from the King to march his forces off to the east, in order to besiege the Roundhead garrison of Taunton.[50] Sir Richard was most reluctant to agree to this command, and it is easy to see why. While the reduction of Plymouth could easily be presented to the Cornish people as a specifically 'Cornish' war-aim, one which would increase the security of the county as a whole, the reduction of far-away Taunton could not. Similarly, while it had been easy to present Grenville's force as a 'Cornish army', intended for the defence of Cornwall, as long as that force remained billeted along the Tamar, it would be much harder to do so once the men had been marched off to Somerset. Even so, the Royalist need for troops at Taunton was desperate, and Grenville was eventually forced to obey. In March he set off to the east with 3,000 soldiers, leaving other units behind to keep up the siege of Plymouth (see Map 4).[51]

When Grenville and his men arrived in Somerset they were at once ordered to join the main Royalist field army under Lord George Goring. Grenville flatly refused, telling the 15-year-old Prince of Wales—then the nominal commander of the Royalist forces in the West—that he had promised the civilian commissioners of Devon and Cornwall that he would not march a mile to the east of Taunton until that town had been reduced.[52] Grenville's refusal was obviously prompted by his own desire to retain an independent command. Yet he may also have realized that if he allowed his 'Cornish army' to become submerged within a much larger Royalist force, the Cornish soldiers would begin to feel that they were no longer fighting in their own interests.[53]

Soon afterwards Grenville's men advanced against Taunton, but before they could move into the assault, Sir Richard himself was badly wounded, receiving 'a brace of bullets' in the groin.[54] The Cornish soldiers were aroused to a quite unusual degree of savagery by this mischance: reportedly 'string[ing] up every man, woman and child who came voluntarily out of the garrison, and threaten[ing] to put all to the sword when they got within'.[55] The sheer depth of devotion which

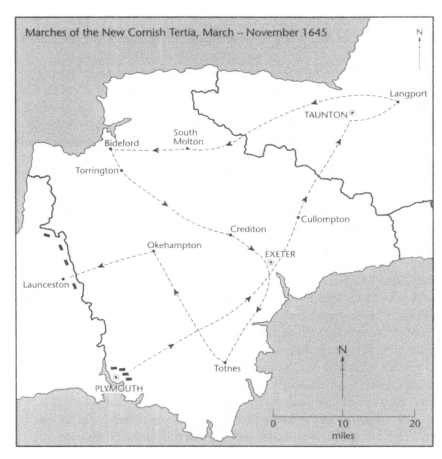

Map 4

Grenville inspired in his fellow-countrymen is made clear. The Prince's council were well aware of 'the strong feelings of loyalty which Grenville's subordinates had for him and their reluctance to serve under anyone else'.[56] Accordingly, they took considerable pains to ensure that Grenville, wounded as he was, should give his personal seal of approval to the man who had been chosen to replace him as commander of the Cornish troops: Sir John Berkeley, Governor of Exeter. These precautions had little effect. According to Hyde, who was himself a member of the council, Grenville pretended to approve of Berkeley's appointment, but, before leaving the Cornish encampment, secretly told his officers to ignore Sir John's commands.[57] Berkeley was soon reduced to despair by the attitude of the Cornish troops, complaining 'that those soldiers brought to Taunton by Greenevill every day mouldered away; and he had reason to believe it was by his [Grenville's] direction'.[58] When Berkeley was replaced by Lord Goring in July, moreover, the situation went from bad to worse.

The Cornish soldiers may not have liked Berkeley, but they positively hated Goring. According to Hyde, this was largely because of the actions of Goring himself:

> [who had] most unskilfully irreconciled [the Cornish troops] to him by continual neglects and contempts of them, as he would usually before Taunton, when he viewed his foot, clap an Irishman, or one of those soldiers who came out of Ireland, . . . on the shoulders, and tell him, in the hearing of the rest, that he was worth ten Cornish cowards.[59]

That a deep antipathy between Goring and the Cornish soldiers existed can hardly be doubted—Goring himself admitted as much[60]—yet Hyde's explanation of how these feelings had first come about seems a little simplistic. Whatever else he was, Goring was a skilful commander, and he would hardly have sought to antagonize troops as good as the Cornish had already proved themselves to be for no reason. If Goring did indeed make the sort of comments which Hyde alleges, it was probably because he had come to realize that the Cornish troops who had been put under his command were pursuing their own, narrowly Cornish, agenda, and thus—as far as the King's wider cause was concerned—that they were indeed less reliable than mercenary troops obtained from Ireland and elsewhere. It did not need hard words from

Lord Goring to make the Cornish troops mutinous and inclined to desert. By June 1645 they had already been marched far from Cornwall, deprived of their own country-born leader and lumped in with a disorderly, polyglot, 'foreign' army—one which largely consisted, moreover, of the very type of Royalist horsemen with whom they had so often quarrelled in the past. Under these circumstances, it is scarcely surprising that desertion became rife. By the beginning of July, less than a third of the Cornish troops whom Grenville had initially brought with him to Taunton were left.[61]

The Prince's council was seriously alarmed by the steady stream of desertions from the Cornish regiments, and Grenville, by now recovered from his wounds, was ordered to return to Taunton and take charge of them. Before he could do so, Parliament's New Model Army inflicted a shattering defeat upon Goring at Langport. Over the next few days the remnants of Goring's beaten army fled westwards in great disorder. During this helter-skelter retreat, the remaining Cornish troops deserted in droves: by 18 July Goring was complaining that 'most of Sir Richard Greenvill's men' had run away, and hinting darkly that Grenville himself, who was then in Cornwall, had 'sent for them'.[62]

Whether or not this was true, the Cornish element in Goring's army was now becoming very thin indeed. The initial desertions had been concentrated among the New Cornish, Grenville's own former regiments, but by late July the men of the 'Old Cornish' regiments—the veteran units which had been raised in Cornwall at the very beginning of the war—were beginning to disappear as well.[63] On 28 July Goring wrote to the council, bewailing Grenville's disaffection to the service. 'I pray God many of his owne Countrimen, especialy of his owne troopes, be not backward by his example', Goring added, going on to say that 'the Old Cornish slip away dayly, and to morrow morning some have appoynted a rendezvouz of theyre owne accord where I have sent for horse to meet them. I shall deale freely with yt.'[64] These final words are particularly significant. What Goring was admitting, in effect, was that those few Cornish soldiers who remained under his command were beginning to act as an independent force, and had arranged their own muster. Accordingly, Goring had ordered Royalist cavalry units to attend the proposed rendezvous and quash it. That he should have been reduced to such desperate measures indicates just how deep the split between the Cornish and the rest of the Royalist army had become.

In Cornwall itself, meanwhile, the arrival of the Prince of Wales and his court, who were fleeing from the Roundhead advance, had upped the particularist temperature. Prince Charles was not only Prince of Wales, he was also Duke of Cornwall, and from July 1645 onwards Royalist propagandists laid increasing emphasis on this fact in an attempt to maximize Cornish support for the Royalist cause. On 24 July Charles issued a proclamation styling himself 'Prince of Great Brytayne, [and] Duke of Cornwall' and he continued using this title thereafter.[65] As Philip Payton has shown, the Cornish had long cherished a dream that some sort of national resurgence or renaissance would one day take place under 'a duke of Cornwall', so the Royalist decision to play on the Prince's title was nicely calculated to appeal to particularist hopes.[66] Grenville may well have encouraged the Prince in this policy: certainly he is known to have met him at Liskeard in July.[67] Soon afterwards, Grenville was appointed overall commander of the Cornish trained bands, or county militia—a clear acknowledgement of the perceived extent of his influence over his fellow countrymen—and thereafter he and the Prince seem to have worked together to appeal to the 'particularist constituency'.[68]

The Parliamentary advance into the West Country slowed down in summer 1645, giving the Royalists a chance to draw breath. Grenville spent most of this time in drawing together 'the Cornish train-bands and those other [Cornish] soldiers who had run from their colours, neither of which', Hyde acknowledged, 'would march without [him]'.[69] At the same time, he did his best to ensure that all 'foreign' Royalist units were kept out of Cornwall.[70] When the New Model Army finally moved into East Devon in October, Grenville moved to counter the enemy by leading the Cornish trained bands across the Tamar and stationing them at Okehampton. He then set off to fetch the remaining soldiers of the New Cornish Tertia, who had by now retreated into South Devon (see Map 4). Sir Richard and his old 'Cornish commanders' were finally reunited at Totnes, where they held a celebratory feast to mark the occasion, and next day Grenville marched the Tertia back to join the trained bands at Okehampton. Once again, Grenville had succeeded in pulling together an exclusively Cornish army—but his triumph was not to last.[71]

The trained bands had agreed to serve in Devon only for a month and in November they returned to Cornwall.[72] Grenville was prepared for this—he had enough regular troops to maintain his position at Okehampton without them—but what he was not prepared for was the trouble which was about to break out in his rear. Following the renewal of the Parliamentary advance, large bodies of disorderly Royalist cavalrymen had begun to retreat to the west. Grenville (significantly, in the light of his assumed role as defender of Cornwall) had given orders that these men were not to be allowed to cross the Tamar. His commands were regarded with contempt by Lord Goring's men, however, and fierce disputes between Grenville's men and the cavalry began to occur.[73] Around 20 November the Parliamentary general Fairfax reported back to the House of Commons with scarcely disguised glee:

> On Monday last a Lieutenant of the Enemies horse quarrelling with the Cornish foot in Torrington, the dispute grew so hot that his horse was shot under him by the said Cornish, and their quarrel is growne so high, that at Bridgerule Bridge upon Tamar, the countrey people keep a guard, and have barricaded the wayes at divers passes . . . to prevent Goring's men from coming in upon them . . . [and] all the Cornish souldiers that ran away . . . joyne with the countrey in opposing them.[74]

As Fairfax's words make clear, the presence of Goring's Horse had sparked off a major insurrection in North-east Cornwall, one in which Cornish civilians, deserters and regular troops had all taken part. Sir Richard's response to this rebellion was prompt—and instructive. On 21 November, he left Okehampton and marched, with all his forces, back to Launceston. Once arrived here, he effectively allied himself with the insurrectionists, stationing the New Cornish regiments along the Tamar, and issuing them with instructions to keep all 'foreign troops' out of the county.[75] Grenville and his supporters were now at virtual war with Goring's Horse, and it is hardly surprising that the Prince summoned Sir Richard to Truro to explain his actions.[76]

By this time, Grenville had clearly decided that the Royalist position in the West could be saved only through an open appeal to Cornish particularist sentiment, and, in a letter written on 27 November, he attempted to gain the Prince's support for an extraordinary plan, one which, if it had been carried out, would effectively have created a semi-independent Cornwall. According to Hyde, Grenville's advice to the Prince was that 'his Highness should send to the Parliament for a treaty, and should offer, if he [i.e. the Prince] might [keep possession of] . . . his duchy of Cornwall . . . that he would not attempt any thing upon [the Parliament's forces]', 'in plain English, to sit still a neuter between the King and the Parliament'.[77] Had we only Hyde's word to rely upon, we might well be inclined to doubt whether even Grenville would have come up with such a controversial scheme as this. Yet a copy of the original letter survives, and this makes it clear that Grenville's proposals were every bit as radical as Hyde suggests.[78]

Grenville began by lamenting the miseries which the war had brought upon his native county: 'we may too truly say', he observed, that 'his Majesty hath no entire county in obedience, but poor little Cornwall, and that too in a sad condition by the miserable accidents of war, under which it hath long groaned'. There was little hope of Cornwall being able to hold out alone for much longer, Grenville went on, and his advice to the Prince was therefore to make a separate peace with Parliament. He should offer to suspend hostilities, on condition that Parliament agreed to leave those areas of the West Country still held by Royalist forces (i.e. Cornwall and West Devon) under his control. Once this autonomous zone had been created, the Prince should be allowed to live off the revenues of his local estates, while his subjects should 'enjoy a free trade unto . . . the parts beyond the seas without disturbance'.[79] This latter clause suggests that Grenville envisaged a permanent existence for the petty statelet which he was proposing. It is clear, too, that he expected his scheme to be popular with the Cornish people. If the Prince took his advice, Grenville asserted, 10,000 men could be raised at once. And even if 'the proposed way of treating produce not its desired success', he added:

> yet the whole county seeing . . . that his Highness's labour tends only to the preservation of these parts from utter ruin and destruction: I am most confident, that upon a general meeting of the chief gentry of this country . . . the whole body of this country, then finding how far the preservation of their persons and estates are concerned, will unanimously join in the defence thereof.[80]

The Prince's councillors were horrified by this call to establish a semi-independent Cornish state and they refused to consider Sir Richard's scheme. Yet the contents of Grenville's letter soon became public knowledge, and, as he himself admitted, 'occasioned a strange rumour in the world'.[81] To the ordinary Cornish soldiers, by now staring defeat in the face, Grenville's plan must have seemed very attractive. Not only did it hold out the chance of peace, but also of a revived Cornish nationhood—that tantalizing chimera which had for so long haunted local people's dreams. Grenville's proposal was widely discussed and even Roundhead propagandists caught the echoes. 'This I told you would be . . . [the Royalists'] last refuge', sneered one, 'and here now they take up station, as if (when all else failed) they meant to make a petty kingdome of it, and erect a new monarchie . . . At Pendennis or St Michael's Mount', he went on, warming to his theme, 'its but imagining a man were at Whitehall and St James Park. The tin-mines may serve for silver . . . and a Crown too [be] made . . . And all this may be done with a strong phantasie.'[82]

To London newswriters, the idea of Cornish independence seemed laughable, a mere 'phantasie', but to Grenville—desperately trying to keep back the Parliamentarians while simultaneously attempting to bolster his own position within the Royalist hierarchy—'playing the Cornish card' had become more important than ever before. Towards the middle of December 1645, Sir Richard sent:

> several letters to the gentlemen of the county to meet him at Lanson [i.e. Launceston] . . . in which he desired [them] to bring as many . . . of ability as [they] could . . . for that he intended to communicate to them some propositions which he had formerly preferred to the Prince, and though they were not hearkened to there, he believed [they] would be very acceptable to his countrymen of Cornwall.[83]

Having failed to persuade the Prince's council of the merits of his 'independence' scheme, in other words, Grenville was now proposing to appeal over the councillors' heads to the Cornish people themselves. It was a dangerous game, but before Grenville could proceed any further in it, his plans were overtaken by events.[84]

Towards the end of December, it was decided that the Prince should advance against the Roundhead army in person, at the head of the Cornish troops.[85] Grenville accordingly crossed over the Tamar with his own New Cornish regiments and the Cornish trained bands. On 27 December the Prince joined him at Tavistock with more Cornish troops, thus creating a substantial army of some 3–4,000 foot.[86] (Goring's cavalry and the other non-Cornish units were stationed well away to the east, between the Prince and the enemy.) For a third time, then, an almost exclusively Cornish army had been gathered together—and by this crucial juncture of the war, even the Prince's servants were prepared to play on the particularist sentiment which Grenville had used so successfully in the past. It was common practice during the Civil War for sermons to be delivered to the assembled troops on the eve of battle and the text of one such sermon—almost certainly delivered to the Cornish troops at Tavistock in January 1646—has fortunately survived. Written by Lionel Gatford, one of the clergymen in the Prince's entourage, this document is of the highest interest.[87]

Rather unusually for Royalist propaganda, Gatford's words were clearly intended for the humble soldiers as well as the gentlemen officers; the sermon is addressed 'to the valiant and loyall Cornish-men of all rankes and degrees whatsoever'. 'It is acknowledged to your eternall honour, O ye noble Cornwallians', Gatford began, 'that you of this County, both Gentry and Commonalty, have in all these unnaturall warres hitherto behaved yourselves gallantly and bravely, like stout men, loyall subjects and good Christians.' This service would not go unrequited, Gatford declared, adding that 'no doubt, if ever it please God to reestablish the King in his royall throne, some Royal decree or publike act will be established by him . . . for the granting of more than ordinary priviledges and immunities to you and yours, who have done such extraordinary service'.[88] Gatford was careful not to be specific about exactly what form these privileges might take, but his suggestion that special rights would be accorded to all Cornishmen and their families after the war may well have stirred particularist hopes, especially in the light of the 'independence' scheme which Grenville had already mooted. That this was Gatford's aim is strongly suggested by a later passage, in which he declared that, even if the other 'tribes' of England fell away, the Cornish should remain loyal:

> [for] it was twice the valiant loyaltie of the tribe of Judah . . . to cleave to their King, when all the other tribes of Israel . . . revolted from him . . . and this loyaltie of theirs was so well accepted by God, that the tribe of Judah continued a Kingdome and remained in their own land above an hundred yeares after . . . the Kingdome of the ten tribes was destroyed.[89]

What would Gatford's auditors have made of this intriguing passage? On the surface it appears to be an appeal for loyalty and nothing more.

Yet when one considers the context in which the preacher's words were delivered, they take on a new significance. By referring to the Cornish people as a 'tribe', and making a specific comparison between them and the tribe of Judah—who for their loyalty were allowed to remain independent, 'in their own land', for over 100 years—Gatford was surely appealing to the old Cornish sense of difference, and to the old Cornish desire for autonomy. If the Cornish people remained loyal to Charles I, Gatford's words seemed to suggest, then Cornwall's position as a semi-autonomous entity within the wider British state would be secured. The preacher could not afford to make this point explicit, of course—he must have known that he was playing with fire—but there can be little doubt that the sermon was specifically designed to appeal to Cornish nationalist sentiment.

This is nowhere made more clear than in the final peroration, where Gatford not only cited the words of Michael of Cornwall, the thirteenth-century poet who had defended his country against English slurs, but also delivered an explicitly nationalist call to arms.[90] 'You have your naturall-borne Duke, the Illustrious Prince Charles, the Duke of Cornwall to goe in and out before you', Gatford thundered:

> and his very name presages some more than ordinary greatness of gallant achievements: you have under him *your own Country-borne* Lieutenant Generall, valiant and vigilant Sir Richard Greenvill, to conduct and lead you . . . you have also divers other subordinate, but approvedly couragious and expert commanders and officers, together with many old thoroughly tryed common souldiers *of your own flesh and blood* to assist and joyne with you, and there is no small incouragement in that.[91]

Gatford's sermon should probably be seen as the climax of the Royalist campaign to harness Cornish particularist sentiment to the King's cause. His words can only have heightened the atmosphere of fevered nationalism which had already been engendered by Grenville and others, and, under the spur of such heady rhetoric, the morale of the Cornish troops briefly revived. A Roundhead report of 6 January stated that:

> the Prince himselfe . . . is come to Tavestocke with whome the Cornish, having mustered all the Forces that possibly they can draw

together, are resolved to live and dye, and to manifest their ingagement, and more particular interest in him, as often as their discourse is of him, they call him not the Prince but altogether the Duke of Cornwall.[92]

That the troops should have chosen to refer to the Prince by this title is significant, for it tends to confirm that, at this moment of supreme crisis, the old Cornish dream of a national revival, under Cornwall's own duke, had resurfaced amongst the common people.

Before the Prince could capitalize on this swelling tide of Cornish feeling, however, the Parliamentarians launched a decisive assault. On 8 January Goring's cavalry were attacked and routed, forcing the Prince to retreat across the Tamar. Chaos at once began to spread through the Royalist ranks, and as Goring's Horse again tried to make their way into Cornwall, they were resisted for a second time by Grenville's soldiers. The Royalist commanders eventually managed to stabilize the situation by assigning Grenville's men to the Cornish side of the Tamar and ordering the cavalry to remain in Devon.[93] Desperate efforts were then made to resume the advance, but Grenville refused to march. On 16 January he tendered his resignation as Lieutenant-General, stating that 'he should be more serviceable to the Prince's affairs, if he were employed in recruiting the army, and guarding the passes of Cornwall'.[94]

Needless to say, the Prince's council viewed this plan with deep suspicion. 'It plainly appeared now', Hyde later recalled:

> that [Grenville's] drift was to stay behind, and command Cornwall, with which, considering the premises, the Prince thought he had no reason to trust him . . . [for] it was very evident, if he [Grenville] were at liberty, and the army marched out of Cornwall, he would have put himself in the head of all the discontented party, and . . . endeavoured to have hindered their retreat back into Cornwall, upon what occasion soever, and for the present that he would underhand have kept many from marching with the army, upon the senseless pretence of defending their own country.[95]

Such a scheme may have seemed 'senseless' to Hyde, but it would not have seemed so to the Cornish soldiers: had Grenville taken up his position behind the River Tamar, it is hard to doubt that many of them would have joined him. Exactly what was going through Grenville's mind at this time is impossible to say. Nevertheless, Hyde clearly believed that Sir Richard meant to wait until the Royalist army had advanced into Devon, and then to withdraw Cornwall from the war—and in the light of Grenville's activities during late 1645 these suspicions do not seem impossibly far-fetched. Grenville had already indicated that, in his opinion, the war could no longer be won and that the only way to salvage something from the wreckage was to establish Cornwall as an autonomous zone. He and his Cornish troops were already at daggers drawn with the rest of the Royalist army, moreover, and it would not have taken much to turn this deep fracture within the Royalist camp into a formal split. Had Grenville been able to draw Prince Charles to his side—and he had many supporters in the Prince's household[96]; had he been able to exploit the Duke's presence and the threat of imminent invasion to ignite the latent Cornish desire for autonomy, he really might have been able to achieve some sort of Cornish U.D.I.

Whether or not Grenville was really planning such a bold scheme, the Prince's council were by now convinced that he was dangerous and on 19–20 January, he was dismissed from his military commands and imprisoned.[97] At once a storm of protest arose. Thousands of Cornish soldiers petitioned for Sir Richard's release, and there were even whispers of a rebellion on his behalf. He had only to give the word, one of Grenville's officers whispered to him at the time of his arrest, 'the troops . . . would stand by him and follow wherever he led'.[98] Grenville refused to countenance such a step, however, and he ordered his men to obey the Prince's commands. Sir Richard has been praised by his biographers for the restraint which he displayed on this occasion,[99] but it is hard to see what else he could have done. The Prince had made it perfectly clear that he sided with his councillors, rather than with Grenville[100]—and without the support of the Prince, any attempt to establish Cornwall as an autonomous zone was doomed to failure: the Parliamentarians would never have considered negotiating with Grenville alone.

Grenville's arrest appeared to bring all hopes of a separate peace for Cornwall to an end, and following his removal from command, the Cornish troops visibly lost heart.[101] Scores more deserted over the next few weeks, and although many Cornishmen took part in the battle of Torrington in February, this was the last time that they were brought together to fight in significant numbers. After the battle had ended in yet another defeat for the King's commanders, the rapacious Royalist cavalry again fled westwards, and this time there was nowhere else for them to go but Cornwall. Within days 4–5,000 demoralized Royalist horsemen had established themselves in the county—and from this moment onwards, the Cornish people effectively abandoned the King's cause. Whatever they did now, their cherished autonomy had been lost, and it was surely better to surrender to the well-disciplined army of Parliament than to submit to occupation by the 'wicked, beaten' (and no less 'foreign') army of Lord Goring. Thousands of Cornish soldiers laid down their arms during February and in March the Royalist Horse surrendered too. The Prince and Grenville, meanwhile, had both fled abroad.[102] The Civil War in the West was over, and so, to all intents and purposes, were the hopes of Cornish semi-independence which 'Skellum Grenville' had so briefly and tantalizingly conjured up.

If this re-examination of Sir Richard Grenville's wartime career has shed some new light on the man himself, it has also helped to broaden our understanding of the Civil War as a whole, for it has emphasized the extent to which the conflict in the far South-west possessed an ethnic, one might even say a 'British', dimension. As Mary Coate once observed, the 'apparent Royalism' of the Cornish people had in fact concealed 'something more primitive'[103] and from the moment the war broke out the tensions between 'Cornishness' and royalism were clearly apparent. As the conflict dragged on, moreover—and partly as a result of Grenville's machinations—these tensions became much more serious. By August 1645, there were, in effect, two separate Royalist armies in the South-west: the Royalist army proper, under Lord Goring, which was fighting in defence of the King, and the Cornish forces, under Grenville, which were fighting as much in defence of Cornwall as anything else. Despite Goring's desperate pleas for assistance, the Cornish consistently refused to join forces with him during late 1645, and this in itself undoubtedly helps to explain why the Royalists were unable to put up an effective resistance to the New Model Army.[104]

* * *

In October 1645 an Exeter Royalist bewailed the recalcitrance of the Cornish troops and swore that, if they could not display what he termed an 'ordinary allegiance', they should all be hanged.[105] His comment implies a dim realization that the Cornishmen's commitment to the King's cause was extraordinary, unusual, unlike his own. Yet at the same time it implies that, like so many contemporary English observers (and so many later English historians) he was unable to comprehend the precise nature of the divergence which existed between English Royalists like himself and the King's Cornish soldiers. It was Grenville's great good fortune that he was not only able to appreciate this ideological division, but also to exploit it to the hilt—and therein lies the secret of the extraordinary hold which he possessed over his men. In recent years scholars have been anxious to stress the cultural diversity of the British Isles during the early modern period and to argue that the conflict of the 1640s was not just an 'English Civil War', but a 'war of three kingdoms', or even of four nations.[106] Sir Richard Grenville's story reveals that the true picture was more complicated still. Perhaps it is time to start thinking in terms of a 'war of five peoples': English, Irish, Scottish, Welsh—and Cornish.

6

'The Gear Rout'

The Cornish Rising of 1648 and the Second Civil War[1]

In July 1648 John Bond, Master of the Savoy, delivered a thanksgiving sermon to the House of Commons, in which he praised God for the series of victories that the New Model Army had recently won in many parts of England and Wales. The tangled, multi-layered conflict known to posterity as the Second Civil War was still raging, rebel forces were holding out in Colchester, and the Scottish army of the Engagement was marching south, but Bond—anxious to buoy up the Army's allies and to cast down the spirits of its enemies—did everything he could to emphasize the universality of the recent successes. 'The garment of gladnesse reacheth all over . . . the Land', he declaimed, 'the robe [of victory] reacheth from . . . Northumberland in the North, to . . . Sussex in the South . . . [and] from Dover . . . in the East, to Pensands, the utmost part of Cornwall, in the West.' Bond's reference to Penzance would have struck a chord with many of his listeners, for accounts of an insurgent defeat in the little Cornish town had been read out in the House some weeks before.[2] Yet from that day to this, the rising at Penzance, and indeed the entire 'Western dimension' of the Second Civil War, have been largely forgotten.

Most general histories of the period pass over the Cornish insurrection of May 1648 in silence, or in a sentence or two at best.[3] Even Robert Ashton, whose magisterial study of the Second Civil War has done so much to enhance our understanding of the conflict, has little to say about events in Cornwall,[4] and consideration of the rising has so far been left to local historians.[5] This is surprising, partly because the revolt was an important episode in its own right, but also because an

113

analysis of its causes can contribute much to the ongoing debate about the nature of the Second Civil War. Many scholars continue to see that conflict as 'a revolt of the provinces', as a series of essentially localist insurrections, born out of the exasperation that the inhabitants of allegedly inward-looking 'county communities' had felt at unprecedented central interference in their affairs.[6] Others stress the ideological dimensions of the risings, and point to the central role of Royalist activists in planning and directing them.[7] Implicit in both approaches is the belief that what went on in each of the revolts of 1648 was much the same. What has never been considered before is the possibility that, in Cornwall and Wales at least, the Second Civil War may have possessed a specifically ethnic undertow, and that the insurrections in these areas should be viewed through a 'British', rather than a purely English, lens. This chapter will argue that, while the Cornish revolt exhibited many of the same characteristics as those that took place elsewhere, it also possessed a dynamic of its own, and was, in many ways, distinct. To fully understand the events of 1648, it will be suggested, we need to focus carefully on the dissonance that existed between the voices of the various rebel groups.

I

In January 1648 England's Parliamentary rulers faced troubles on every hand. The Scots were planning to invade, Royalist irreconcilables were stirring, and the recent decision to break off negotiations with the captive Charles I had caused the old division in the Parliamentary ranks between 'presbyterians' and 'independents' to resurface. Disturbances were widely anticipated and, at Parliament's direction, the Lord General of the New Model Army, Sir Thomas Fairfax, had begun to provide for the security of the realm. Military command of the West Country—an especially sensitive region—was entrusted to one of Fairfax's most reliable officers, Colonel Sir Hardress Waller. Sir Hardress had family connections in Devon and had spent the winter of 1645–6 campaigning there.[8] He was well qualified to assume the role of military overlord in the West, therefore, and the forces that had been assigned to him were comparatively strong.[9]

Nevertheless, Waller faced a daunting task. Cornwall was notoriously disaffected, while Devon, too, contained many 'malignant' pockets.[10] Opposition to fiscal demands was growing, particularly in Devon, which felt itself to be heavily over-taxed, and even as Waller marched into the county a petition against free-quarter and assessment was circulating.[11] More threatening still was the disaffection among the local garrison troops. In late 1647 Parliament, desperate to reduce the spiralling cost of soldiers' wages, had ordered that all superfluous (or 'supernumerary') troops across the kingdom should be disbanded, and given two months' pay towards their arrears. The soldiers of the western garrisons— including Plymouth in Devon and Pendennis Castle in Cornwall—were offered only half this amount. Enraged, they resolved neither to disband nor to hand over their garrisons until the money which was owing to them had been paid.[12] Confronted with this multiplicity of problems, Sir Hardress can hardly have been cheered by his reception at Exeter, the regional capital. The citizens, already burdened with a permanent garrison, were not prepared to support Waller's men as well, and they made bitter representations to Parliament. Anxious to placate local opinion, Waller ordered most of his men to seek quarter elsewhere.[13] Plymouth was clearly out of the question—the angry garrison had refused point-blank to admit any of Waller's troops[14]—so Sir Hardress quartered his men in the local market towns instead. Over the next few weeks he did what he could to defuse the simmering tension in his western fiefdom. Yet across the Bristol Channel rebellion was already at hand.

At Pembroke Castle in South Wales the governor, John Poyer, had long been growing disenchanted with his political masters, and when, in early 1648, he was ordered to disband his garrison and hand the castle over to another officer, he refused to obey. Instead, Poyer bade defiance to the forces that had been sent to replace him, and demanded that his arrears be paid in full. When these demands were not met, Poyer sallied out of the castle and routed the troops of his putative successor. In the wake of the mutineers' success, other discontented soldiers came flocking in to join them, together with hundreds of local countrymen. By late March much of South Wales was up in arms—and many believed that Cornwall would soon follow.[15] On 26 March it was reported that 'men . . . much fear the West', while the Venetian Ambassador went so far as to aver that 'the people of Wales *and Cornwall* are rising in favour of the King'.[16] He exaggerated, but malcontents were certainly plotting in the South-west—and in Cornwall, as in Wales, mutiny had broken out among the local garrison troops.[17]

The trouble centered on Pendennis Castle, where Colonel Richard

Fortescue and his men were refusing to disband until they had been paid their arrears. According to one source, the mutiny began when the garrison soldiers seized on the 'commissioners appoynted to pay and discharge them⸴ . . . and brought them prisoners into the Castle'. The kidnapping of civilian commissioners was a tactic that had often been employed by mutinous soldiers before,[18] but Fortescue's refusal to give up the castle to Fairfax's appointee seemed more ominous. One source suggested that his defiance had been directly inspired by Poyer's example, while another claimed that the discontented soldiers in Cornwall were 'holding out a hand to the governor of Pembroke'.[19] Hints of a connection between Fortescue and Poyer can hardly have failed to alarm MPs, and they ordered Fairfax to 'take speedy and effective care for disbanding the forces . . . at Pendennis'. Fortescue remained defiant, and on 13 April he sent a letter and a 'representation' to Parliament.[20]

For a week affairs in Cornwall hung in the balance. One gleeful Royalist averred that 'Pendennis hath declared against Parliament and Hardress Waller lyes at a distance, unwilling to provoke the Cornish who are well-affected'.[21] Royalist excitement was understandable: had military mutiny and civilian discontent come together in Cornwall as they had already done in Wales, the central regime would have faced a formidable challenge. Fortunately for Parliament, Fortescue was prepared to come to terms; his letter agreed to hand over Pendennis, providing that certain conditions were met. The Colonel's missive was read out to the House on 18 April, after which it was ordered that his arrears should be paid, that he should be awarded a gratuity, and that he should be especially recommended to Fairfax 'for some employment'. The sense of relief was palpable, and Cromwell himself was given the task of finding Fortescue a suitable military post.[22]

Whatever the mood may have been in London, the officer in charge of negotiations on the ground, Colonel Robert Bennett, was clearly taking nothing for granted until the castle had been given up. Bennett, who had performed sterling service for Parliament during 1642–6, was the governor of St Michael's Mount and the fort known as 'the Dennis', near Helford. He was also a fervent supporter of the Army and an assiduous record-keeper: his surviving papers throw much new light on the Second Civil War in the West.[23] By dint of frantic borrowing Bennett had managed to accumulate enough money to pay four months' arrears to the soldiers in Pendennis, and when Fortescue's men finally marched out of the castle on 29 April everything passed off peaceably. Bennett clearly felt that the mutineers had taken advantage of him, however, for he complained in his private accounts that he had been forced to pay several former soldiers at officers' rates. Significantly, Bennett had dared not expostulate, owing to 'the high mutiny of the soldiers' and 'the ill being of the people'.[24] Clearly, fears of a conjunction between the discontented Cornish populace and the mutineers persisted.

Nevertheless, with Fortescue's men disbanded and a reliable garrison installed in Pendennis, Sir Hardress had good reason to believe that he had averted the threat of trouble in Cornwall. The news from Wales also appeared to be good. Writing from Bodmin on 2 May, Waller informed Bennett that 'it is thought Poyer is beaten, and his forces nothing to what was reported'.[25] Encouraged by this (false) intelligence, Waller crossed back into Devon, and rejoined his infantry at Tavistock, already 'resolving . . . to looke eastward'. On 6 May Lieutenant-Colonel Edward Salmon left Tavistock for Exeter, at the head of six companies of Waller's foot.[26] Before Sir Hardress could follow, storm-clouds began to gather across the Tamar. Later that day, Waller was forced to go to Saltash to discuss a message from the Sheriff of Cornwall, Edward Herle, concerning the activities of 'divers malignant gentlemen'. Herle had long been keeping a watchful eye on these men, and now—'by reason of the greate resorte that was made unto them & their late fixing of Armes'— he feared that they 'speedely meant to desturbe the peace of the county'. Waller promptly issued warrants for the plotters' arrest, and within a week several had been apprehended. So anxious did the Parliamentarian administrators of Cornwall remain, however, that they dared not lodge their prisoners locally but prepared to send them up to London instead, lest their presence 'hazard the peace of the county here'.[27]

As if Waller did not have enough to contend with in Cornwall, worrying intelligence now reached him from Exeter, where Salmon had been refused permission to quarter his troops. The town governors, still smarting from their last experience of free-quarter, not only gave Salmon 'very ill words', but told him that if Fairfax himself

> had come as . . . [he] did they would have kept him out. And supposeing it not too late, the Mayor did with all speade send to shutt the gates, according to which command three were immediately shutt, but the soldiers being neare, the shutting of the fourth gate was prevented, at which they marcht in.

The soldiers may have got into the city, but the inhabitants still refused to admit them to their houses, prompting Salmon to lament that 'hee should not be able to quarter the souldiers without putting the Towne in Blood'.[28] Seriously alarmed, Waller now rode to Exeter himself, eventually arriving on 12 May, by which time the Chamber had begun to back down and to make arrangements for quartering Salmon's men. The citizens remained deeply resentful, however, and again complained to Parliament.[29] Meanwhile, far to the west, the long-anticipated storm was about to break.

II

On 16 May the deliberations of the Cornish county committee (the group of Parliamentarian gentlemen who administered local affairs) were interrupted at Launceston by the arrival of a merchant named Anthony Gubbs, who had come to warn them of an imminent rising in his home town of Penzance. The committee clearly took Gubbs's words with a pinch of salt, for soon afterwards he set off disconsolately for home again. That very night, insurgent forces began to rise in the countryside around Penzance, while in the nearby town of Helston many of the inhabitants 'vapoured most terribly' against friends of the Parliament.[30] By dawn a substantial rebel force was assembled in Penzance, and from here the insurgents moved off to confront the garrison at St Michael's Mount, a couple of miles to the east (see Map 5). The rebels' initial intention was to surprise the Mount, but the garrison had been informed of their approach. By the time the insurgents arrived at the adjoining town of Market Jew, the castle had been put in a state of defence. Shortly afterwards, John St Aubyn of Clowance and two other Parliamentarian gentlemen rode into Market Jew (Marazion) to 'parley' with the insurrectionists.

St Aubyn had already sent a messenger hurrying to the east for reinforcements, and was clearly playing for time. He managed to get the meeting postponed until Saturday and the rebels returned to Penzance.[31] Thus it was that when Anthony Gubbs finally arrived home he found his worst fears had been realized, and that the local malcontents were now 'with many hundred more grow[ne] to a head, & . . . lodged in our towne'. Wheeling about, Gubbs made his way to nearby St Ives where his son, Joseph, lived and told him to ride to Waller for help. Gubbs then returned to Penzance, where he was seized by the insurgents, and

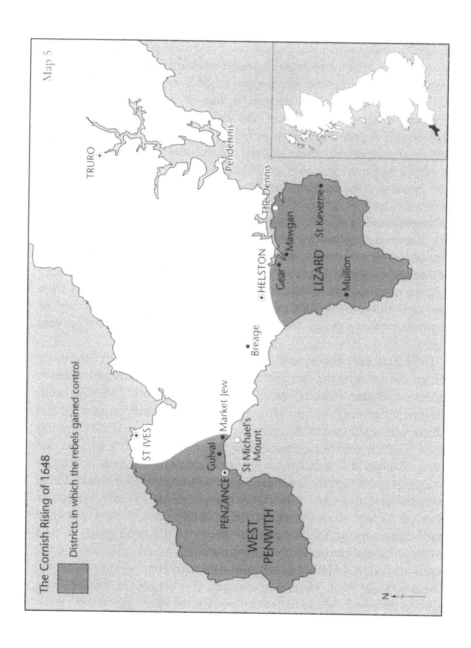

The Cornish Rising of 1648

Districts in which the rebels gained control

Map 5

TRURO

Pendennis

The Dennis

HELSTON
Gear
Mawgan
St Keverne
LIZARD
Mullion

Breage

ST IVES

Guival
Market Jew
St Michael's
Mount
PENZANCE
WEST
PENWITH

N

his goods confiscated 'for the supplie of ther rebellion'. Soon afterwards the rebels demanded that Gubbs give them £300, and, when he refused to comply, pronounced sentence of death on the terrified merchant.[32]

While Gubbs languished in prison, the insurgents established a gunpowder magazine in the market-place and triumphantly beat up their drums.[33] The rebels had high hopes of assistance from neighbouring towns at this point, and the people of St Ives were thought to be particularly sympathetic. Significantly, one of the first reports of the rebellion to appear in London had claimed that 'the disaffected to Parliament [are] risen in *two* places in Cornwell, viz, at Pensance, and St Ives'.[34] The claim that there had been a full-scale rising in St Ives was incorrect, but it is clear that local Parliamentarians regarded the town with extreme distrust, for on 19 May, St Aubyn rode across rebel-held territory to St Ives, in order 'to quiet them [there] who were suspected to have a hand in the confederacy'. It is probable that the rebels were also expecting assistance from the market town of Helston, where serious unrest had already manifested itself, but here too they were to be disappointed. On Thursday evening a party of thirty Parliamentarian soldiers marched into Helston on their way to the Mount, and were prevailed upon by a local supporter to stay, thus pre-empting an insurrection that a group of disaffected townsmen had planned for that night.[35]

The rebels' failure to secure St Ives and Helston was made all the more serious for them by the fact that their enemies had now begun to react. In Devon, Waller—clearly rattled—had issued a call on 17 May for 'well-affected volunteers' to join him, and soon afterwards he crossed the Tamar with a substantial force.[36] Yet Waller's men would take time to arrive, and the one hope of crushing the rebellion swiftly lay with the scattered units that had already been stationed in Cornwall when the trouble began. Chief among these were two troops of Horse that Waller had sent into Cornwall earlier that year, and the County Troop (or 'Sheriff's Troop') under Edward Herle.[37] Within days, all three units had made their way into the West, where they joined a small group of foot soldiers under Colonel Bennett and prepared to advance against the rebels. On 20 May Herle and Bennett arrived in Helston with some 400 Horse and 120 Foot. That same evening, they set off for Breage, a few miles to the north, where they quartered for the night. Herle was clearly anxious to engage the rebels as quickly as possible, and by 9 p.m. on the following day he had advanced with his cavalry as far as Mr Harris' house at Kenegy, just a mile or two east of Penzance. From here he sent an anxious message to Bennett (whose men had got no further than the Mount) urging him to hurry and stressing the need to procure intelligence from the rebel camp. The best way of gaining such information, Herle suggested, would be to employ 'a townsman [of Market Jew] or souldier of the Mount. . . who may pretend to run away to them, and to stay with them till he can learne their strength and resolucions'.[38]

If any Parliamentarian spy did make his way into Penzance that night, he would have found that the rebels' numbers were still swelling. The insurgent leaders had sent out 'their warrants to the Westerne Parishes . . . to raise men' and fresh recruits had been coming into the town from the surrounding countryside all day, bringing arms and ammunition with them. Even after Herle arrived at Kenegy, reinforcements continued to come in to the rebels, including a group of nine men who arrived in Penzance from Towednack on the morning of 22 May.[39] By noon that day the rebel force had grown to between 300 and 500 men.[40] The insurgents were confident of still further accretions of strength, more-over, for, having learned of Herle's advance, they had despatched an emissary to the Lizard peninsula, 20 miles to the south, in order to bring the people of that district to their assistance. The individual charged with this mission, Captain Thomas Pike, had set off from Penzance by boat that morning, and he 'landed upon the sand by the Looe [Bar]' near Porth Leven a few hours later. From here Pike made his way 'unto the South to raise them'—and the speed with which local men rallied to him suggests that the insurgents of the Lizard were following a pre-laid plan. According to the Parliamentarians, 'their plot was to [march north and] come into the reare of our forces that evening'.[41]

As the rebellion caught fire in the south, events were rapidly moving to a climax in the north, where Bennett and Herle were preparing to advance on Penzance. The insurgents had already erected makeshift fortifications around the town, and now they hastened to man these defences; a witness later deposed that one Robert Pascow had 'led on a p[ar]tye of musketers to lyne the Hedges against the Parliament forces'. Bennett cannot have relished the prospect of carrying out an assault against prepared positions, and he summoned the insurgents to surrender. Those within the town—buoyed up by the hope that their allies would at any moment fall upon Bennett's back—refused to listen to his overtures: they were 'very desperate, [and] would accept noe terms'.[42] Bennett was left with no alternative but to attack and, shortly after noon, his soldiers 'fell resolutely on'. According to John Moyle, a member of the Parliamentarian county committee, the fighting at the barricades raged for some time, until 'after neere two houres dispute, with the losse of only two of ours [killed], & four or five wounded, the enemies were totally scattered, [losing] about 60 or 70 slaine, some drowned [&] sixty taken'.[43] Routed, the surviving rebels took to their heels, many of them managing to elude their pursuers among the maze of ancient field-boundaries that still today surround Penzance.[44]

It was a dangerous time to be abroad in West Penwith, and when Alexander Daniel (a resident of Larigan, who had earlier been put under house-arrest by the rebels) attempted to ride into Penzance to congratulate Bennett on his victory he was confronted by 'a bloody soldier, who held up his musket to knock me on the head'. Daniel somehow managed to escape unhurt, but his ordeal hints at the tidal wave of violence and disorder that now engulfed Penzance.[45] The town had been taken by storm, and was thus a legitimate target for plunder. The victorious soldiers set about the work with a will and had soon stripped the entire town. Reminiscing many years later, a trooper recalled that he had had '5 gallons of English coin, silver & gold, and pieces of Eight . . . measurd out to him as his share'. One awestruck contemporary claimed that 'the souldiers never had such plunder since they were souldiers', adding that 'the town is utterly undone'. Moyle confirmed this picture: 'the towne . . . [is] exquisitely plundered', he laconically informed a correspondent. Only Anthony Gubbs, who had been reprieved from almost certain death as a result of the Parliamentarian victory, had his house and goods spared.[46]

While the soldiers pillaged, news arrived that fresh rebel forces were gathering near Helston. Alarmed, Bennett and Herle set about reassembling their scattered troops, but it was obvious that this would take time. Impatient of delay, an unnamed Helston man (who had ridden with Bennett to Penzance, and who subsequently composed the most detailed account of the 1648 rising) set off to reassure the townsfolk that help was on its way. Once arrived in Helston, he ordered bonfires to be lit and bells rung out for the victory at Penzance. On the face of it these demonstrations of public joy were purely celebratory, but there can be little doubt that they were primarily intended to hearten Parliament's supporters, and to cast down the hearts of Helston's pro-rebel faction. Nor was the impact of the measure limited to the town itself, for as the bells pealed out and the '*feux de joie*'—their flames visible for miles around—blazed up into the night-sky, those who were on the point of stirring in the surrounding countryside may well have had second thoughts. Certainly, the district around Helston remained in a quavering quiet that night. But further to the south the rebels were gathering strength, and news soon reached the town that 120 insurgents were assembled in Mullion churchyard.[47]

This intelligence put Helston's Parliamentarian faction 'in a pittifull fright', as the anonymous chronicler later confessed. 'We procured a watch', he recalled, 'and all that we dare trust . . . [in the town] were not above 20, and all the muskets were but 15, [so] the mayor, my selfe, and the rest of our magistrates, watched in person all night.'[48] Luckily for Helston's trembling defenders, no attack materialized. At five o'clock next morning one Renald Loggett sent a letter to Herle from Helston, informing him of the rebels' overnight movements. Instead of striking directly north, they had marched eastwards from Mullion to the town of St Keverne, gathering up recruits as they went. 'The country there aboute fales in to them', Loggett reported, while 'all the honest men in them p[ar]tes are inforced to flee.' As a result, the rebel force had grown very considerably during the night. 'They are in number, as [is] coniectured, 4 or 5 hundred & well armed', Loggett went on, and 'if you doe not make haste, it is doubtfull whe[ther] they do attempt the Dennis or not.'[49]

The possibility that the insurgents might try to capture this little fort (which had been built by the Royalists in 1644, and subsequently provided with a small Parliamentary garrison) had doubtless already occurred to Herle.[50] By the time Loggett penned his letter, the sheriff's forces were already hurrying south. Meanwhile the insurrectionists themselves had begun to edge north. Towards noon on 23 May, word reached Helston 'that there was a great body of rebels at Maugon Church Towne', two miles to the south. The rebel strength was now put at 300 foot and 40 horse, less than Loggett had feared, but still quite formidable enough to overwhelm the handful of pro-Parliamentarians in Helston, who were 'struck in amazement' by the news. Yet the town magistrates kept their nerve. By sending out horsemen to confuse the rebel scouts they managed to delay the advance of the main insurgent body until Herle could arrive. Towards six that evening Herle's Horse and Foot swept into Helston and almost at once moved out against the insurrectionists.[51]

The first skirmish took place at Mawgan Church, where the Parliamentarians 'charged on', killing several rebels. From here, they advanced to the insurgents' main position, which lay half a mile away 'at Trevilian's Barn, on the top of the hill above Geare Bridge'. Two accounts of the engagement that followed survive. The first was written by the anonymous Helston man, and is very brief: 'our Horse and Foot fell on bravely', he wrote, '[and] routed them with the hurt only of one man.'[52] The second is that of the eighteenth-century historian Richard Polwhele and is based on an unknown source, almost certainly an oral tradition. Polwhele's account of the episode runs thus:

> A number of men under the command of Mr Bogans of Treleage in St Keverne . . . had . . . posted themselves in a most advantageous position at Gear . . . with an apparent determination of defending that important pass. But the Parliament troops advancing, and showing themselves in much greater force than was expected, Major Bogans' men deserted him without coming to action. Some betook themselves to the Dinas, the greater part dispersed, and Major Bogans himself fled to Hilters Clift, in St Keverne, and concealed himself in a cave in the rocks.

The incident had never been forgotten in the vicinity, Polwhele added, and 'is still remembered . . . by the name of the Gear Rout'.[53]

Obviously, Polwhele's account must be treated with caution. His claim that the rebels held the Dennis, and that the fort was later besieged by the Parliamentarians, is not borne out by contemporary evidence. In this respect, at least, it seems likely that Polwhele's informants had got the events of 1648 confused with those of 1646 (when the Dennis was indeed invested).[54] More generally, though, Polwhele's account is convincing. His statement that the St Keverne rebels were led by a local gentleman seems eminently plausible; his description of the engagement as a 'rout' tallies with the account of the Helston chronicler, while his assertion that most of Bogans's men fled without fighting is supported by Moyle's comment that only 'seaven or eight' rebels were killed at the Gear.[55] Polwhele's description of how Bogans fled to St Keverne also ties in neatly with other evidence. According to the Helston chronicler, the Parliamentarians pursued the fleeing rebels throughout that night 'unto St Keverne and all the south [parts]', killing and capturing many in the process. The troopers were unable to account for all the insurgents, however, for 'some of the principall firebrands', finding themselves trapped upon the sea-coast by the pursuing troopers, 'were so desperate, that scorning mercy, they joyned hand in hand and violently run themselves into the ocean, where they perished in the waters'.[56] Others again went to ground in the surrounding countryside, and were still said to be 'lurking in ye cliffes and in Tinne pitts' a week later.[57] Polwhele's statement that Bogans hid on the sea-coast near St Keverne seems perfectly credible, therefore—especially as one of the other rebel leaders is known to have concealed himself in the same way.[58]

The Gear Rout marked the end of the Cornish rising. Within hours, Hardress Waller rode into Truro and at once set about restoring order in the far West. On 24 May he wrote to Parliament, assuring MPs that the insurgents had been dispersed and some 200 prisoners taken. The task of interrogating the captured rebels had already begun, and five days later, the newly appointed 'Committee for Troubles' moved from Truro to Helston 'for ye better inquiring . . . [into] the authors and causes of the Insurrection'.[59] As the few remaining rebel fugitives were either captured or made their escape, any residual threat to the Parliamentary authorities disappeared, and the committee-men were able to proceed with their investigations unhindered. The final part of this chapter will attempt to follow in the Parliamentarians' footsteps, by identifying as many as possible of the insurgents and exploring the complex web of hopes, fears, and resentments that had prompted them to risk their lives upon so desperate a cast.

III

Mary Coate, the only previous historian to have examined the rising in any depth, was able to identify twelve men who had been involved in the insurrection: seven who had helped to plan it and five who had acted as rebel 'captains'. By drawing on a wide range of sources which Coate missed (most notably the Bennett papers, which include a set of interrogatories administered to rebel prisoners) it is possible to expand this list to fifty-eight, and to correct several mis-identifications. Names can now be ascribed to perhaps one in twenty of those who took part in the rising: a far higher proportion than usual for early modern rebellions. Included among these fifty-eight men were a servant, a butcher, two ministers, three soldiers, and no fewer than nineteen gentlemen. (The occupations of the others are unknown.) The prominence of gentlemen in the sample is interesting and proves that the rising was by no means a purely popular revolt, but should not be taken as evidence that the insurgent host was a mere rabble of gentility. In the wake of the rising the Parliamentarians were obviously more anxious to identify the rebel leaders than anyone else, and as a result it is the gentry participants who emerge from the historical record with the greatest clarity.

What is intriguing about these gentlemen is not so much their social status as their political allegiance. Coate noted, accurately, that the chief plotters had been Royalist sympathizers and that the insurgents at Penzance had been led by 'some inferior royalist officers'.[60] If anything, this underplayed the importance of militant Cavalierism in the rising. A thorough re-examination of the evidence reveals that almost all of the rebel leaders were ex-Royalist officers. Thus, of the seven gentlemen-plotters identified by Herle before the rebellion began—John and Richard Arundell, Sir Arthur Basset, Robert Harris, Sir John Trelawny, Jonathan Trelawny and Charles Trevanion—at least six had previously served as regimental commanders in Charles I's army.[61] Those who commanded the rebel forces on the ground were also ex-Royalist officers, though of a slightly lower rank. Hannibal Bogans, the leader of the insurgents at Gear, was a former Royalist major.[62] So was Christopher Grosse of St Buryan, later acknowledged to have been 'chief . . . in the insurrection at Penzance'.[63] Grosse's six main confederates—Robert Coleman, 'Mr Jones', William Kiegwin, Martin Maddern, Thomas Pike, and 'Mr Tresillian'—had all served as Royalist majors or captains.[64] So had another of those implicated in the rising, Neville Blight of Carnedon, while the 'Captaine Pendarvys' who was arrested near Penryn on suspicion of having been with the rebels in Penzance was probably William Pendarves of Roscrow, yet another ex-Royalist officer.[65]

Robert Ashton's conclusion that 'the leadership of the English risings of the Second Civil War was overwhelmingly Cavalier' is thus strongly borne out by the evidence from Cornwall: indeed, the Cornish rebel leaders would appear to have been even more overwhelmingly Cavalier than were their counterparts elsewhere![66] Of all the rebel 'captains', only two are *not* known to have served in the army of Charles I: an obscure individual named 'Glover' who helped to command the Lizard insurgents,[67] and Thomas Flavell, Vicar of Mullion, who—following in the footsteps of an earlier generation of West Cornish rebel clerics—put himself at the head of his parishioners and led them into battle. Flavell (whose participation in the rising has gone unnoted by previous scholars) was clearly a remarkable man. A renowned exorcist and layer of ghosts, his own shade is said to have troubled the parish of Mullion long after his death. As late as the nineteenth century, the spot where his spectre had finally been laid to rest was still pointed out to the curious: some measure, perhaps, of the local reputation which Flavell had enjoyed during his lifetime.[68]

For the purposes of the present discussion, Flavell's most important attribute was not so much his aptitude with bell, book and candle as his stout royalism. Described by Walker as 'a man of singular Courage and Boldness', he was a thorn in the side of Interregnum governments, and is said to have 'vowed never to shave off his beard until the return of his Majesty to his Kingdoms'.[69] There can be little doubt that this hirsute warrior-priest was at least as much of a Cavalier as were the other rebel leaders. As one would expect, far less evidence survives about the rank and file, but there are clear hints that, in Cornwall (as in many other places) ex-Royalist soldiers formed the core of the rebel forces in 1648.[70] John Pierce, leader of the Helston malcontents, had been a sergeant to the Royalist Colonel Collins.[71] A rebel scout named Calenso killed at St Mawgan may well be identifiable with one of the two men of the same name listed in the Royalist garrison at the Dennis in 1644. Thomas Chirwin, Roger Ellys, and Thomas Nighton—all middle-ranking rebels in Penzance—are known to have been 'chiefe actors' for the King in 1642–6. And many of those who rallied to Hannibal Bogans in 1648 must surely have served under him four years before, when he had commanded the Royalist militia of St Keverne.[72]

The picture that begins to emerge, therefore, is of a rising of ex-Royalist officers and soldiers, run along military lines and orchestrated from the top. Moyle spoke of a pre-arranged 'designe', or plot, 'universall in our County, [&] long transacted at Trerise [the home of the ultra-loyal Arundell family] and elsewhere', while Gubbs blamed the rebellion on months of pre-planning by former Royalists.[73] But the insurrection could never have attained the proportions it did without the support of the West Cornish countryfolk. Contemporary testimony makes it clear that the inhabitants of West Penwith and the Lizard peninsula rallied to the insurgents *en masse*. The 300–500 men who gathered at Penzance and the 300–400 who came in from around St

Keverne represented a large proportion of the adult male population of those two districts—and the insurgents had many well-wishers in Helston and St Ives as well. It is clear that the rebellion attracted support from across the spectrum of West Cornish society, and that in Cornwall, as in most other parts of the realm in 1648, the insurgent forces were made up of Cavaliers and countryfolk combined.[74]

What were the rebels' motives? The short-term causes of the insurrection are clear enough. First, the initial success of Poyer's rebellion had fostered an atmosphere of growing anticipation among the local Royalists and had encouraged them to hasten preparations for a revolt of their own. Second, Herle's discovery of the Royalist plot, and his subsequent drive to apprehend the conspirators, had made it plain to the Cornish Cavaliers that if they did not act quickly they would be prevented from acting at all. Third, rumours of trouble in Exeter— confirmed by Waller's hasty departure for that city on 12 May—had aroused extravagant hopes that the 'Key of the West' was about to come out in open rebellion against the Parliament.[75] Finally, the erection of a maypole—that most potent of Royalist symbols[76]—in Penzance on 15 May had provided an opportunity for discontented elements to gather, and was later said to have been 'the occasion' of all the trouble which followed.[77] (In this respect, Penzance's experience mirrored that of Bury St Edmunds, Suffolk, where the erection of a maypole had led to 'a great combustion' a few days before.[78])

Far harder to pin down are the underlying causes of the insurrection. Unlike most other insurgent groups in 1648 the Cornish rebels did not issue a manifesto, and this helps to explain why previous scholars have been content to state that the rising was a 'Royalist' one, and to leave matters there.[79] That the over-riding aim of the Cavalier officers who led the rebellion was to restore the King to power need hardly be doubted. Yet even among this group, other, less purely ideological motives can be discerned. The revolt of Major Grosse, for example, was explicable not only in terms of his zeal for the royal cause, but also of his resentment at Parliament's failure to grant him and his men a gratuity, which they had been promised when they agreed to surrender the Isles of Scilly in 1646.[80] And matters are made more complicated by the fact that the Cornish rebel leaders (like many of their counterparts elsewhere) evidently strove to conceal the true extent of their own 'Cavalierism'.

Despite the lack of a written manifesto, some intriguing hints survive as to the sort of political programme which the rebel leaders publically espoused. Shortly before the rising began Sheriff Herle reported that attempts were being made by Royalist activists 'to get hands to Poyer's declaration' in Cornwall. This can only have been a reference to the manifesto which Poyer had issued in March, and the conspirators' decision to adopt this document is revealing.[81] As Ashton has observed, Poyer's Declaration was 'emphatically mainstream'; it displayed 'an equal concern for the rights of the king and the privileges of Parliament'.[82] By choosing to adopt this document, the Cornish rebel leaders sought to present themselves not so much as Cavalier intransigents as Royalist moderates. And bearing this in mind, the fact that Grosse and Pike told a local man 'thatt the service that they weare in was for King and Parliament' is intriguing.[83] The rebel leaders' appropriation of this slogan—first used by supporters of Parliament in 1642—confirms that they wished to appeal to as wide a constituency as possible.

The Cavaliers' use of the language of moderation may well have helped them to win over a handful of ex-Parliamentarian soldiers. Among the rebels taken at Penzance were two men who had been 'formerly imployed in the Parlament service under . . . Captain Keates'. Keates' company had been disbanded and paid off in 1647, so resentment over arrears seems unlikely to have been an issue in this case: possibly the two men had been genuinely convinced by the rebels' arguments. But the only *serving* Parliamentary soldier who is known to have deserted to the rebels did so primarily because he believed that the insurgents would pay his arrears; John Perne of Market Jew later confessed that 'he went to the enemy att Penzance by the perswation' of others who told him 'that he should have . . . [his] 2 moneths pay'.[84] Such illusory promises were made to soldiers all over the realm during 1648.[85]

As well as appealing to the soldiers, the insurgents also capitalized on the resentment which existed against them. The Helston chronicler noted that, when the rebels first rose, 'they pretended that they were threatned and wronged by the Mount soldiers, and took up armes to defend themselves, but this', he added sceptically, 'was a meer pretence'.[86] His cynicism may have been partially justified, but there can be little doubt that in West Cornwall, as elsewhere, anti-military feeling was running high. In February a local man had made bitter complaint against his treatment by troopers, who had 'threatned to cutt [his] throte except [he] should doe accordinge to there will'. A visitor to Penwith later claimed that it was the presence of the Mount soldiers which had first 'made the country people to grumble', while the fact that a Goldsithney man 'violently strooke a souldier of the Mount' during the rebellion tends to confirm that there was genuine popular hostility towards the garrison.[87]

Resentment against taxation was another major grievance which helped to propel many into the rebel camp; it was later reported that the insurgents had supposed 'yt all the Land would have followed their example, and have risen against the Parlament. . . by reason of the great burdens & taxes that were imposed on the people for the maintenance of the Army'.[88] Once the rebellion was underway, fear of punishment also proved an important incentive; Grosse warned his anxious listeners that 'the party that did appose the Towne [of Penzance] . . . did intend to plunder & burne [it]'.[89] In their desire to protect their homes and families, then, their hatred of taxation and their antipathy towards the soldiery, the Cornish rebels—like those who rose in many other parts of the kingdom during 1648—clearly shared a great deal in common with the Clubmen of 1645–6.[90] Yet were there any peculiarly local factors at work?

So far, little evidence has emerged to suggest that there was anything distinctively 'Cornish' about the rebellion of 1648; that the rebel bands that gathered at Penzance and St Keverne were in any way different from the 'ill-assorted bod[ies] of royalists . . . ex-supernumeraries . . . and local clubmen' that rose in other parts of the kingdom during the Second Civil War.[91] The rebels possessed a similar agenda to insurgent groups elsewhere, they expressed the hope that sympathizers from other parts of the realm would join them, and they are said to have 'imagined that what they there att Pensance did was ye sence of ye whole kingdom'.[92] Nor were the rebels themselves exclusively Cornish: Flavell was originally from Somerset, while several of the other participants were Devonians. There was even a 'Blackmoore' among the rebel host: Captain Pike's man-servant, Martin, who was unfortunate enough to be captured in arms near Penzance.[93]

It would not do to present the rebellion of May 1648 as an exclusively Cornish affair, therefore. But it should not be forgotten that the central government's relationship with Cornwall was quite exceptionally strained, even by the standards of 1648. Cornwall had been perhaps the most strongly Royalist district in the entire kingdom during the First

Civil War and thousands of Cornishmen had flocked to the King's banner, creating bitter resentment in the hearts of many English Parliamentarians. Such feelings had lingered long after the war was over, and in 1647 it was seriously proposed that the Cornish should be forbidden to elect MPs to Westminster 'until such time as it shall appear that their former Enmity and Rancour be laid aside'.[94] This suggestion was not adopted, but there can be little doubt that the 'foreign' Parliamentary soldiers stationed in Cornwall after the war behaved with particular insensitivity towards their reluctant hosts.[95] Unsurprisingly, then, the Cornish remained notoriously hostile to Parliamentary rule after 1646—and it seems probable that this hostility was most virulent of all in the far west of the county, where the ancient Cornish language and culture continued to cling on by its fingertips and local people nursed 'a secret envy' against the English. It has been argued in the preceding chapters that the notorious rebelliousness of this region during the Tudor period was partially explicable in terms of its inhabitants' desire to defend the religious and cultural practices which served as the symbols of Cornish nationhood.[96] Did a concealed resentment against English cultural hegemony—accentuated in 1648 by the protestantizing, centralizing policies of the Parliamentary regime— similarly contribute to the Cornish rising of the Second Civil War?

It is impossible to be sure, but the evidence is suggestive. We should note, first of all, the links which existed between the Cornish and the Welsh rebels in 1648. One contemporary claimed that the Cornish first rose 'by example of the Welch', and it is fascinating to speculate as to exactly what ordinary Cornish (and, indeed, ordinary Welsh) rebels may have perceived the underlying aims of Poyer's rebellion to be.[97] Poyer's Declaration—which, as we have seen, the Cornish rebels adopted—was a Royalist document, but it also spoke of the need to defend the Book of Common Prayer *in Welsh*, one of the most visible symbols of an English willingness to accept Welsh difference, while many, perhaps most, of his followers were Welsh-speakers.[98] Poyer's multi-hued rebellion had a definite Celtic tinge to it, therefore, and it might not be going too far to suggest that in 1648 (as in 1642?) the West Cornish decision to rise for the King was partially prompted by a desire to join with their brethren across the Bristol Channel in defiance of the meddlesome English Parliament.

There are other hints that ethnic tensions helped to fuel the rebellion. First, the insurrection was entirely confined to that small area of

Cornwall in which the old language was still spoken—'those westerne heathen partes' as John Moyle contemptuously referred to the districts around St Keverne and Penzance.[99] Second, a number of the rebel leaders were former officers of Sir Richard Grenville: the Royalist commander who had emerged as the champion of Cornish particularism during 1644–6.[100] Third, the Parliamentary soldiers who defeated the rebels subsequently staged a victory parade through the streets of Penryn in which they carried, impaled upon the points of their swords, 'three silver balls used in hurling'.[101] Hurling, a wild type of handball, was looked upon as 'a sport peculiar to Cornwall' during this period, so the significance of the soldiers' action is obvious.[102] The public violation of the hurling balls was a symbolic declaration of their triumph, not only over the insurrectionists, but over traditional Cornishness itself. Finally it is worth noting that, according to the testimony of one ex-rebel, the insurgents had been joined at Penzance by a butcher named 'Curnowe'. *Kernow* is the Cornish-language name for Cornwall, and it is tempting to suggest that—like the John Somerset who led a Somerset Club rising in 1645 and the man named Christmas hurt in a riot in favour of yuletide festivities at Ipswich in 1647—Curnowe may have been particularly remarked upon because his name helped to symbolize the rebel cause.[103]

The insurrection which shook the far west of Cornwall in May 1648 was a complex phenomenon. At first sight, it appears to have been a purely Royalist rising: led by ex-Royalist officers, supported by ex-Royalist soldiers, and espousing broadly Royalist ideals. There are clear parallels here with the situation in Essex, where as the late Brian Lyndon has shown, the Second Civil War was above all a resumption of the conflict of 1642–6.[104] Yet within the main stream of recrudescent Cavalierism there were other important currents. It is probably no coincidence that, of all the risings that occurred in 1648, the one that the Cornish revolt most closely resembles is that which occurred in North Wales, for in both regions there lurked a visceral resentment against English overlordship, a resentment which could, from time to time, break forth into sudden violence.[105] The opposition to centralization that existed in Cornwall and Wales was of a quite different order to that which existed in the shires of England, and the rebels' evident concern for 'Cornishness' should not be taken as an uncomplicated manifestation of 'county communitarianism'. Popular hostility to soldiers, free-quarter, heavy taxation, and so forth certainly helped to fuel the West Cornish rebellion, but it was a combination of aggressive royalism and defensive 'Celticity' that lay at its core—and, ironically, helped to seal its fate.

The defeat of the rebels can be attributed to many things; to Herle's watchfulness, to Gubbs's warnings, and to the speed with which local Parliamentarian commanders reacted. Yet most serious of all was the insurrectionists' failure to reach out to potential allies. None of the Cornish garrisons came over to them, despite the manifest discontent among the soldiery, and this meant that the insurgents were denied a secure 'place of retreat' of the kind that proved so vital to Poyer in Wales. Nor was any support forthcoming from Devon, even though resentment against taxation and free-quarter in that county was intense, and Plymouth and Exeter continued to defy Waller's orders. Not a single prominent ex-Parliamentarian is known to have joined the rebels, in fact, in striking contrast to the situation elsewhere. It is tempting to conclude that, despite the best efforts of the rebel leaders, the public face of the May 1648 rising remained just too ultra-Royalist and too ultra-Cornish to attract any widespread support beyond the Cornish-speaking heartlands of the far West—and that therein lay the chief reason for its failure.

7

William Scawen

A Seventeenth-century Cornish Patriot

Present-day scholars and speakers of Cornish owe an immeasurable debt to William Scawen: the seventeenth-century antiquarian who devoted his latter years to the study of the dying language. Scawen it was who ensured that the unique exemplar of the fifteenth-century Cornish passion poem, *Passio Christi*, was translated into English and preserved for posterity: Scawen it was who industriously gathered up and recorded traditional Cornish proverbs and sayings; and Scawen it was who—by encouraging his Cornish-speaking friends and relatives in the far west of Cornwall to begin writing letters to each other in Cornish— effectively founded the first 'school' of Cornish language enthusiasts during the late seventeenth century.[1] Scawen may fairly be regarded as the founding father of the modern Cornish language movement, then, the man who did more than any other to ensure that a corpus of traditional Cornish literature was transmitted to future generations.

Remarkably, no detailed account of his life has ever been published. Most general histories of Cornwall refer to Scawen only in passing, if at all, while even the handful of scholars who have devoted serious attention to his writings on the Cornish language have made little attempt to engage with the individual who compiled them.[2] Scawen's re-emergence from the obscurity in which he has languished for the past 300 years is long overdue. This chapter sets out to tell the neglected story of William Scawen's life, to explore his views on Cornish language and history, and to consider what those views reveal: not only about the man himself, but about conceptions of Cornish nationhood and identity during the turbulent years of the seventeenth century.

Map 6

I

William Scawen was born in November 1600, the eldest of the ten children of Robert Scawen (*c.*1562–1627) and his wife Isabella, daughter of Humphrey Nicoll of Penvose.[3] The Scawens were a gentry family of distinguished lineage, who had been established at their mansion house of Molenick in St Germans parish, in the extreme south-east of Cornwall (see Map 6), for at least three centuries, while the Nicolls were among the most influential and well-connected of Cornish gentry clans.[4] As one would expect, the young William enjoyed the classic upbringing of an early modern gentleman. He appears to have been schooled in East Cornwall, and in his early teens he went up to Queen's College, Oxford. Having matriculated at Queen's in 1617, Scawen entered Lincoln's Inn two years afterwards, where he presumably learned the basic principles of law and estate management.[5] Ten years later his father died and William took over the family estates.[6] The bulk of the Scawen family lands were situated in St Germans and the neighbouring parish of Menheniot, but William also inherited properties scattered across the whole of East Cornwall, from Tintagel in the north to Golant, near Fowey, in the west (see Map 7).[7] He was now in a position to start a family of his own and in *c.*1635 he married Alice Sawle, the twenty-year old daughter of Nicholas Sawle, of Penrice, Esquire. 1636 saw the birth of the couple's first son, William, and other children followed later.[8]

Of Scawen's character and interests during his youth little is known. His later writings show that he possessed an intimate knowledge of the tract of countryside which stretches between the Tamar and the river Fowey: a knowledge which, it seems fair to suggest, he is more likely to have acquired as a young man than in middle or old age.[9] A man of his social status could hardly have escaped the burdens of local office and Scawen's subsequent recollections of having attended shire elections and Stannary convocations in the great hall at Lostwithiel—a building which was destroyed in 1644—indicate that he had taken an active part in county affairs before the Civil War.[10] The fact that, in 1630, his celebrated fellow-parishioner Sir John Eliot of Port Eliot—then a prisoner in the Tower—chose Scawen (alongside Sir Bevill Grenville and four others) to serve as one of his executors demonstrates that William was already regarded locally as a figure of some substance[11]— and also hints that, like many other Cornish gentlemen, he may not have been entirely uncritical of royal policies during the troubled 1620s.[12]

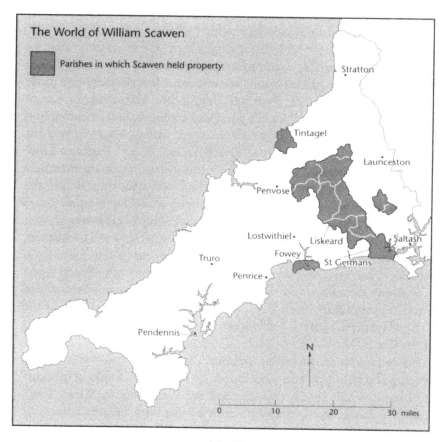

Map 7

Clear evidence that Scawen was opposed to the financial expedients of the Personal Rule emerges from what is apparently his earliest extant letter, a missive sent to Eliot in June 1631, in which he speaks disparagingly of 'courtiers', glories in his own refusal to pay his knighthood fine, and assures Sir John 'that as you suffer for others, so there are some others that suffer for you, amongst which is your servant, W.S'.[13]

Scawen's friendship with Eliot might lead one to assume that he would have been predisposed to favour the cause of Parliament during the Civil War. So might his family connections. Isabella Scawen's uncle was none other than John Pym, and during the 1620s Pym appears to have acted as patron to William's younger brother Robert, securing him a place in the service of the Earl of Bedford, who was later to become notorious for his opposition to the Personal Rule.[14] Perhaps more important still, Isabella's father and brother were prominent members of the East Cornish puritan network, which was later to underpin the Cornish Parliamentarian party.[15] Yet there must have been other influences acting on Scawen too. His father-in-law, Nicolas Sawle, later declared for the King.[16] So did Piers Edgcumbe, a rich local gentleman, whose mansion house of Mount Edgcumbe lay just a few miles from Molenick, and who was soon to become—if he was not already—one of Scawen's closest associates. By 1639, moreover, Scawen's brother had parted acrimoniously with Bedford and entered the household of the Earl of Northumberland: a nobleman who was then regarded as a friend of the Court.[17]

Scawen had a foot in either political camp, then, and it is not clear which party he supported—or, indeed, if he was yet thinking in terms of parties—when he decided to stand for Parliament in March 1640. Scawen's name was eventually returned for two constituencies, St Germans and East Looe, and in April he set off for Westminster (where he chose to represent the former seat[18]). Nothing is known of the part which Scawen played in the brief and inglorious assembly known to posterity as the Short Parliament. The experience cannot have been wholly uncongenial to him, however, for in autumn 1640 he stood for election again. This time his Parliamentary ambitions were to be thwarted. Although his name was again returned for St Germans the result was disputed and—thanks to the intervention of the Cornish MP Sir Richard Buller and his sons in the House of Commons—effectively decided in favour of Scawen's rival.[19] This episode—recently described by Anne Duffin as a prime 'example of the godly organising to secure the return of a puritan MP'[20]—provides the first clear indication of Scawen's pro-Royalist, or at least anti-puritan, leanings. It also demonstrates the formidable political influence which was wielded by the proto-Parliamentary gentry of South-east Cornwall.

Throughout 1641 and early 1642 this faction, led by the Bullers of Shillingham, dominated the countryside around Molenick. Their local critics had little choice but to lie low—and this is what Scawen appears to have done. Beyond the fact that he took the Protestation at St Germans in February 1642, we know little of Scawen's activities between January 1641 and October 1642.[21] No doubt he heard—and approved? —of his father-in-law's decision to sponsor a pro-Royalist petition in May 1642, and received—with disdain?—the news that his brother had followed his patron into the Parliamentary camp a few weeks later.[22] Yet as the great Parliamentarian families of South-east Cornwall tightened their grip on power in the region during summer 1642, and moved into close alliance with the Roundheads of Devon—who had established a garrison at Plymouth, just across the Tamar from St Germans[23]— Scawen can scarcely have failed to realize that any outright expression of dissent on his part would have put him in considerable danger. Not until Sir Richard Buller and his Roundhead allies had been ejected from Launceston by the massed ranks of the sheriff's *posse* in October did it become possible for Parliament's enemies in South-east Cornwall to declare their hands.[24]

In the wake of Buller's retreat, Piers Edgcumbe and other 'well-affected people of the parts about Millbrook'—the little town which lies on the river near Mount Edgcumbe—sent a message to the sheriff asking for protection against the Plymouth garrison.[25] A troop of Royalist dragoons was accordingly sent to Mount Edgcumbe and, emboldened by their presence, Edgcumbe and Scawen embarked upon what was clearly a pre-arranged scheme to muster the local militia in support of the King. As soon as the dragoons had taken up their quarters, an eyewitness later recalled:

> Mr Edgcumbe beinge Collonel of a Regiment of ye Trayned Bands
> . . . did, together with . . . Mr Scawen his Lieutenant Collonel[26]
> . . . cause his Regiment with some Companies of Volunteeres to
> bee drawne into the . . . Towne of Millbrooke, and did there settle
> a Garrisson, which hath ever since . . . bin maintayned, and
> Commanded by them for ye Kinge against ye Parliament.[27]

Scawen was appointed Governor of Millbrook, and for the next six months he and his men were to play a vital role in defending South-east Cornwall from enemy attack. In January 1643 they took part in the battle of Braddock Down, where an invading Parliamentary army was crushed, and three days later they assisted in the Royalist recapture of Saltash.[28] Following the near-collapse of the Parliamentary cause in the West in summer 1643, pressure on the Royalist defences along the Tamar effectively ceased. Scawen now became involved in a plot to capture St Nicholas Island, a Parliamentarian outpost in Plymouth Sound. The Island's governor was Sir Alexander Carew, grandson of the celebrated Cornish antiquarian Richard Carew, and a near neighbour of Scawen's before the war.[29] Carew had begun to entertain doubts about the wisdom of his decision to join the Parliamentarians and, in August, he 'found means to correspond with some of his old friends and neighbours in Cornwall, and by them to make a direct overture to surrender . . . [the] Island to the King'.[30] There can be little doubt who these 'old friends and neighbours' were. A witness later deposed that Carew had been 'chiefly drawn and seduced to have effected that plott' by Edgcumbe and Scawen, and added that the two Royalist commanders had 'caused divers boates to bee made ready att Cawsand to have carried in Souldiers . . . from thence to the aid of the said Baronet'.[31] Unfortunately for Carew, the Parliamentarians got wind of the plot. The governor was arrested, shipped off to London and, a year later, beheaded on Tower Hill.[32] Scawen had inadvertently helped to lead his former friend to the executioner's block.

By early 1644 the Parliamentarians had recovered from the low point of the previous summer and were again beginning to make life uncomfortable for the Cornish Royalists. In May the Plymouth garrison mounted a surprise attack on Millbrook, briefly forcing Scawen's soldiers out of the town,[33] and two months later the Earl of Essex launched a full-scale invasion of Cornwall. As Essex's troops poured across the Tamar, Sir Richard Grenville—now in overall command of the Royalist forces in Cornwall—ordered the garrisons of Millbrook and Saltash to pull back towards the west and join his army. Edgcumbe and Scawen hurried to obey[34] and they and their men were soon encamped near Truro.[35] Within days Grenville's army set off to join the King, who had by now entered Cornwall in pursuit of Essex. On 10 August Grenville occupied Bodmin, linking up with the King's forces and effectively trapping the Parliamentarians around Lostwithiel.[36] Almost at once Edgcumbe and Scawen began to edge back still further towards the east, clearly anxious to liberate their own small corner of Cornwall from enemy control. In a letter sent to the King from Liskeard on 15 August, Edgcumbe, Scawen and other local gentry loyalists not only demanded that they be sent troops to help them drive the Parliamentarians out of Saltash but also complained bitterly of the conduct of the Cavalier Horse.[37]

It was the first hint that a latent tension might exist between Edgcumbe and Scawens' zeal for the royal cause and their loyalty to their own county, and when the requested troops failed to arrive the two men appear to have taken matters into their own hands. In a letter sent to Edgcumbe on 28 August, the King complained that 'wee have received Advertisement that yourself, your Lt. Colonell and divers of the officers and souldiers of your Regiment have lately gonne home from our Army and deserted the service thereof'.[38] The King commanded Edgcumbe to reassemble his men and return with them to the royal camp, but there is no evidence that his command was obeyed. Instead, Edgcumbe and Scawen appear to have marched back to Mount Edgcumbe, relieved the small garrison which they had left behind there in July,[39] and settled down to re-establish control over the surrounding area. Had they been secretly encouraged in their disobedience by Sir Richard Grenville? Certainly, their behaviour at this time seems curiously reminiscent of that which Sir Richard himself was to display a few days later when, following the eventual surrender of the Parliamentary army at Lostwithiel, he ignored a royal order to pursue the fleeing Roundhead cavalry, and stopped instead to capture Saltash.[40]

Fortunately for Edgcumbe and Scawen—and, indeed, for Grenville too—the King, basking in the unaccustomed glow of martial triumph, readily forgave his Cornish commanders for their recent misdemeanours. On 8 September he ordered that ammunition should be supplied to the newly re-established garrisons of Millbrook and Mount Edgcumbe, while six days later Grenville was reappointed commander of the Royalist forces besieging Plymouth.[41] Over the following winter Scawen continued to act as Governor of Millbrook. Grenville instituted a tight blockade of Plymouth during this period and Scawen and his men may well have crossed the Tamar in order to participate in assaults on the town defences. That Scawen did, at some time, experience the peculiarly intimate nature of Civil War siege warfare is made clear by his subsequent writings. He was later to recall that 'in the . . . Civill War, wee began to make some use of . . . [the Cornish language] upon the Runnagates [i.e. Cornish Royalist deserters] that went from us to the contrary parte, from our opposite works: and more wee should have done, if the enemy had not been Jealous [i.e. suspicious] of them, and prevented us'.[42] This statement is important, not only because it proves that the Cornish tongue was used in the field by the King's Cornish soldiers, but also because of what it reveals about Scawen himself. Clearly, by 1645–6 at the latest, Scawen—who had been born and brought up in the wholly English-speaking district of East Cornwall—had begun to take an interest in the Cornish language. It seems fair to suggest that this interest may have been initially kindled when he found himself fighting alongside men from the Cornish-speaking districts of West Cornwall in the Royalist army.

Scawen's wartime service was by no means restricted to the military sphere. As he was later to confess, he combined his role as a militia officer with 'other severall imployementes' on the King's behalf,[43] and he is known to have served as a Royalist commissioner of Oyer and Terminer and as Judge of the Cornish Vice-Admiralty Court.[44] Some indication of Scawen's growing local influence is provided by the fact that, in April 1645, he was one of the four Cornish commissioners who attended the Prince of Wales at Bridgwater in order to discuss the creation of a new Royalist army in the West.[45] Yet as the King's cause began to falter during late 1645—and as Lord Goring's plundering bands of Cavalier horsemen began to fall back towards the Tamar—Scawen, like many other Cornish Royalists, began to reconsider his position. By early 1646, Scawen—along with Piers Edgcumbe, Colonel William Coryton of Callington and a number of other East Cornish gentlemen—was involved in a secret correspondence with the Roundhead commanders in Devon.[46] These covert discussions were soon to bear rich fruit for the Parliamentarians.

In February 1646 the New Model Army forced the passage of the Tamar at Stratton and launched its long-awaited invasion of Cornwall. As it did so, Sir Ralph Hopton ordered the Royalist units which had been stationed along the line of the river to retreat towards the west and regroup.[47] Yet Edgcumbe, Scawen and the other commanders of the trained-band regiments of South-east Cornwall refused to obey. Instead they entered into formal negotiations with Sir Thomas Fairfax, and, in a treaty concluded at Millbrook on 5 March, agreed to surrender themselves, their men and garrisons, and indeed all 'the Easterne part of Cornwall' to the Parliament.[48] It was a defection which effectively signalled the withdrawal of Cornish support from the King. 'The prosperous endeavours' of these 'Gentlemen of interest', Fairfax wrote next day, '[has] given such a progresse to our affaires in these partes as nothing more could have advanced [them]', and in the wake of the Millbrook treaty all but the most fanatical of the Cornish Cavaliers abandoned the Royalist cause.[49] Deprived of the Cornish infantry whom he had counted on to assist his cavalry, Hopton now had little choice but to surrender, and on 15 March he laid down his arms.[50] The startling speed of the Royalist collapse had owed much to the earlier defection of the East Cornish militia officers. Indeed, one Parliamentary witness claimed that the defection of 'these gentlemen' had been 'the speciall meanes of the submission of this whole County, which soone after followed'.[51] Small wonder that Royalist die-hards regarded the officers who had surrendered at Millbrook as renegades, while Fairfax extolled them as men to 'be lookt on with more then an ordinary eye of favour'.[52]

On 6 March Scawen and his fellow-officers laid down their arms and took the National Covenant.[53] Soon afterwards they petitioned to compound for their Royalism on the favourable terms which they had been promised by Fairfax, but almost at once ran into difficulties.[54] Because the Millbrook treaty had been a verbal agreement, rather than 'a formall capitulacion', doubts were cast upon its legitimacy by the Parliamentary sequestrators, and over the next three years the Cornish militia officers became embroiled in an interminable battle to have the original terms confirmed. Thanks in part to Fairfax's personal intervention, Scawen eventually managed to get his fine reduced by half in 1649, but this was a far cry from the full 'immunity' for his estate and person which he had originally been led to expect.[55] Nor did this put an end to his troubles, for—although he appears to have withdrawn from public affairs between 1646 and 1660[56]—he is known to have been imprisoned for a time in Pendennis Castle: presumably as a suspected Royalist.[57] Small wonder that Scawen later nursed bitter memories of the Interregnum, and of the state-sponsored 'Beagles' who had quested after his person and property during 'those troublesome times'.[58]

The restoration of the Monarchy in 1660 transformed Scawen's political fortunes. Rather surprisingly, his wartime defection to the Parliamentarians appears to have been forgiven, if not altogether forgotten, in the wake of Charles II's return, and Scawen now found himself enjoying handsome rewards and favours of the sort which were commonly accorded to veteran Cavalier officers by the new regime. Thus he was reappointed to the County Bench, restored to his former rank of Lieutenant-Colonel in the militia and, most gratifying of all, elevated to the highly prestigious and lucrative position of Vice-Warden of the Cornish Stannaries.[59] Scawen was also recommended for the projected order of the Royal Oak and, during the 1670s, appointed as County Collector of the Cornish Hearth Tax.[60] For the rest of his life, he was to remain a highly respected member both of county society and of the local Anglican-Tory elite: two groups which were, in any case, practically co-terminous in late seventeenth-century Cornwall.[61]

Public duties undoubtedly took up much of Scawen's time during the post-Restoration period, but increasingly—and perhaps especially after the death of his wife in 1664[62]—he devoted himself to private study. There are hints that, even before the Civil War, Scawen had possessed a reputation as a man of learning—or at least as one who wished to appear learned: in 1640 a disgruntled neighbour had waspishly described him as 'a man yt accounts himselfe a witt'.[63] Yet the passionate interest which Scawen was subsequently to evince in the Cornish language appears to have been a relatively late development. As we have seen, Scawen's first known encounter with Cornish-speakers had taken place during the Civil War and he was later to confess that he had not applied himself to the study of the language until he was 'growen far up into yeares'.[64] Taking all the evidence together, it seems probable that Scawen first began to devote himself to the subject during his fourteen years of enforced absence from public life between 1646 and 1660. This suggestion is given credence by Scawen's later account of a conversation he had had with Robert Foster, the Judge of the Western Circuit, at Launceston Assizes, sometime between 1660 and 1663.[65] That the subject of the two men's conversation should have been the precise derivation of the place-name Launceston—a name which Scawen assured the Judge was not of Saxon origin, but derived instead from 'the Cornish original . . . Leostofen'[66]—makes it clear that, by this date at the very latest, Scawen had begun to turn his mind towards the elucidation of the ancient language and history of Cornwall.

Scawen's fascination with this subject derived, at least in part, from his possession of the medieval Cornish manuscript poem *Passio Christo*. The processes by which this poem had originally come into Scawen's hands remain obscure, as indeed does the precise date at which he had acquired it. What is clear is that Scawen—who after 1660 made strenuous efforts to recover further documents written in Cornish, but to no avail[67]—eventually came to believe that the manuscript in his keeping was the last surviving remnant of the ancient Cornish language. It was this conviction which caused him to preserve the poem as, in his own words, a 'precious Reliq', and to make what provision he could for the manuscript's safety after his own death.[68] Initially he toyed with the idea of sending it to the Bodleian Library, but later thought better of this scheme, fearing—perhaps justifiably—that the manuscript would simply 'have layen useless there, and nothing come of it'. Instead, Scawen resolved to keep the document in his own possession and to arrange for the text to be translated into contemporary Cornish and English by various more or less learned men of his acquaintance, Cornish–English bi-linguals, who lived in the far west of Cornwall.[69] Thus matters rested until the late 1670s, when Scawen—by now very aged, but still full of mental vigour—received the crucial spur which would finally galvanize him into composing a formal treatise on the Cornish tongue.

During the Launceston Assizes of 1678, which Scawen attended as usual, talk in the Judge's Chamber turned to the 'loss or decay' of the Cornish language, prompting Lord Chief Justice North to enquire of the assembled Cornish gentry 'whether there were anything written in it now remaineing'? At least one man denied that there was, but Scawen hastened to refute him, and excitedly informed the Lord Chief Justice of the manuscript in his own possession. When North expressed himself 'earnest for a sight' of this, Scawen took the Judge at his word, and promised to provide him with a copy of the poem when he next visited Cornwall on circuit. Over the ensuing months, Scawen devoted himself to preparing a version of the text—complete with scholarly 'additions'—for the Judge's perusal. Illness and fatigue dogged his progress, though, and eventually seem to have confined him to the house: thus preventing him from travelling to the Assizes and from keeping his rendezvous with the Lord Chief Justice.[70] Nothing daunted, Scawen spent the early 1680s converting the materials which he had amassed for North's benefit into a manuscript treatise entitled *Antiquities Cornu-Brittanic: . . . [or] Memorials of . . . the Primitive Speech of Cornwall*, several different versions of which are still extant today.[71]

Scawen's own master copy of this work (which is the fullest and most complete version, and is now preserved in the Cornish Record Office) is divided into four separate sections. The first of these—headed 'A

Complaint for the Decay of the Cornish Speech'—is in fact a good deal more ambitious than this modest title suggests, for it provides the reader with what is, in effect, a brief history of the Cornish people from the earliest times right up to Scawen's own day. The second—entitled 'The Causes Assigned to the Cornish Tongues Decay'—is a lengthy discussion of the various factors which Scawen believed to have been responsible for the language's decline. The third section—which Scawen clearly regarded as the centre-piece of the entire volume—consists of a translation of the *Passio Christo* into contemporary English and Cornish verse. The fourth and final section—entitled 'Observacouns on the Tongue'—is something of a mixture, and includes a number of general remarks on Cornish history, language and folklore. Scawen appears to have completed the main text of the treatise in around 1685, but he continued to scribble additional notes in the margins—in an increasingly crabbed and indecipherable hand—right up until his death.[72] This finally occurred at St Germans in November 1689, as Scawen was approaching his ninetieth year.[73]

Scawen's monumental treatise—which is well over a hundred pages long, and draws on a splendidly eclectic mixture of classical authorities, original documents, printed historical works, personal reminiscences and second-hand oral testimony in order to support its various arguments—provides as rich a discussion of the question of Cornish identity from a contemporary Cornish standpoint as we are ever likely to get. Yet, strange as it may seem, this fascinating document has been almost entirely neglected by previous historians of Cornwall. Most have been familiar with only part of Scawen's *oeuvre*—a variant copy of his original manuscript, which was first printed as a pamphlet in the 1770s, and then reprinted in a general history of Cornwall in the 1830s.[74] This somewhat confused, and confusing, text—which appears to be a preliminary draft of the *Antiquities*—does not convey the true radicalism of Scawen's vision. In the following pages his views will be considered, in their full complexity, for the first time. An attempt will then be made to relate them to the chequered and, at first sight, rather puzzling course of Scawen's own political career.

II

Perhaps the single most important insight to emerge from William Scawen's writings is the fact that he considered himself to be not an

Englishman, but a Briton. An eighteenth-century antiquarian described the Scawens as 'an antient and *mere British* family'—meaning that their line was of 'pure Cornish' descent, with no admixture of English blood—and this statement perfectly sums up (indeed, probably derives from) William Scawen's own view of his lineage.[75] He was fiercely proud of the 'Ancient Brittish Blood' which he believed to run through his own veins and those of his Cornish fellow-countrymen and women: he was puzzled and dismayed by the tendency of so many seventeenth-century Cornish gentlemen to regard their British ancestry with indifference, if not outright embarrassment; and he looked to the records and traditions of former ages to reveal not only what the Britons had been in the past, but also what they might one day be again.[76]

'Things Primitive are usually purest. . . which by time, inobservation and intermixion grow insiped' Scawen remarked at the beginning of his treatise, and—as this opening salvo might lead one to expect—the historical view which subsequently unfolds is that of a primordial British Eden gradually undermined by the passage of the years and the infiltration of 'ruder [foreign] nations'.[77] Scawen was in little doubt that the Britons had been the 'Aborigines', or original inhabitants, of these islands, and he painted a glowing picture of the life of universal felicity which they had enjoyed before the coming of the Romans.[78] Scawen believed that the members of the ancient British 'race' or 'nation' (he used the two terms interchangeably) had possessed their own sophisticated set of laws and customs, as well as their own language; he believed that they had been physically distinct from other peoples by virtue of their 'excellent beauty and form'; and he believed that—thanks to the instruction of the druids who had made up their priestly caste— they had excelled all other peoples in terms of scholarship and learning too.[79] Scawen even went so far as to suggest that, while the druids had undoubtedly been pagans, their knowledge of philosophy, morality and divinity had been such that they might fairly be regarded as the precursors of the early Christians: as preliminary instructors sent by God to prepare the British people for 'the attaining afterward of a more full and Caelestiall knowledge'. Scawen's view of the Britons as God's chosen people was here made plainly manifest.[80]

If Scawen was convinced that the ancient Britons had been a uniquely virtuous race, he was also unable to shake off the—frankly partisan— suspicion that those who had lived in the far South-west had been the most virtuous of them all. Indeed, he claimed to have it on the authority of the classical historian Diodorus Siculus that the inhabitants of the South-western peninsula had been a people 'of courteous humanity . . . [even] more than others of the [British] nation were observed to be'.[81] Scawen was understandably reluctant to make dogmatic pronouncements about the precise nature of the political and territorial divisions which had existed in the British Isles before the arrival of the Romans, but—following the authority of Geoffrey of Monmouth and others—he clearly inclined to the view that the island which would later become the two kingdoms of England and Scotland had then been divided up between four ruling dynasties: those of England, Scotland, Wales—and Cornwall.[82] If Cornwall had indeed been an independent kingdom 'in times long forepast', Scawen mused, 'we had then need . . . to have fayth that it was then of a farr greater extent than now it is', and he went on to posit a vanished 'Super Cornwall': the boundaries of which had stretched eastwards into Devon as far as Exeter and westwards into the Atlantic as far as the Scilly Isles, via the legendary 'drowned lands' of Lyonesse.[83]

It was the failure of the 'petty kings' of the Britons to sink their differences and unite against the common foe, Scawen believed, which had finally brought an end to the golden age of British power and enabled the Romans to conquer the island. Even so, he hastened to add, it had been 'no easy nor quick conquest', and the Britons 'were never totally vanquished till their neighbours . . . came as auxiliaries to the Romans in great swarms against them'.[84] Roman rule, once established, Scawen appears to have viewed as relatively benign. No doubt this was chiefly because it was during the Roman ascendancy that Christianity had first been introduced to the British Isles. Scawen, like many of his Welsh contemporaries, believed that the Britons had 'embraced Christianity . . . very earely . . . eaven near [to] the apostles times'.[85] He ascribed the British people's precocious acceptance of the Christian faith chiefly to the preparatory work of the druids, who, by spreading their own 'smaller . . . rays of illuminations' throughout the land, had rendered the inhabitants 'more capable of enjoying a greater [light], when the Bright Star of righteousness of the East should arise in his Humanity'.[86]

Scawen held that, once the true light of Christ had finally dawned, Britain had swiftly become one of the most important strongholds of the new faith. It was no coincidence, he suggested, that Britain should have produced the world's 'first Christian King', nor that, with the support of 'the Brittish Legions', the half-British governor of the province, Constantine the Great, should have become 'the first Christian Emperour'.[87] Scawen took it for granted that the British 'race' had been immeasurably strengthened by its gradual infusion with the Christian faith. Indeed he believed that, when the power of Rome eventually began to wane, the revitalized Britons might well have been able to recover their 'lost [political] libertie' and establish a glorious Celtic-Christian imperium in these islands, if only they had been left to their own devices.[88] That no such British Utopia had, in the end, been achieved in the post-Roman period Scawen ascribed to the onset of '*Malum ab Aquilone*': 'Evil from the North'.[89]

It is the 'unchristianed Northern Nations', the Angles and the Saxons, who are the villains of Scawen's work.[90] He repeatedly condemns these peoples in the most violent terms: as 'pagans', 'invaders', 'ravishers' and 'oppressors'.[91] He describes how, having first arrived in Britain as auxiliaries, the Anglo-Saxon mercenaries later turned on their erstwhile masters and seized more and more land for themselves. He repeats the ancient legend that the Saxons treacherously slew many hundreds of the British leaders near Stonehenge, and adds bitterly 'no doubt after them, abundance more [were] openly made away [with]'.[92] He tells of how those Britons who continued to resist were 'forced by the oppression of the Saxons to fly into Wales and Cornwall', while everywhere else 'the Brittish Laws, Customes and Liberties' were snuffed out and the light of true religion extinguished.[93] A black veil of savagery now descended across the land, in Scawen's retrospective vision, as British men were slaughtered, British women defiled and British children sold into slavery by the Saxons. So determined were the invaders to obliterate all traces of British culture, Scawen claimed, that they even cut out the tongues of the British women whom they had forced into marriage, so 'that their children might not learne their speech'.[94]

Only in Wales and Cornwall had the Britons been able to resist. Here, the ancient British kingdoms of the pre-Roman period had been resurrected, while new British champions had arisen to combat the encroaching Saxon hordes. Pre-eminent among these, of course, had been King Arthur—not only a Cornishman, Scawen trumpeted, but 'one of the worthies of the world'—who had 'fought many successful Battles against the Pagan Saxon and Infidels, for liberty, truth and religion'.[95] Thanks to the efforts of Arthur and the other British war-leaders, Scawen averred, 'our Ancestors here [in Cornwall] and our brethren in Wales, retained in a good measure Christianity, when those then unchristianed nations oppressed it and us'.[96] Scawen's account of the titanic struggle which he supposed to have been waged between Christian Britons and Anglo-Saxon pagans during the Dark Ages was an overtly partisan one: he was fully prepared to upbraid the Saxon 'heathens' in the most reproachful terms. When it came to discussing what had transpired between the two peoples in the wake of the Anglo-Saxons' conversion to Christianity, however, Scawen became far more circumspect. It was no part of his intention, he protested at one point, 'to utter any . . . hard terms against . . . those . . . nations that then received the Gospell', and this may help to explain why he failed to provide any account of how the Cornish had eventually been defeated by the (Christian) West Saxons and incorporated into the nascent English state, limiting himself instead to the cursory aside that 'we cannot deny our being conquered, and our subjection'.[97]

Scawen's reticence on this crucial subject, which must surely have been of absorbing interest to him, did not simply reflect an unwillingness to speak harshly of fellow Christians: it also reflected an anxiety not to be seen as overtly anti-English. We should remember that Scawen's treatise was originally composed for the edification of an English judge—and that any explicit attack upon the English nation by a Welsh or Cornish writer during the early modern period might well have been construed as seditious. Scawen took good care to clear himself of any such imputation. 'God forbid', he expostulated, 'that I, who endeavour to doe right to the Brittans, should vilifie or despise any of those other peoples . . . whome the Royall or Gentle blood . . . hath incorporated in this Land'.[98] It was a noble sentiment—but despite Scawen's claim that he bore no malice towards the English, or indeed towards any other nation, the cloven hoof of Anglophobia is frequently to be discerned beneath the hemline of his text.

Indirect criticisms of the English—and more specifically of the way in which the actions of the English government, and the influence of English culture, had helped to accelerate the decline of traditional Cornish identity—can be found on almost every page of the *Antiquities*. Scawen bemoans the decision of the (English) Church to order that all young people should 'learn the Lords Prayer . . . in English', for example, and condemns the decision of the (English) Parliament not to take 'the like care . . . for us as for our Brethren in Wales' when it authorized the translation of the Book of Common Prayer into Welsh, but not Cornish, in 1563.[99] Scawen did not go so far as to accuse the English of attempting to impose their culture by force on a uniformly hostile populace: he was all too well aware of the fact that large numbers of Cornishmen and women had long been anxious to embrace the perceived benefits of Englishness. Nevertheless, Scawen plainly regarded the processes by which so many of his compatriots had been encouraged to abandon their ancient customs—and especially their language—as an insidious form of English cultural imperialism.

Many Cornish place-names in the vicinity of Molenick had been 'wrested away' as a result of their proximity to Devon, Scawen declared—adding darkly, 'as . . . other things [have been], by like accidents, in the eastern parts of the county'.[100] Elsewhere in his writings, he complained that Cornish place-names had 'suffered much violence along the river [Tamar] from Devon side'; criticized the Devonians for having 'stolen away . . . many of the antient British names and intruded upon us many strange ones' and fulminated against the way in which the Cornish language had been 'infected', 'invaded', 'disfigured' and 'eaten up' by English.[101] Scawen's deep sense of resentment against the English for having 'undermined' the Cornish tongue emerges from a comment which he made towards the end of his treatise. After having stated that the English language had now, itself, become 'adulterated and degenerate', he added bitterly 'it is some parte of a Revenge, that they which have corrupted others should be altered and defiled in themselves'.[102]

Scawen's distaste for the English nation is nowhere made more explicit than in those passages of the *Antiquities* which deal with the vexed question of rebellion. As we have seen, Cornwall had been shaken by a whole series of violent popular insurrections during the Tudor period, and this in turn had led to the Cornish people acquiring a reputation for rebelliousness and disloyalty. A propensity for sedition was scarcely something to boast of in early modern England, and during Elizabeth's reign Cornwall's gentry leaders had been reluctant even to mention the revolts in public. Scawen—who was anxious not to 'cast any scandall or offence upon his country'—might well have been expected to leave this peculiarly delicate subject alone. Yet he could not quite bear to. Instead, in one of the most intriguing passages of the *Antiquities*, he delivered himself of a decidedly schizophrenic judgement on the Cornish rebels of 1497: on the one hand condemning them as 'vain' and 'misguided' men whose actions had made 'themselves . . .

ridiculous, and their country discredited', while on the other praising them for their exemplary conduct on their march to Blackheath—and even seeming to imply that, like the Welsh rebels of the medieval period, they had been rebelling against English overlordship (see Appendix 3). Would it be going too far to suggest that the first view represented 'the official Cornish gentry line' on the Tudor rebels, while the second more nearly represented Scawen's own opinions?

Scawen had not only acknowledged the skeleton of rebellions past which lurked in the Cornish family cupboard, he had come perilously close to shaking it by the hand. This was not a road down which it would have been politic for him to have proceeded very far, however, and in the succeeding sentence he abruptly changed tack. Rather than attempting to palliate the offences of the 1497 rebels, Scawen now sought to shift the imputation of intrinsic rebelliousness away from the Cornish and onto their English neighbours. To this end he naturally drew first of all upon the evidence of the Civil War. During 1642–6, Scawen somewhat unctuously reminded his readers, it had been the Cornish who had persisted in their obedience to 'his late Majestie of blessed memory, Charles I, when his rebellious and ungratefull [English] people, unworthy to have so good [a] Prince to reigne over them, impiously rose up against him'. It had been England, not Cornwall, in other words, which had then been 'the Rebellious parte of . . . [the] kingdome'.[103] Nor should this situation have occasioned any particular surprise, he implied, for matters had ever been thus, and the contrasting behaviour of the Cornish and English peoples during the Civil War had simply mirrored the contrasting behaviour of their ancestors.[104]

The Britons had always been supremely loyal subjects, declaimed Scawen, and far more obedient 'towards their Princes, than others have been since, who have gotten upon themselves . . . by their often rebellions, bad terms abroad in the world, under the name of *Reges Anglice* [i.e. English Kings]'.[105] Here Scawen was almost certainly referring to what one Royalist commentator of the 1640s described as the 'old saying' that 'the King of England is a King of Devills, because of their disobedient murmurings, and often rebellion'.[106] Scawen then unleashed the triumphant asseveration that:

It was a Truth sadly pronounced by Mary Queen of Scots a little before she was put to death, who was then heire apparent of the Kingdom of England . . . that the English had often murthered their Kings (as they also did afterwards her Grandson King Charles the Martyr), which she might also have pronounced of the Scots . . . as well as the English, but we find it not so said of the Brittaines.[107]

In the political climate of the post-Restoration period, it is hard to think of an argument which could have been better calculated to heap ignominy and shame upon the English while simultaneously exalting the Cornish.

III

As these references to the execution of Charles I help to make clear, Scawen's treatise is suffused with memories of the Civil War and Interregnum. But what does the text reveal about the author's own attitudes during that period? Without the evidence of the *Antiquities*, Scawen's political progress—from youthful critic of the government in 1631, to ardent Royalist in 1642–5, to defector from the King's Army in 1646, to Cavalier grandee in the years after 1660—might plausibly be interpreted as that of a mere opportunist, a man anxious to adhere to whichever side was in the ascendant, a Cornish Vicar of Bray. Yet viewed in the light of Scawen's own writings, that progress transforms itself into something very different. Elsewhere in this book, it has been argued that Cornish royalism was a unique amalgam: the product of a widespread conviction to the west of the Tamar that the cause of the Crown was inextricably tied up with the cause of Cornishness itself. Scawen's writings provide powerful support for this thesis—and suggest that his own political career, far from being unprincipled or opportunistic, was governed, throughout, by a fierce sense of Cornish patriotism.

Previous chapters have argued that the Cornish rallied to Charles I in 1642 partly because they regarded him as 'the King of Great Britain, the defender of the rights and privileges of *all* his subject peoples', rather than of those of the English alone. Scawen clearly subscribed to just such a view: he went out of his way to praise the Stuarts for having reassumed the title 'King[s] of Great Brittain'.[108] Previous chapters have argued that the Cornish Royalists' determination to preserve the Duchy and Stannary organizations partly reflected their belief that these institutions helped to 'set Cornwall apart from the rest of England'. Scawen averred that the creation of the Duchy of Cornwall had 'proclaimed to posteritie . . . the blood, name and speech of the ancient Brittish to be eminent in . . . [this] place'.[109] Previous chapters have argued that many Cornish Royalists saw the Civil War in terms of a quasi-national struggle between Cornwall and England. Scawen took enormous pride in what he termed '*our* Battle at Stratton . . . where the Rebels . . . were . . . defeated by the *Cornish only*', and positively exulted in the fact that during 'the late Civil Wars . . . *wee in this County* susteined for four yeares time the whole power . . . of the Rebellious Part of all the Kingdome [i.e. England], invading us with severall great and well formed Armies'.[110]

It could be countered, of course, that what Scawen wrote in the 1680s may not have reflected what he had actually thought in the 1640s: that his Cornish patriotism was simply a later affectation, which had had no bearing whatsoever on his original decision to side with the King. But such a suggestion seems inherently unlikely. Scawen's first surviving letter, written when he was only 30 years old, hints that he had already come to see the world in terms of virtuous 'Cornish men' versus duplicitous 'strangers'[111]—and if one accepts that this was the case, then the apparent contradictions of his later career become readily explicable. Thus, it may be argued, his sympathy for Eliot in 1631 sprang from a dislike of Court meddling in Cornwall, while his declaration for the King in 1642 reflected his perception of the Royalist party as the party of 'Cornishness'. Similarly, his temporary desertion of the King's army in 1644 may have reflected not only a natural desire to secure his estates from plunderers of either side, but also a readiness to put specifically Cornish war aims—in this case the re-establishment of control along the Tamar frontier—above those of the Royalist war-effort in general. Scawen's defection of 1646, moreover—on the face of it, the most remarkable of his all tergiversations—may be explained in precisely the same terms, as a reconsideration of the context in which that defection took place will help to show.

Thoughts of deserting the Royalist cause first seem to have been aroused in the Cornish officers who later surrendered at Millbrook by a letter which Fairfax sent to the Sheriff of Cornwall in September 1645. Couched in such a way as to suggest that the Parliamentarians regarded Cornwall almost as a foreign country, it threatened the Cornish with bloody punishment if they continued to support the King, but promised leniency if they would 'drive . . . the enemy out of your country . . . call home . . . the forces you have sent them . . . [and] stand upon your guard to defend yourselves . . . from any further oppressions . . . or invasions'. The letter—which clearly sought to build on the growing tensions between the Cornish and the King's English supporters—also appeared to imply tha't, if the Cornish did as they were told, no Roundhead troops would be permitted to cross their borders (see Appendix 2). There can be little doubt that this intriguing document helped to inspire Sir Richard Grenville's subsequent proposal (discussed in Chapter 5) that Cornwall should withdraw itself unilaterally from the war. What Scawen and his brother-officers in the Cornish trained bands thought of their commander's scheme can only be guessed at. What is clear is that, following Grenville's imprisonment in January 1646, any lingering hopes that the Cornish forces might be able to continue to hold the line of the Tamar against hostile 'strangers' of *both* camps—vengeful Parliamentarians and licentious Royalist Horse alike—must have been finally dashed.

It seems unlikely to be coincidence that it was just two days after Grenville's arrest that the East Cornish Royalists first entered into negotiation with the Roundheads.[112] There is a very strong possibility, in other words, that Edgcumbe, Scawen, Coryton and their co-conspirators were not just seeking to save their own skins during early 1646, but also to take up the baton which had been dropped by Grenville, to extricate Cornwall from a conflict which could no longer be won, and thus to save the Cornish people from the long-threatened Parliamentarian revenge. Certainly this is what they later managed to achieve, whether by accident or design, at Millbrook, for the agreement which they came to there amounted—in its practical consequences, if not in its formal terms—to a separate Cornish peace treaty. In its wake, thousands of Cornish soldiers laid down their arms and the whole of East Cornwall was occupied without bloodshed. Scawen and his fellows had without doubt betrayed the King's cause—but in doing so they had helped to preserve Cornwall itself from utter disaster. Once again, it seems fair to suggest that Scawen's actions may have been at least partially explicable in terms of local patriotism. His instant elevation to the ranks of the Cornish Cavalier elite after 1660, moreover, strongly suggests that most of his former comrades approved of what he had done—and thus that, in the final analysis, they, like him, put Cornish patriotism above party loyalty.

* * *

William Scawen was by no means a typical seventeenth-century Cornish gentleman. He was far more learned than most of his East Cornish gentry neighbours, he was far more proud of his supposed British ancestry, and he was infinitely more concerned about the decline of the Cornish language. Yet this does not mean that he was merely an isolated eccentric whose views on Cornish identity can be safely dismissed. On the contrary, it is precisely *because* Scawen was an untypical Cornish gentleman—one who was anxious to celebrate Cornish ethnic difference, rather than to apologize for it and to play it down, as so many of his social equals did—that his work is so crucially important. Scawen was prepared to acknowledge, albeit circumspectly, the presence of deep-rooted Anglo-Cornish tensions which his gentry neighbours usually found it expedient to ignore. In addition, thanks to his contacts in the far west of Cornwall, Scawen was able to draw heavily on the folklore, language and customs of the Cornish-speaking westerners— those who had always been most resistant to English cultural dominance—and to weave their attitudes and perspectives into his own writings. In consequence Scawen's *Antiquities Cornu-Brittanic* is the one surviving document which gives sustained expression to the subversive counter-tradition of early modern Cornwall: to that secret current of resentment against English overlordship which is otherwise glimpsed only fleetingly in the historical record—and then almost invariably in a hostile context. Behind Scawen's scholarly cadences, it seems fair to conclude, we may still catch the voice of a vanished people whispering to us across the centuries.

8

'A Monument of Honour'

The Cornish Royalist Tradition after 1660

Perceptions of what it meant to be Cornish were transformed forever as a result of the Civil War. During the 1640s the traditional view of the Cornish as an inherently rebellious people—a view which had been deliberately revived by Roundhead propagandists following what they saw as Cornwall's 'revolt' against the Parliament in 1642—had begun to be challenged by a new and opposing 'Royalist' view; one which saw the Cornish as a race of super-loyal subjects. The Restoration of the Stuart monarchy ensured that it was the latter view which would eventually prevail and from 1660 onwards Cornwall's former notoriety for rebelliousness was increasingly overlain by its newly won reputation for constancy and fidelity to the Crown. The Anglican divine Thomas Fuller nicely captured this shift in attitudes when he wrote of the Cornish in 1662 that 'it must be pitied that these people . . . have so often abused their valour in rebellions . . . however, the[y] . . . have since plentifully repaired their credit by their exemplary . . . loyalty in our late Civil Wars'.[1]

In the wake of the Restoration, the Cornish did all they could to turn this novel reputation to good account and to reap the rewards of their wartime service. The 1660s have been well described as a time of 'exaggerated loyalty' in Cornwall, as local gentlemen vied to outdo each other in the display of pro-Royalist sentiment, and in boasting of their previous sacrifices for the Cavalier cause.[2] The same was true across the length and breadth of the kingdom, of course. Yet the evidence suggests not only that preoccupation with the events of the Civil War was even more obsessive in post-Restoration Cornwall than it was everywhere else, but also that—thanks to Cornwall's unique experiences during that

157

conflict—a unique retrospective vision of the Civil War developed to the west of the Tamar. This vision, which was both fiercely Cavalier and fiercely Cornish, may conveniently be labelled the Cornish Royalist tradition. It served, at one and the same time, to celebrate Cornish conservatism and regional distinctiveness in the past, to underpin Cornish conservatism and regional distinctiveness in the present and to perpetuate Cornish conservatism and regional distinctiveness into the future. For a century after the Restoration, this partisan assemblage of shared memories and myths helped to shape the ways in which Cornish people defined themselves, and it continues to retain a vestigial influence even today. The present chapter tracks the development and continued evolution of the Cornish Royalist tradition from 1660 to the twentieth century, and considers the nature of its relationship to Cornish identity as a whole.

I

At the heart of the Cornish Royalist tradition lay three fundamental tenets. The first was that Cornwall had been almost unanimously Royalist between 1642 and 1646. The second was that the Cornish Royalist leaders in general, and Sir Bevill Grenville in particular, had been personifications of the pure Cavalier spirit. The third was that the Cornish Royalist Army had been not only exceptionally courageous and successful but exceptionally pious and well-disciplined as well: that it had been a true 'Christian Army'. All three of these tenets were firmly rooted in the events of the 1640s—and, as we shall see, two of them, at least, were given permanent physical expression in the years after 1660.

That the great majority of Cornish people had indeed favoured the King's cause rather than Parliament's between 1642 and 1646 could scarcely have been doubted by anyone who was familiar with the war's events. The initial uprising against the Parliament in 1642, the desperate struggle against the much larger Roundhead armies in 1643, the violence meted out to Essex's soldiers in 1644: memories of these episodes and many others like them stood as lasting testament to the sheer strength of support which Charles I had enjoyed in Cornwall. There had been Cornish Parliamentarians, of course, especially among the gentry, but after 1660 it would have been in few people's interest to have insisted on this fact. Those former Roundheads who lived on into Charles II's reign had good reason to maintain a low profile. Their Royalist and neo-

158

Royalist neighbours, basking in the glow of Cornwall's reputation for ultra-loyalty, had similarly good reason to play down what limited degree of support had existed for the Parliament in the county. The political imperatives of the post-Restoration period thus served to strengthen the impression of unanimous Cornish Royalism which had already been established by the events of the war itself.

What did more than anything else to foster the retrospective notion that Cornwall had been a wholly Royalist district, however—and to ensure that this was the view which was transmitted to posterity—was the fact that it appeared to be supported, from beyond the grave, by the testimony of 'the Martyr King' himself. Most students of Cornish history, and, indeed, of the Civil Wars in general, are familiar with the letter of thanks which Charles I sent to the Cornish people in September 1643. Copies of 'the King's declaration' still hang in many Cornish churches today, and are frequently noted in guide books[3]—but, rather surprisingly, the story of how this document came to be so prominently displayed in the county's churches in the first place has never been told.[4]

The genesis of Charles I's decision to send a letter of congratulation to the Cornish should probably be traced back to the very beginning of the Civil War in the South-west. From the moment that the ordinary people of Cornwall rose up *en masse* to eject the Parliamentarians from their county in October 1642, their local gentry leaders had assured them that their actions would be well 'represented . . . to his Majestie, who wee doubte not will in due tyme make knowne how much he values . . . [your] affection and service' (see Appendix 1).[5] (Was the issue of this statement by the Royalist gentry in part an attempt to exorcize the ghosts of 1497 and 1549, and to reassure their neighbours that, on this particular occasion, a popular rising in Cornwall would not be regarded by those in authority as an act of rebellion?) We may presume that, soon afterwards, the leaders of the Royalist party in Cornwall duly requested Charles I to make public acknowledgement of his Cornish subjects' service. Certainly, this is what the King himself subsequently chose to do.

In a proclamation issued from Oxford on 13 March 1643 Charles declared 'that . . . we shall alwaies remember the singular courage of Our County of Cornewall, and . . . their notable Zeale and Affection to us'.[6] This was high praise indeed, but during the following summer— as the Cornish Army built on its original success by conquering most of South-west England for the King—some may have begun to feel that more lavish commendations still were called for. On 7 September the Cornish Army crowned its achievements so far by capturing the city of Exeter; the 'centre, heart and head of the West'.[7] Word of this latest triumph was carried swiftly eastwards and on 9 September it reached the encampment of the King's main field army at Sudeley Castle in Gloucestershire, where, according to an eyewitness, the news caused 'great joy' among the Royalist soldiers.[8]

The King's decision to compose a formal letter of thanks to the Cornish people was clearly a direct response to this heartening news (although Charles may also have been influenced by the continued pleas of Cornwall's gentry leaders for greater recognition of their countrymen's services).[9] Next day, the King published a 'declaration unto all his loving subjects of . . . Cornwall' from Sudeley—and the latter part of this remarkable document is worth reproducing in full. Having praised the Cornish for their loyalty and for their many victories, Charles's letter ends with the ringing declaration:

> That as We cannot be forgetful of so great Deserts, so We cannot but desire to publish to the World and perpetuate to all Time the Memory of these Their Merits . . . And to that end We do hereby render Our Royal Thanks to that Our County, in the most publick and lasting manner we can devise, commanding copies hereof to be printed and published, and one of them to be read in every Church and Chapel therein, and to be kept forever as a Record in the same; That as long as the History of these Times and this Nation shall continue, the Memory of how much that County hath merited from Us and Our Crown may be derived with it to Posterity.[10]

This document, as Charles made clear in an effusive letter to the Cornish gentry written on the following day, was intended to 'fix . . . a perpetuall Marke of meritt uppon that our county'[11]—and no communication like it was ever directed to any other part of the King's dominions. That the declaration was ordered not only to be printed but also to be displayed in every parish in Cornwall 'forever' shows that the King's intention was to make its message permanent in a way that that of the earlier proclamation had not been. And although it has been suggested that Charles did not keep his promise to have the declaration published, this allegation can be swiftly disproved.[12] Not only was the printing of the King's letter reported at the time in both the Royalist and Parliamentary press, but several printed copies of the declaration itself, published at Oxford on or around 15 September, still survive (see frontispiece).[13]

From Oxford, bundles of the newly printed document were presumably sent down to Cornwall for general distribution. A copy is certainly known to have been put up in at least one Cornish church soon afterwards: in November 1643 the town authorities of Launceston paid two shillings for 'a fram[e] for the Kings declaration hangine in the church'.[14] Few sets of churchwardens' accounts survive for Cornwall for the 1640s, but it would appear that Launceston's example was universally followed, for when the New Model Army finally conquered Cornwall in 1646, the invading Parliamentary soldiers found copies of the King's letter 'hanged up in every church in the Country'.[15] What happened to these documents during the Commonwealth and Interregnum remains a mystery. We must presume that few, if any of them, remained on public display. Many must have been destroyed by the Parliamentarians, others may have been concealed by local people. Following the Restoration, however, the King's letter once again became a legitimate focus for Cornish pride—and over the next fifty years it established itself as the central, sacred text of the Cornish Royalist tradition.

Historians have tended to assume that the impressive painted copies of the declaration which still survive in many Cornish churches today— variously executed on wooden boards (see Plates 6 and 7), plaster panels and, in one case at least, on canvas[16]—date from the 1660s.[17] This may well be so in some cases, but, as we shall see, a number of the surviving examples in fact appear to be rather later. Quite possibly, then, it was paper versions of the declaration—whether the original printed broadsides or hand-written copies—which were most commonly met with in Cornish churches during the late seventeenth century. What is clear is that, in almost every parish, the declaration was returned to the position of public honour which it had occupied in 1643–6. An observer wrote in 1732 that the King's letter 'may be read at this Day within the walls of almost all the Churches and Chapels in the county', and his subsequent comment—that the text provided indisputable proof both of the 'Heroick Virtue' of the Cornish and of 'the Universality of their Loyalty'—nicely illustrates what he, for one, believed the central message of the declaration to be.[18]

If the ringing words of the King's declaration helped to underpin the retrospective notion that Cornwall had been an entirely Royalist county, they also helped to preserve the memory of the Cornish Royalist leaders, for Charles' letter made sorrowful reference to the fact that the Cornish Army's victories had been accompanied by 'the Loss of some Eminent persons, who shall never be forgotten by us'. Cornish people studying the declaration in later years would have known at once whom the King had meant. Of all the officers of the Cornish Army slain during 1642–3, the most publicly lamented had been Sidney Godolphin, killed at Chagford in February 1643, John Trevanion and Sir Nicholas Slanning, killed at Bristol later in the same year, and above all, Sir Bevill Grenville, slain at Lansdown, near Bath, in July 1643. All four had been regarded as just and honourable men during their own lifetimes and all four became elevated to the status of heroic martyrs for the Royalist cause after their deaths. In 1683 an elderly husbandman who had served as a common soldier in Grenville's regiment recalled that he had been engaged at Lansdown 'when his heroyicke colonel Sir Bevill Grenvill was slayne' and referred, with almost equal regret, to the deaths of 'the valiant Sir Nicholas Slanning, Colonel Godolphyn and Colonel Trevanion'.[19] Twenty years later the Devon biographer John Prince recorded the mournful distich on the four men which is still remembered today:

[Gone] the four wheels of Charles' Wain,
Grenvile, Godolphin, Trevanion, Slanning slain.[20]

Of these four pillars of the Royalist cause, it was Grenville who enjoyed the greatest reputation, both in his own lifetime and posthumously. The head of one of Cornwall's most distinguished gentry families—the Grenvilles had been established at their ancestral seat of Stowe, in Kilkhampton parish in the extreme north-east of the county, for well over three centuries—Sir Bevill had formerly been a vocal critic of the Court.[21] By 1640, however, his sympathies were firmly behind the King, and from the beginning of the Civil War, Grenville had been regarded as the most important and influential of Charles I's Cornish supporters. It was Grenville who was believed to have done more than anyone else to raise Cornwall for the King in the first place, Grenville who was held to have inspired the great Cornish victories at Braddock Down and Stratton, and Grenville who—by leading his pikemen in a desperate assault against Parliamentary troops in prepared positions at Lansdown, an assault which was ultimately successful, though it led to his own death—was credited with having delivered the Cornish Army from almost certain destruction. Grenville's suicidal courage at Lansdown, combined with his undoubted personal qualities, earned him a place of exceptional honour in the Royalist pantheon. Within weeks of the battle, a collection of elegies lamenting his death had been published at Oxford, and almost every subsequent Royalist account of the war in the South-west paid glowing tribute to his valour, his resolve, and, above all, his loyalty.[22]

Following the Royalist defeat in 1646 Grenville's reputation fell into temporary abeyance but with the Restoration his stock soared. Sir Bevill's eldest surviving son, Sir John Grenville, had been one of the most trusted servants of Charles II during his period in exile, and when the King returned to the throne, rewards and offices were showered upon him. During 1660–1 John Grenville was appointed Lord Lieutenant of Cornwall, Lord Warden of the Stannaries, Steward of the Duchy of Cornwall and Governor of Plymouth, as well as being created Earl of Bath and Viscount Lansdowne (a title specifically chosen to commemorate Sir Bevill's wartime service).[23] Throughout the next thirty years, Bath's pre-eminent position in South-western society ensured that the cult of his father's memory would continue to grow. He himself encouraged this process by hanging a splendid portrait of Sir Bevill in the magnificent classical mansion which he had built on the site of his father's old house at Stowe during the 1680s.[24] It might not be going too far, indeed, to see the new house itself as a monument to the memory of Sir Bevill, who, as William Scawen later wrote, had ensured 'by his [own] death' that 'his children . . . [would] attain . . . to the Top of a great honour'.[25]

Grenville's burgeoning reputation as an archetypal Cavalier hero was one in which almost all Cornish people could take pride, and as time went by he not only came to be seen as the greatest of Cornwall's wartime leaders, but as the very personification of Cornish royalism. His loyalty and that of his family (which was proverbial—in 1654, Sir Bevill's brother Sir Richard had boasted that 'all my ancestors since the Conquest . . . [were] ever constantly for the services of the Crown'[26]) became conflated with the wartime loyalty of Cornwall itself. His personal courage and integrity became emblematic of that of the entire Cornish Royalist officer corps. And his genuine piety, which even the Parliamentarians were forced to concede, became both a symbol of, and a partial explanation for, the legendary piety of the Cornish Army as a whole. 'Sir Bevile wished that his Army were all of them as good as his Cause', wrote David Lloyd in 1667, 'he disciplined [them] to piety . . . and strictness . . . [and] there were fewer oaths among them than in any Army . . . in England.'[27]

The Cornish Army's reputation for godliness and good discipline, the third of the conceptual props on which the Cornish Royalist tradition rested, was by no means the invention of Sir Bevill's post-Restoration hagiographers. It dated back to the very beginning of the Civil War, and was attested to by Royalists and Parliamentarians alike. As early as October 1642 a Roundhead correspondent in Plymouth had candidly acknowledged that Hopton's troops were guiltless of 'any mischiefe or great spoile', while in May 1643 the Parliamentarian officer James Chudleigh, a prisoner of the Cornish Royalists, had averred that 'I never saw any army freer from vice, nor more religiously inclined, than I perceive the whole genius of this army to be'.[28] Later that same year a Parliamentary journalist had noted that the King's English-Irish troops mocked the Cornish soldiers as 'puritans', an epithet which was also applied to their leader, Sir Ralph Hopton.[29] And even as late as summer 1645, by which time the war was plainly lost to the King and discipline among the bulk of his troops had all but broken down, the Cornish had continued to be praised for their good conduct. A petition drawn up by the Clubmen of Devon and Somerset at this time had claimed that the Cornish troops of Sir Richard Grenville were as well governed as those of the New Model Army itself.[30] It is hardly surprising that many Royalist sympathisers should subsequently have come to believe that the remarkable military successes of the Cornish army had been a direct result of their unusually pious and well-disciplined bearing: that, as Lloyd expressed it, 'the sobriety of this Army . . . made them valiant'.[31]

That the Cornish troops had indeed been remarkably valiant, almost everyone agreed. During the post-Restoration period, former Royalist officers frequently extolled the valour of the Cornish Army. Thus Captain Richard Atkyns of Gloucestershire, who had served alongside Hopton's forces in 1643, recalled in 1669 that 'the Cornish Foot . . . were the very best foot that ever I saw, for marching and fighting' and termed the Cornish troops who had participated in the storm of Bristol 'as gallant men as ever drew sword'.[32] As one might expect, veteran Cornish officers were more fulsome still in their praises. Colonel Richard Arundell, who had served in the Cornish Army throughout the war, recalled with evident pride 'how prosperous and successfull that

Army was (as long as theire owne officers lived to command them)', and averred that the Cornishmen's services 'cannot be forgotten, [as] by the Battle of Stratton, the taking of Exeter, Bath, Bristoll . . . and the long and sad sieges laid against Plymouth and Lyme'.[33] William Scawen was no less proud, and descanted at length on 'that famous Defence of the Cornish att Lans-Downe . . . where a small stand of Cornish Pike entertained the fierce assault of the whole body of the Rebels horse more then once, chargeing upon them, whome they continually withstood and forced off '.[34]

Scawen, like Lloyd, clearly believed that the Cornishmen's virtuous conduct had prompted God to endow them with special courage—and nowhere was this view better expressed than in the writings of Charles Hammond, an Englishman who had served as a captain in one of the Cornish regiments, and who penned an account of the Cornish Army's wartime services during the 1670s. 'Pray enquireth of the worst of our Enemies', Hammond declaimed:

> how . . . [the soldiers were] governed, when they were first raised, and how God prospered them, being but 5 regiments of Foot and very few Horse. The chief commanders [were] the Lord Mohun, Sir Bevil Greenfield, Sir Nicholas Slanning, Coll. Godolphin, Coll. Trevanion, and others, which . . . most of them lost their lives in the service, [and] their officers and soldiers under them were as well instructed to fear God as to honour and serve the King. Oaths was held so abominable amongst most of the officers, that the soldiers durst not swear an oath before them. Likewise [we] went to prayers before we went to fight, if possible we had time. The soldiers durst not command for a cup of beer, much less then to Robb, Plunder and Spoyl their Quarters . . . and for their undaunted valour . . . it was very well tryed several times . . . as . . . at Stratton . . . where . . . we went to prayers . . . before we fought them, and that strengthened our Forces, and Armed our soldiers with undaunted Resolution: in a word, no courage like a Christian courage.[35]

II

Such depictions of the Cornish Army as a Christian militia, one which had been led by saint-like officers in defence of a devotedly loyal county, held the field almost unchallenged in Cornwall throughout the period 1660 to 1700. It is easy to see why this should have been so, and why the Cornish Royalist tradition which these images served to define should have met with such eager acceptance. First, the tradition was a politically advantageous one: one which, during the 1660s and 1670s at least, seemed likely to win Cornwall special favour with the central government. Second, it was a credible tradition: a retrospective vision of the Civil War which was built upon judicious exaggeration rather than on wholesale invention, and was thus relatively easy to swallow. Third, it was a socially conservative tradition, one which reinforced the existing hierarchy by preaching the necessity of obedience to one's superiors and respect for private property, and was therefore bound to commend itself to the local gentry. Fourth, it was, nevertheless, a genuinely popular tradition: one which celebrated the wartime service of many thousands of ordinary Cornishmen as well as of their officers, and thus enabled members of both groups to look back on the war with equal self-satisfaction. Fifth, it was a unifying tradition: one which brought the vast majority of Cornishmen and women together in a shared sense of pride at their common loyalty and sacrifice during the 1640s.

The Cornish Royalist tradition served another, less obvious, but perhaps even more important, purpose too. By encouraging the belief that Cornwall had been uniquely, almost preternaturally, loyal during the 1640s while the English counties to the east had been riddled with Parliamentarianism and rebelliousness, it powerfully reinforced notions of Cornish distinctiveness and fostered the development of a new conception of Cornish identity: one which was based upon unswerving, near-fanatical support for the Crown and the established Church. This reinvention of Cornish identity had important politico-religious consequences. Popular conviction that to be Cornish was to be ultra-loyal surely helps to explain why post-Restoration Cornwall was, in the words of K. Feiling, '[the] most famous and individual of Tory territories', a region in which Tory electoral victory was practically guaranteed.[36] Such conviction must also have stiffened Cornwall's remarkable resistance to the spread of religious dissent: as late as 1700, 'Cornwall's population of over 100,000 contained only one dissenter to every hundred inhabitants'.[37] Thus the intimate association which had been established between Cornishness and Cavalier-conformity during the 1640s helped to ensure that Cornwall would remain both fiercely Tory and fiercely Anglican for decades to come.

Potent as the Cornish Royalist tradition was, it could not hope to entirely drown out other, competing versions of Cornwall's Civil War history—or at least not while many veterans of the 1640s remained alive. Throughout the late seventeenth century 'official' depictions of Cornwall as a unanimously Royalist county continued to be implicitly contradicted at grass-roots level by the personal recollections of hundreds of Cornishmen and women who had either supported the Parliament themselves, or had known others who had. Depictions of the Cornish people as boundlessly enthusiastic in the King's cause were similarly undermined by hidden memories of forcible conscription into the royal armies, of mass desertion from the trenches before Plymouth and Taunton, and of fierce opposition to plundering Royalist troopers. The tales recorded by the early eighteenth-century antiquary William Hickes of popular resistance to Lord Goring's cavalry at St Ives in 1646 may serve as a case in point.[38] Hardest of all to reconcile with the Cornish Royalist tradition, perhaps—in its official version at least—were those memories which suggested that, far from having been motivated by selfless loyalty to the King, the Cornish had in fact been fighting primarily in their own interests: in defence of Cornish autonomy and identity.

Recollections of such episodes as the Cornish troops' refusal to march eastwards with the King in 1644 or the separate Cornish peace-treaty signed at Millbrook in 1646 were, in their own way, even more subversive of the Cornish Royalist tradition than were memories of the few occasions when Roundhead recruiters had enjoyed a modicum of success in Cornwall. Such occasions could be convincingly dismissed as aberrations: short-lived and unsuccessful demonstrations of support for Parliament which were unrepresentative of the mainstream of Cornish opinion. The tensions between the King's Cornish supporters and the Royalist party as a whole, on the other hand, had been central to Cornwall's wartime experience. They had been visible throughout the war, had grown much more serious as time went on, and had frequently been sustained and exacerbated by that central icon of the Cornish Royalist tradition—the Cornish Army itself (see Chapters 4 and 5). To have admitted to this during the post-Restoration period would have been to have admitted that Cornwall's wartime allegiance had been conditional, rather than absolute—and thus to have demolished the central premise of the cult of Cornish Royalism.

The whole question of Cornish cultural distinctiveness, in fact, was a deeply problematic one for post-Restoration Royalist commentators. William Scawen's retrospective vision of the Civil War in the South-west as a conflict between the 'ever-loyal' Cornish and the 'rebellious' English—'unworthy to have so good [a] Prince [as Charles I] to reigne over them'[39]—might well have commanded support among the fiercer sort of Cornish patriot, but it was hardly likely to appeal to English Tories, or indeed to that increasing number of Cornish folk who were by now coming to regard the Cornish identity as primarily a regional, rather than an ethnic, one. Members of both these latter groups preferred to see Cornwall not as *sui generis*, but as a role model for other English counties: as a glowing example of the way in which those counties could and should have behaved during the Civil War. Reminiscences which suggested that Cornwall's wartime behaviour had been, at least in part, a product of ethnic difference obviously tended to undermine this vision and would have been most unwelcome in orthodox Tory circles.

Dissonant voices like those of Hickes and Scawen continued to challenge the dominant orthodoxy throughout the late seventeenth and early eighteenth centuries. But as the generation of the 1640s gradually died away, and as impressions of the Civil War came, of necessity, to be increasingly founded on the authority of written sources and inherited tradition, rather than on that of personal recollection, the Cornish Royalist tradition became ever more firmly established as the 'truth' about Cornwall's Civil War history. At the same time, it became ever more simplified, romanticized and even, one might venture to suggest, 'Anglicized'. The second half of this chapter will explore how the tradition evolved after 1700, and will focus in particular on the three individuals who arguably did most to influence that process: the first and most important of them being Edward Hyde, Earl of Clarendon.

III

The publication of Clarendon's monumental *History of the Rebellion* in 1702–4 may be regarded as the event which set the Cornish Royalist tradition in stone. Begun soon after Clarendon's flight to Jersey with the future Charles II in 1646, but not completed until the 1670s, the *History* was perhaps the most influential of all studies of the Civil War and certainly the work which did most to shape the historical view of eighteenth-century Tories.[40] Partially based on Clarendon's own wartime experiences (he had spent the last year of the conflict in the West Country, as a member of the Prince of Wales' Council) the *History* essentially reiterated the established Royalist view of Cornwall's wartime behaviour. Clarendon repeated the claim that Cornwall had been an exceptionally Royalist county. He sang the praises of the Cornish troops and their leaders, observing that 'the fame of their religion and discipline was no less than of their courage'. Finally, he paid extravagant tribute at the shrine of Sir Bevill: averring that 'he was indeed an excellent person, whose activity, interest, and reputation, was the foundation of . . . [all that was] done in Cornwall' during the Civil War.[41] Such plaudits resulted in Grenville being included among the select band of eighteen Royalist 'champions' whose portraits appeared, grouped around a depiction of Charles I himself, in early editions of Clarendon's work (see Plate 8)— and thus contributed still further to Grenville's burgeoning cult.[42]

Clarendon's *History* was also highly influential in that it finally dislodged Grenville's brother, Sir Richard, from his—already somewhat precarious—place in the pantheon of Cornish Royalist heroes. As has been shown elsewhere, Sir Richard had been a key figure in Cornwall during the Civil War. Following his brother's death, Sir Richard had inherited Sir Bevill's mantle as the champion of Cornish Royalist sentiment, and he had remained the undisputed favourite of the Cornish troops until his removal from command in January 1646. Grenville's dismissal sparked off bitter protests in Cornwall: indeed it was widely believed at the time to have been the final straw which alienated the Cornish from the King's cause. Following the defeat of the Royalist armies in the West, moreover, and Sir Richard's flight abroad, he had remained, for a number of years, the perceived leader-in-exile of the Cornish Royalist cause. Many of his old officers had taken part in the Cornish rising of 1648, and in 1650 Cavalier conspirators attempting to engineer a fresh insurrection in the county had informed the Royalist leadership 'that Sir Richard [Grenville's] presence in Cornwall was essential to the success of their enterprise'.[43]

Grenville died in October 1659, just a few months short of the Restoration, but memories of his wartime activities continued to command respect among many Royalists—and especially, perhaps, in Cornwall—for decades to come. In 1667 David Lloyd appended a glowing pen-portrait of Sir Richard to the lavish encomium on Sir Bevill in his Royalist martyrology.[44] Long after this, Colonel Edward Roscarrock, one of Grenville's former subordinates, continued to tell of how Sir Richard had enjoined his mutinous officers and men to 'a strict obedience to the commands of the Prince' at the moment of his 'unjust' dismissal in 1646.[45] And as late as 1704, the grieving relatives of Hugh Piper of Launceston caused his funerary monument to be emblazoned with the proud statement that he had 'served in the Civil Wars as a Ensign, Lieutenant and Captain, under Sir Richard and Sir Beville Granville, Knights, at the siege of Plymouth [and] at the battles of Stratton and Lansdowne'.[46] This inscription neatly demonstrates the way in which, at the start of the eighteenth century, Sir Richard and the long, bloody and ultimately unsuccessful siege of Plymouth remained— to some, at least—as much a part of the 'approved' version of Cornwall's Civil War history as did Sir Bevill and the famous Cornish victories of summer 1643.

Yet to mainstream Tories and neo-Royalists, Sir Richard had always been something of an embarrassment. His personal vindictiveness, his quarrelsome nature and his well-known taste for atrocity made it impossible to present him as a 'true Christian knight' in the mould of his brother. More awkward still was the fact that he had frequently evinced a willingness to put Cornish interests above those of the Royalist war effort as a whole, and towards the end of the conflict had even proposed that Cornwall should withdraw from the hostilities altogether. Sir Richard was the very embodiment of that turbulent, particularist spirit which had lain just beneath the surface of Cornish Royalism, in other words, and this was reason enough for many post-Restoration English conservatives to see him as a subversive figure whose wartime prominence was best forgotten. The publication of Clarendon's *History* greatly reinforced such attitudes. Clarendon had been a bitter personal enemy of Sir Richard's, and his book was in part a deliberate attempt to blacken Grenville's name. By launching a series of violent attacks upon Sir Richard's character—and by implying that he had eventually been dismissed because he was plotting to betray the King's cause— Clarendon dealt a mortal blow to Grenville's reputation as a Cornish Royalist champion. After 1704 Sir Richard was effectively 'written out' of the Cornish Royalist tradition, and his memory became increasingly eclipsed by that of his brother.

Clarendon's *History* both inspired and infuriated the man who, after Hyde himself, was to prove the most influential figure in the retrospective construction of the Cornish Royalist legend. Born in 1667, George Granville (as he always preferred to spell his name) was the eldest son of Sir Bernard Grenville, himself the fourth son of Sir Bevill. Throughout his childhood, the young George was clearly surrounded by memories of the illustrious part which his family had played in the Civil Wars. He later recalled that Martin Lluellin's epigram on Sir Bevill, taken from the collection published at Oxford in 1643, had been 'often repeated to me as a boy', while it is evident that both his father and his uncle, John Grenville Earl of Bath, had frequently regaled him with tales of their own wartime adventures in the service of Charles II.[47] That George grew up to be an ardent admirer of the old Cavalier cause, a high Tory in his politics and a bitter opponent of religious dissent comes as little surprise. In 1685, aged only 18, he begged his father to permit him to serve against the Duke of Monmouth's rebels, and in 1688 he sought similar permission to enlist in James II's forces against William of Orange, reminding his father that 'my Uncle Bathe was not so old when he was left among the slain at the battle of Newbury'.[48]

Dismayed by the outcome of 'the Glorious Revolution', Granville spent the years between 1688 and 1702 'in literary retirement', devoting himself to the composition of plays and poems.[49] Following the accession of the Stuart Queen Anne in 1702, however, Granville entered public life and quickly rose to become a figure of great political significance in the South-west, where he succeeded the Earl of Bath as chief manager of the Tory electoral interest in Cornwall. Granville's pride in Cornwall's rock-solid Toryism was immense and in 1702 he boasted that the county 'never sent up a heartier set of gentlemen then now, for out of the four and forty [newly elected Cornish MPs] there are but two exceptionable persons'.[50] Granville himself was elected as MP for Fowey in 1702, while in 1710 he and his fellow Tory candidate, John Trevanion—both fervent supporters of the high churchman Dr Sacheverell—were chosen as Knights of the Shire for Cornwall amidst cries of:

> Granville and Trevanion, sound as a Bell,
> For the Queen, the Church and Sacheverell.[51]

In the triumphant Tory administration of 1710 Granville was made Lord Treasurer, and in 1711 he was created Lord Lansdowne, a title which, given its Civil War connotations, he must have especially savoured. But Granville's political eminence was not to last. In 1714 Queen Anne died and was succeeded by the Hanoverian George I, who favoured the Whigs. In the general election which followed the Tories, deprived of the all-important support of the Crown, suffered a catastrophic defeat: a defeat which was as absolute in Cornwall as it was everywhere else. West of the Tamar, 'a Tory supremacy of 40 members to 4 in the last Parliament of Anne was transformed by the return of . . . [33 Whigs to 11 Tories] in the first Parliament of George'.[52] Routed at the Cornish hustings, Granville found himself out of favour at the Court too, and in October 1714 he was dismissed from his post as Treasurer. Desperate to recover his political fortunes, Lansdowne now became involved in a nationwide conspiracy to place the exiled Pretender, James Edward Stuart, on the throne, and it is almost superfluous to add that it was to Cornwall—that perceived stronghold of Stuart loyalism and Grenville family interest—that Lansdowne chiefly looked for support in his intended rebellion. Henceforth, he was to lay repeated public stress on the connections which had existed between his own family, the Cornish people and the Stuart dynasty in the past as he strove to engineer a similar alliance in the future.

This process had begun even before Granville's fall from power. In 1714 he had erected an impressive stone monument to mark Sir Bevill Grenville's final resting place in Kilkhampton Church. That Granville chose to embellish this structure with extracts from Clarendon's encomium on Sir Bevill reveals the extent to which the *History of the Rebellion* had already begun to influence contemporary perceptions of Cornwall's role in the Civil War.[53] Soon afterwards Granville erected a second monument on Stamford Hill, in neighbouring Stratton parish, to commemorate the great Royalist victory which had been won there in 1643. The central tablet proclaimed that 'In this place ye army of ye Rebells . . . received a signall overthrow by ye Valor of Sir Bevill Granville and ye Cornish army on Tuesday ye 16th May 1643' (a statement which, it will be noted, not only memorialized the purely Cornish composition of the army which had triumphed at Stratton, but also implied that Sir Bevill, rather than Sir Ralph Hopton, had been its chief commander).[54] By thus commemorating the actions of one of the greatest heroes of the Stuart cause, Granville was not only expressing conventional family pride: he was also hinting at his own distaste for the Hanoverian regime.

By summer 1715 Granville was the acknowledged leader of the Jacobite party in England and preparations for a major rising in the South-west were almost complete. The government had long been keeping the plotters under observation, however, and in September its agents struck, arresting Lansdowne together with many of his co-conspirators.[55] Soon afterwards an abortive insurrection took place in Cornwall when a small group of Cornish Jacobites proclaimed James III at St Columb.[56] This affair, the last rebellion to take place in Cornwall during the early modern period, was also the least well supported. The Pretender's local supporters were swiftly hunted down and Cornwall played no further part in the events of the 1715 or, indeed, in any subsequent Jacobite rising. This is somewhat surprising, for Cornwall's long tradition of Tory-Episcopalianism, its even longer tradition of resistance to central authority, its remoteness from the Whig heartlands of South-east England, its poverty, its rusticity and its still lingering Celticity might all have been expected to lead, ineluctably, to its becoming a hotbed of Jacobite activism. That this did not, in fact, happen may well have reflected the accelerating pace of Cornwall's cultural assimilation with England—though lack of organization among the movement's local gentry leaders may also have played its part in queering the Jacobite pitch in the far South-west.[57]

Lansdowne—who was released from the Tower in 1717, but who continued to work in the Pretender's interests thereafter—long remained hopeful of harnessing the Cornish Royalist tradition in the Jacobite cause.[58] In 1723 he caused yet another monument to Sir Bevill to be erected: this time on Lansdown Hill, on the spot where the Royalist commander had met his death. The monument, which took the form of an imposing stone column, was dedicated by Granville not to Sir Bevill alone but 'to the immortal memory of his renowned and . . . valiant Cornish friends, who conquered dying in the Royal Cause, 5 July 1643'.[59] Granville clearly hoped that this dedication would infuse the Cornishmen of his own day with what he fondly believed to have been the fierce Stuart loyalism of their forefathers, but in this he was to be disappointed; Cornwall remained stubbornly quiescent throughout the 1720s. Nevertheless, Granville returned to the theme of Cornish Royalism towards the end of his life, when he wrote a vindication of Sir Richard Grenville against the attacks which had been launched upon him by Clarendon and others.[60] This work made little impact on the general public, and it was Clarendon's portrait of Sir Richard which continued to hold sway when Granville finally died in 1735. But if Granville's literary effusions proved ephemeral, his architectural legacy was to exert an abiding influence.

The monuments which Granville erected at Kilkhampton, Stratton and Lansdown gave permanent physical expression to the Cornish Royalist tradition. Together with the (soon to be ruined) mansion house at Stowe, they created a landscape of remembrance through which Sir Bevill's shade would continue to flit for centuries to come. It is at least possible, moreover, that Granville's imposing memorials in brick and stone directly inspired other, more humble, memorials in wood and plaster, for, of the few dated examples of the King's declaration which survive in Cornish churches today, all were painted in the early 1700s. Thus the copy at Launceston is known to have been painted and re-framed at some time between 1717 and 1732, while that at Calstock is dated 1735 and that at Camborne 1736.[61] The fact that the painted copies of the declaration in at least two other churches are entitled 'His Majesties Grace['s] letter to the County of Cornwall *after the death of Sir Bevill Granvill*' strongly suggests that these examples, too, date from the early eighteenth century—by which time the legend of Sir Bevill had already become well established—rather than from the immediate post-Restoration period, when the precise context in which the letter had been sent would still have been widely remembered.[62]

Ironically, these painted boards—so redolent of the Tory-Anglican ascendancy in Cornwall—were erected on the very eve of that ascendancy's final collapse. During the 1740s the Wesleys launched the first of the great Methodist preaching campaigns in Cornwall and over the following decades tens of thousands of Cornish folk began to drift away from the established Church.[63] At the same time, the rapid expansion of tin and copper mining heralded the era of industrialization in Cornwall and changed the nature of local society forever. By the end of the eighteenth century a new conception of Cornish identity had been forged; one which was based not on politico-religious conservatism and cultural isolation as it had been in the past, but on Methodism, incipient political liberalism and 'technological advance'.[64] In the process, the great majority of the ordinary people of Cornwall became irrevocably divorced from the old Anglican-Royalist tradition. Yet even as the Cornish Royalist tradition lost its grip upon the common people of Cornwall, so its hold upon the literary middle classes, both in Cornwall and elsewhere, continued to grow.

That this was so was chiefly due to the burgeoning cult of Sir Bevill. Some indication of the rate at which Grenville's posthumous reputation grew during the eighteenth century may be gleaned from the writings of the Devonian John Prince. In 1701 Prince published a collection of historical biographies entitled *The Worthies of Devon*. As one would expect this book had little to say about Sir Bevill, a Cornishman, although when dealing with the Devon branch of the Grenville family Prince did refer in passing to Sir Bevill's 'renowned action . . . at Lansdowne'.[65] In an unpublished sequel to the *Worthies*, however—a work which was completed in 1716 and heavily influenced by Clarendon's *History*— Prince was a good deal more effusive, referring to 'that Immortal Hero Sir Bevil Grenvil'.[66] And by the time a second, revised edition of the *Worthies* was published in 1809, Grenville had been transformed from a bit-player into the star of the entire piece. His portrait now graced the front papers of the book, while Prince's original three-line digression on Sir Bevill had been expanded by the nineteenth-century editors into a glowing three-page encomium.[67]

By now, earnest literary pilgrims had begun to make their way to the sites most closely associated with Grenville's life. So great was the number of visitors who thronged to Lansdowne's monument on Stamford Hill that, at some time prior to 1817, the landowner felt obliged to dismantle the structure 'in order to prevent the injury which the field sustained'.[68] This regrettable action did nothing to diminish Grenville's fame. Rather, it had the opposite effect, for the inscribed tablet which had formed the centrepiece of the original structure was now set up on the wall of the Tree Inn, in Stratton town, where it was more conveniently accessible to passers-by.[69] By the mid-nineteenth century, Stratton, Kilkhampton Church and the ruins of Stowe had all become recognized stopping-off points along what was, in effect, a tourist trail through 'the Grenville Country' of north-east Cornwall. The folklorist Mrs Bray set out to visit all three places in 1845[70] and many others were soon to follow in her footsteps, attracted not only by the sites themselves, but by the writings of the man who was to inspire the final baroque flowering of the Cornish Royalist tradition: the Reverend R.S. Hawker, vicar of Morwenstow.

IV

Born into a clerical family in Plymouth in 1804, Robert Hawker was ordained in 1831 and presented to the living of Morwenstow, a neighbour-parish of Kilkhampton, in 1834. Always a reactionary at heart—he was to write in 1868 that 'I have no Radical or Liberal tendencies in my nature. So far as taste and judgement go, my mind is cast in the Old Conservative mould'[71]—Hawker was one of those many nineteenth-century Anglicans who 'looked longingly to the Stuart Church' as a symbol of vanished social and religious harmony.[72] Bitterly hostile to religious dissent, he was an admirer of Archbishop Laud and introduced many ceremonies redolent of Laudian church practice into his services.[73] Although most of Hawker's youth was spent to the east of the Tamar, he quickly developed an elective affinity with Cornwall, which—like Lansdowne before him and many others since—he idealized as a stronghold of traditional values in a world of flux and change. Hawker was especially fascinated by Cornwall's past, which, again like Lansdowne, he regarded as a rich source of inspiration for conservatives in his own day, and, in the many songs, ballads and stories which he wrote over the course of his long life, he frequently drew upon—and distorted—Cornish history in order to provide models for contemporary emulation.

Hawker's methods are well illustrated by the story of 'Trelawny', or 'The Western Men': a ballad which he wrote in his early twenties. First Hawker appropriated what appears to have been a genuinely old scrap of doggerel verse relating to the arrest of the Cornish MP John Trelawny for breach of Parliamentary privilege in 1627:

> And must Trelawny die?
> And shall Trelawny die?
> We've twenty thousand Cornish Boys,
> Will know the reason why![74]

Next Hawker altered, either subconsciously or deliberately, the context of the piece, by claiming that it related to the imprisonment of Bishop Jonathan Trelawny for refusing to agree to James II's proposed toleration of religious dissent in 1688. Finally, after having recast 'Trelawny' into a hero after his own heart, Hawker embedded the original verse within a wholly new poem written in a plausibly archaic style. The resulting composition—a rousing paean to Cornish stout-heartedness and independence of spirit—was acclaimed from the moment of its first publication, grew ever more popular thereafter and eventually established itself as the Cornish equivalent of the Marseillaise.[75] So great has been the impact of Hawker's ballad upon the popular imagination, indeed, that even today one may often hear it claimed not only that the song is an authentic late seventeenth-century composition but even that a Cornish insurrection in support of Bishop Trelawny actually took place!

Hawker himself, a man for whom the boundary between fact and fiction grew increasingly hazy as time went by, soon came to believe implicitly in his own fabrication. In a sermon prepared for an episcopal visitation in 1845 he posed the rhetorical question 'Can we ever forget that day of glory in our annals when the strength of 20,000 Cornish hearts arose . . . to set their Bishop free?'. Yet his subsequent plea to his audience—to similarly support their own Bishop 'so ye may be found worthy to inherit the praise and the blessing of the good old Cornish name'—shows that Hawker fully appreciated the contemporary applications to which the 'Trelawny myth' might be put.[76] By conjuring up the ghosts of the 'Church and State' Cornishmen of the late seventeenth century, he believed, it might yet be possible to inspire a return to the 'good old Cornish' values which they had, allegedly, embodied, and to turn back the clock to the days before John Wesley had—in Hawker's own very telling phrase—'corrupted and degraded the Cornish character'.[77]

Given Hawker's intellectual preoccupations, his historical bent and his residence in that district which had long been established as the spiritual home of the Cornish Royalist tradition,[78] it was almost inevitable that he would eventually turn his pen to the subject of Sir Bevill Grenville. In 1861 he wrote, apparently at the entreaty of one Miss Harris of Hayne, 'a theme of the Cavaliers called Sir Beville', or 'The Gate Song of Stowe'.[79] Clearly intended to repeat the success of 'Trelawny', 'Sir Beville' was couched, like its predecessor, in a vaguely seventeenth-century style and incorporated, like it, a fragment of genuinely old verse. In its central concerns, too, 'Sir Beville' closely resembled 'Trelawny'. An exhortation to the people of Cornwall to rise 'one and all' for 'the King and the land' against the forces of evil—in this case personified by 'dark Cromwell'—it bore witness to Hawker's lifelong love affair with that idealized form of Cornish patriotic sentiment which he regarded as the eternal buttress of the old socio-religious order in the far South-west.[80]

Flushed by the success of his ballad on Sir Bevill, Hawker returned to the theme of Cornish Royalism in 1866, when he composed a paper for the periodical *All the Year Round* entitled 'Anthony Payne: A Cornish Giant'.[81] The inspiration for this piece evidently came from C.S.

Gilbert's *History of Cornwall*, first published in 1817, which contains a brief but racy account of Payne: a prodigious youth from Stratton who had been 'the . . . favourite attendant of John, eldest son of Sir Beville, afterwards Earl of Bath'.[82] Hawker took this story and—indulging to the full what his tactful son-in-law was later to term his 'inventive faculty'[83]—'improved' upon it: claiming that Payne had been Sir Bevill's servant rather than Sir John's, ascribing personal qualities to him which Gilbert had attributed to other men, and fleshing out the bones of the original account with a collection of 'traditions' relating to Payne's adventures during the 1640s—'traditions' which Hawker had almost certainly invented himself. Hawker's most audacious stroke was to include within the article an entire letter, purportedly written by Payne to Lady Grace Grenville in July 1643, which gives a tear-jerking account of Sir Bevill's death at Lansdown and of the valour allegedly shown thereafter by his 14-year old son, as, mounted upon his father's horse, he had led the Cornish troops to victory (see Plate 10).[84] This document Hawker claimed to have copied from an original discovered by his first wife at Stowe Barton.[85] Needless to say no trace of the alleged letter has ever been found since.

The 'Payne' who emerges, fully formed, from this fantastical article is an intriguing construct. Proudly Cornish, immensely brave and strong, yet always deferential to his social superiors, he may be regarded as an idealized model of a Cornish Royalist soldier: the perfect counterpart to Hawker's scarcely less idealized portrait of that archetypal Cornish Royalist leader, Sir Bevill. Hawker's apoplectic reaction to the 1867 Reform Bill makes it difficult to believe that, in an age of increasing democratization, he had deliberately set out to furnish the Cornish Royalist tradition with a low-born hero figure of the type which it had previously lacked.[86] Yet this was precisely the effect which his article was eventually to have. Hawker's vision of Cornish Royalism proved remarkably enduring and during the half century which followed the vicar of Morwenstow's death, in 1875, the fame of Anthony Payne— 'the Falstaff of the West'[87]—grew almost to rival that of Sir Bevill himself.

Although denounced almost at once by scholars as a forgery[88], 'Payne's letter' quickly established itself in the public mind as a genuine historical document. It was widely admired—one Victorian essayist termed it 'the fine[st] story . . . told . . . since first men began to slay each other'[89]—and frequently reprinted, and it continues to be gravely cited in works of historical scholarship even today.[90] The anecdotes about Payne which Hawker claimed to have derived from local tradition were swallowed more uncritically still, and incorporated wholesale into many subsequent anthologies of Cornish folklore.[91] Fresh literary accretions soon began to grow up around Hawker's initial myth, moreover. A popular Cornish poet wrote a verse tribute to Payne, celebrating the fear which he had inspired in all 'Roundheads', while a wholly new story began to circulate that Payne had assisted Queen Henrietta Maria during her sojourn in the West in 1644.[92] This was the invention of tradition with a vengeance.

Why should 'Hawker's Payne' have exercised such a strong appeal? The existence of an apparently genuine portrait of the historical Payne— one which Gilbert had discovered in c.1815, and which was presented to the Royal Institute of Cornwall in 1889 at the height of the excitement sparked off by Hawker's article[93] (see Plate 9)—undoubtedly helped to impress the giant's image on the popular imagination. A copy of the painting was later commissioned by the owner of the Tree Inn at Stratton, the house where Payne was said to have died, where it may still be seen to this day: yet another physical memorial of the Cornish Royalist tradition inscribed on the north-east Cornish landscape. This portrait aside, the success of Hawker's creation appears to have rested chiefly upon the vigour and plausibility of his own literary style, and upon his instinctive feel for the sorts of ideas and images which were most likely to appeal both to Cornish patriotic sentiment, and to that brand of highly sentimentalized Cavalierism which was cherished by late nineteenth-century conservatives of all sorts.

Hawker's writings on Grenville and Payne updated the Cornish Royalist tradition for the Victorian age, and permitted it to enjoy a last romantic efflorescence between 1870 and 1930. When Mary Coate, the first serious historian of seventeenth-century Cornwall, arrived upon the scene in the 1920s she found that tradition still strongly entrenched, and in her seminal book on the Civil War in Cornwall, published in 1933, she went out of her way to stress the extent to which the legend which had grown up around the Cornish Royalist party had blinded 'later generations' to the complexities of the war beyond the Tamar.[94] Miss Coate's carefully researched work may be regarded as the cock's crow which finally broke the 300-year-old spell of the Cornish Royalist tradition, and banished it from the historiographical centre-stage.[95] Henceforth, the existence both of Cornish Parliamentarians and of widespread local hostility to the war itself would be recognized by all serious students of the conflict. Yet if Coate had disinterred two of the historical secrets which had lain buried for so long beneath the imposing monument of Cornish royalism, she had only partially uncovered the third: namely, that the success of the Royalist party in Cornwall had been inextricably bound up with the question of ethnic difference. Perhaps it is only with the late twentieth-century rediscovery of this, the deepest secret of them all, that a stake may finally be said to have been driven through the Cornish Royalist tradition's heart.

Conclusion

Reflecting in later years on his *Tudor Cornwall* (1941)—without doubt, the single most influential history of early modern Cornwall to have been published during the last century—A.L. Rowse observed that the central concern of that book had been 'the process of tension, struggle, adjustment' by which the Cornish were eventually absorbed 'into the mainstream of English life'.[1] The pieces contained within the present collection have explored that self-same process, but they have set it within a broader chronological framework and approached it from a significantly different angle. Rowse was the first academic historian to give proper consideration to the subject of Cornish 'difference'— indeed, he remains one of the comparatively few to have done so to this day—but the historiographical tradition in which he wrote was still, essentially, a Whiggish one. Rowse held that the process of Cornish cultural absorption into England had been 'inevitable'. He believed that by around 1600 that process had been largely completed and he was confident that, on the whole, this had been 'a good thing'. It was the Anglicizing, Protestantizing, 'forward-looking' Cornish gentry who were the heroes of Rowse's book, rather than their traditionalist opponents and those whom he frankly termed 'the stupid and backward-looking peasantry'.[2] In this respect, as in so many others, Rowse was the intellectual and spiritual heir of Richard Carew, the gentleman-antiquary who died at Antony, in South-east Cornwall, in 1620 and whose *Survey of Cornwall* (1603) has, for almost 400 years, been regarded as the definitive literary portrait of the society in which he dwelt.[3] Yet Carew was not the only Cornish antiquary of his generation—and Carew's is not the only ideological prism through which the history of early modern Cornwall may be viewed.

Where Carew spoke for that powerful section of local society which regarded the decline of the traditional Cornish language and culture with equanimity, or even with outright satisfaction, William Scawen—in his unpublished *Antiquities Cornu-Brittanic* (*c.*1688)—spoke for that smaller, less vocal, but nonetheless significant strand of local opinion which regarded the erosion of the separate sense of Cornish identity with regret, and hoped that that process might somehow be reversed.[4] The tide of history may eventually have swept over those who were opposed to cultural assimilation with England—but this does not mean that their actions and opinions should be ignored. In many ways, I have followed in Scawen's footsteps during the course of researching and writing this book, just as Rowse followed in Carew's. Although several of the earlier chapters were completed before I became aware of the *Antiquities'* existence, the collection as a whole attempts to do very much what Scawen did: to tell the story of early modern Cornwall from the point of view of those who sought to perpetuate the Cornish sense of difference, rather than from the point of view of those who sought to undermine or to suppress it. The characters who have taken centre stage—Scawen himself, Sir Richard Grenville, the rebels of 1548–9, the Royalists of 1642–6, the doomed insurrectionists at the Gear, even Lansdowne and Hawker in the eighteenth and nineteenth centuries— may all be regarded as champions of Cornwall's continued claim to a unique and distinctive identity: they may all, in their different ways, be regarded as 'West Britons'. This book argues that the tradition which they embodied has the right to be considered as a separate thread within the tapestry of the 'new' British history.

* * *

During the Interregnum, a group of men from the West Cornish parish of Sennen flatly refused to obey a zealously Protestant 'way-warden' when he ordered them to cart away an ancient stone cross so that it could be used to mend a hole in a road. As the warden himself later recalled, one man averred that not even three yokes of oxen would be able to budge the stone, while a second observed that the shaft served as a guide to travellers, and a third 'said in Cornish that it was a Holy Cross, and if it was good before, it is good now'. Faced with this implacable opposition, the warden abandoned his attempts to remove the cross from its accustomed position, 'by reson wher of', he concluded his story exasperatedly, 'itt lieth there to this day'.[5] Dogged traditionalism, extreme religious conservatism and continued adherence to that ancient Cornish tongue by means of which subversive sentiments could (usually) be voiced in public without fear of detection to the central authorities: this was the combination of forces which had underlain Cornish rebellions for well over a century, and which—as this anecdote makes clear—retained the power to spark off popular protest as late as the 1650s. It was a conjunction which would soon disappear for ever, but one which had, in its time, given pause to both princes and parliaments. It is a conjunction which surely deserves to be remembered today.

Appendix 1

'A Gratulacion to Cornish Men'

A letter sent by a group of Cornish Royalist gentlemen to the parish constables, 1642

This previously unnoted letter dates to the period immediately after the Parliamentarians had been thrown out of Cornwall by the Sheriff's posse in October 1642 (see Chapter 4). Sent by a group of local Royalist gentlemen to the parish constables, who were ordered to read it out in church, the document congratulates the Cornish people on 'the greate Cheerefullnes' with which they had rallied to the King's cause, and assures them that Charles I himself will be informed of their 'affection and service'. The letter is significant not only for what it reveals about the sheer strength of Cornish support for the King at the beginning of the Civil War, but also because it foreshadows the famous Royal 'Declaration' which was sent to the Cornish in the following year.

[On back: 'Gratulacion to Cornish men']

Mr. Constables,

The greate Cheerefullnes that wee observed in the Countries readye repayre uppon the legall Commaund of the Sheriffe for Raysinge the Posse Comitatus cannott passe awaye without speciall notice. And as they testified theire loyaltie and love to theire Kinge and Countrye in that Action, soe wee shall retaine a faithfull memory of an Acte soe much tendinge to the publique peace, in makeinge the adverse partye see the affection of this Countye and what they muste expect if peace followe not, whereunto this apparance hath given a greate beginninge. Wee desire you to publishe in all the Churches within your hundred our thanckes by theise to the Countye, And assure them that wee shall represent theire forwardnes not only in theire former willingnes but in the perticuler soe seasonablie performed to his Majestie whoe wee doubte not will in due tyme make knowne how much he values theire affection and service, And thus Rest,

Your loveinge freinds

Warwick Mohun,
John Grills,
John Arundell of Trerise,
Hen. Killigrew,
Ezechiell Grosse,
Tho. Bassett.

[Undated, but clearly October 1642.]

[Source: DRO, Tremayne MSS, 1499/M/4/3, 'Parliamentary Papers', no. 4. Reproduced by kind permission of Mr J.W. Tremayne and the DRO.]

Appendix 2

The Parliamentarian Summons to Cornwall

A letter to the Sheriff of Cornwall from Sir Thomas Fairfax and Oliver Cromwell, 1645

This letter was sent to the Sheriff of Cornwall by Sir Thomas Fairfax and Oliver Cromwell, the two chief commanders of the New Model Army, as they prepared to advance into the West Country in September 1645. It urges the Cornish people to abandon the King's cause, to 'call home' their soldiers from the king's armies and 'to drive the remainder of the enemy out of your Country'. An artful mixture of threats and blandishments, the document warns the inhabitants of Cornwall that, if they continue to resist the Parliament, they will be 'dealt withal in the severest way of war', but at the same time holds out the hope that, if they eject the King's troops as they have been instructed to do, they will be 'secured from any invasion or incursions of the Parliament's forces'. Couched, throughout, in terms which suggest that the Cornish were regarded as semi-autonomous players in the conflict, this letter very probably helped to inspire Richard Grenville's 'independence scheme' of November 1645 (see Chapter 5). It certainly played an important part in paving the way for the eventual Cornish surrender at Millbrook in March 1646.

For the High Sheriff of the County of Cornwall and the well affected Gentry, and Inhabitants of that County.

Whereas, besides the great and frequent supplies of men, money and other aids to the enemy which have been raised out of your County above others, to the sad continuation and often reinforcing of the unnatural war against the Parliament, we are given to understand, that the restless enemies of your and our and the Kingdom's peace, being (through God's late returning mercies to us all, and the blessing of the forces of the Parliament) driven almost out of all other parts of the Kingdom and destitute of all dear supplies from elsewhere (save that little angle which you possess) do yet persist by all the ways of art and violence, to draw out from amongst you some fresh supplies and reinforcement of their broken forces, whereby they may once again appear in the field to disturb the peace of the Kingdom, and continue and renew the miseries of it by a further war, we being equally careful to prevent (if possible) your ruin or further sufferings as the kingdom's further troubles, have thought good to admonish you and declare to you, as followeth:

(1) We desire you would be, and we pray God to make you once at last sensible of the interest of Religion, and of the rights and liberties of yourselves and the rest of the people of England, of which the power and authority of Parliaments hath been in former ages and is ever like to be (under God) the best conservatory and support, and which by this unnatural war against the Parliament and that in a great degree by the aids your Country hath afforded thereunto, have been so much endangered: And if now at last you shall appear sensible thereof, we shall be willing to believe of you, and be glad we may have occasion so to represent you to the Parliament and Kingdom. That the great aids you have formerly afforded the enemy against them, have been only forced or drawn from you by violence or deceit or those that God has suffered hitherto to be possessed of the power over you.

(2) As we believe you have had by this time sufficient sense and experience of the violence and oppressions (besides all other wickedness) of that party so we advise you timely to consider how unlike you are in humane probability to bear and maintain their war alone against the rest of the Kingdom, that is now by God's blessing almost cleared to the Parliament, how heavy the burden is like to be to you in the prosecution of such a war alone, and how great calamity may befall you in the issue of it.

(3) If God shall see good to set those considerations home upon your hearts and incline you to endeavor the freeing of yourselves from the yoke you have been under, from the burden and danger that may befall you, and from the guilt of so much mischief and trouble to the Kingdom as the prolonging of such a war, when otherwise likely to be happily ended. And if upon these considerations you shall apply yourselves to drive the remainder of the enemy out of your Country, if you shall call home, and (as much as in you lies) withdraw, from the enemy the forces which you have sent them, and forbear for future to afford them any more aids or contribution, but stand upon your guard to defend yourselves and country from any further oppressions, plunderings, or invasions, you shall not only be allowed therein, but countenanced and assisted, as you shall desire, by the Parliament's party; and be secured from any invasion or incursions of the Parliament's forces, unless you shall desire any of them for your assistance. You shall likewise have free trading and commerce by sea and land to all places, and with all persons that are not in hostility against the Parliament, and shall have for money what supplies of arms or ammunition you shall need for your said defence. But if, notwithstanding this offer, you shall persist to aid the enemy any further, you

must expect and be assured when God shall give leisure and opportunity (as yourselves thereby will give occasion) for the Parliament's forces to come down amongst you, that you shall be accounted and dealt withal in the severest way of war as the most eminent and obstinate disturbers and retarders of the Kingdom's peace, now by God's mercy in a fair way to be speedily settled. Yet hoping better of you for the future (which we shall be glad to hear of) we remain,

From before Bristol,
Sept. 8, 1645

Your assured friends,
Tho. Fairfax
Oliver Cromwell.

[Source: W.C. Abbot, *The Writings and Speeches of Oliver Cromwell, Vol. I, 1599–1649* (Harvard, 1937), pp. 372–3.]

Appendix 3

Extract from William Scawen's *Antiquities Cornu-Brittanic*, *c.*1688

This intriguing passage from William Scawen's late seventeenth-century treatise on Cornish history and identity illustrates the curious mixture of shame and admiration with which the author regarded the Cornish rebels of 1497 (see discussion in Chapter 7). At the same time, it illustrates the fierce, whole-hearted pride which Scawen took in the exploits of the Cornish Royalists of the 1640s—and his conviction that, in behaving as they did, the King's Cornish supporters had been following in the footsteps of their valiant British ancestors.

Tho' [Cornwall] were heretofore honour'd with the Title of one of 4 Dinestyes, yett it is but a small County in Respect to others next Conjoyn'd. True it is that our Brethren in Wales being a greater Body of Men, and larger Territory, had long and often contentions in former times for their Libertie & Regalitie, but in vaine. Much vainer it would have been in us to have attempted [it], should we have had minds to have done so generally; though some few of us being misguided in some bad times have endeavoured to make themselves unfortunate and ridiculous, and their Country discredited. Such as was that in K:[ing] H:[enry] 7[th's] tyme in partaking with a Counterfeit which we are ashamed to thinke of. Yet where the greatnes of the offence, and the vanity of that sudden Enterprise (not for Liberty), seemes to be somewhat extenuated [is] by this, that it is observ'd, that in their march (which was a long one) from Cornwall to Black-heath, there was no spoyle done, nor any complaint made [against them by any] of the Countries through which they past. And in that after their twice suppression, they quietly went home, where is our best being.

Tis enough for us to say, that we followed the Examples of ye former Ages of the Brittans, persisting in our Obedience. Yett withall to speake a little of our services (not boasting neither, where our duty is concerned) and particularly, that in the late Civill Wars on behalf of his late Majestie of blessed memory, Charles 1, when his rebellious and ungratefull People, unworthy to have so good [a] Prince to reigne over them, impiously rose up against him, Wee in this County susteined for four yeares time, the whole power (upon the matter) of the Rebellious parte of all the Kingdome, invadeing us with severall great and well formed Armies. And what wee did elsewhere in other Counties with our forces (God assisting) reducing them to obedience (temporall compliance att least) may be better spoaken of by others (who received the benefitt thereof) then written by me as things memorable. Amongst others, that famous defence of the Cornish att Lans-Downe may not be forgotten, where a small stand of Cornish Pike entertain'd the fierce assault of the whole body of the Rebels horse more then once, chargeing upon them; whome they continually withstood and forced off, and thereby recovered the King's Army, which was before worsted, into a new Rally, and fresh heart againe; to the great animation of all the Loyal Party, and the encouragement of his Majestie, to whome, as the present Benefitt was great, so was also his contentment in heareing the mentioning of it ever afterward.

To be satisfied of the truth of this famous exploit, if any should doubt it, the Inquisiters need goe no farther then to the Enemy themselves, who have sufficiently given testimony thereto, lookeing upon it with admiration, [and] acknowledging it such a service [as] they never saw the like. Amongst others, by Sir Ralph Knight, a Cromwellian, I have heard it magnified in more particulars, then wee ourselves could recite. But least this . . . digression, be thought . . . inexcusable, the Reader may be pleased to consider, that this [anecdote] is not improperly placed here among these Memorials . . . [of Cornwall, for] as faces doe answeare in Glass, [so] men may in some sort see what our former Progenitors were, by such marks remaining in their Posterity, and find these like [to] those before.

[Source: CRO, F2/39 (William Scawen's Cornish Manuscript), ff. 27–29. Reproduced by kind permission of the Cornish Record Office.]

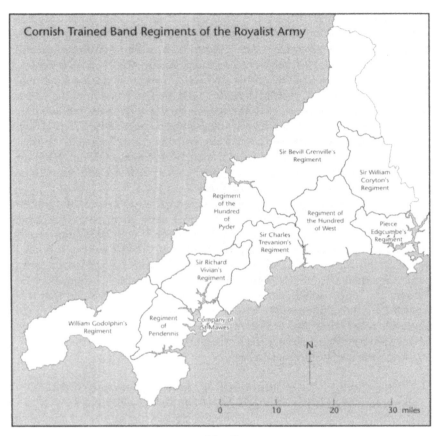

Map 8

Appendix 4

Officers of the King's Cornish Infantry Regiments, 1642–1646

How 'Cornish' were the King's Cornish armies? This appendix lists all the officers of the rank of Ensign or above who are known to have served in Royalist infantry regiments raised in Cornwall during the Civil War. For those who are interested in such things, it also includes a brief account of each regiment's wartime service. Of the 394 men whose names appear below, no fewer than 303 (77%) can definitely be shown to have been Cornishmen, 40 (10%) to have been Devonians and just 13 (3%) to have come from elsewhere in England (for the 38 remaining individuals it has not yet proved possible to establish a county of origin). These figures serve to illustrate the remarkable homogeneity of the King's Cornish infantry regiments.

The sheer number of Royalist officers which Cornwall produced is also very striking. If one adds to the 303 names listed below the 84 Cornish officers who are known to have served in Royalist cavalry regiments: the 30 Cornish officers who are known to have served in Royalist infantry regiments raised elsewhere in England (chiefly in Devon), and the 25 more Cornish officers who are known to have served the King in an uncertain capacity, one arrives at a grand total of 442 men. Only one other county in the kingdom—Yorkshire—supplied as many men to the Royalist officer corps as this, and in proportional terms none did. Most of these men survived the war, moreover. When one bears in mind Joseph Jane's comment, made in 1647, that 'there have not died so few as 100 [Cornish] gentlemen and officers' in the King's service it becomes clear that Cornwall must have supplied Charles I with well over 500 officers in all: a huge figure for such a small county.

List of regiments

1. Colonel Jonathan Arundell's Foot 194
2. Colonel Richard Arundell's Foot 195
3. Colonel William Arundell's Foot 196
4. Sir William Coryton's Foot 196
5. Sir Peter Courtenay's Foot 197
6. Sir William Courtenay's Foot 197
7. Colonel Piers Edgcumbe's Foot 198
8. Colonel William Godolphin's Foot 198
9. Sir Bevill Grenville's Foot 200
10. Sir Richard Grenville's Foot 202
11. Lord Mohun's Foot 203
12. Sir Nicholas Slanning's Foot ('The Tinners') 205
13. Colonel Jonathan Trelawny's Foot 207
14. Colonel Lewis Tremaine's Foot 208
15. Sir Charles Trevanion's Foot 210
16. Colonel John Trevanion's Foot 210
17. Sir Richard Vivian's Foot 212

1. Colonel Jonathan Arundell's Foot

New Cornish Regiment, of Sir Richard Grenville's army. The regiment was probably raised in September–October 1644. It served at the sieges of Plymouth (1644–5) and Taunton (1645), and at the battles of Langport and Torrington. The unit surrendered at Pendennis in August 1646.

Colonel
Jonathan Arundell   of Cornwall [*RO*, pp. 6–7].
Lieutenant-Colonel
??? Robinson   of Cornwall [mentioned in *IO*].
Captains
Richard Blewitt   of Cornwall [*IO*].
George Collings   of Cornwall (also listed under Sir Richard Grenville) [*IO*].
Peter Courtenay   of Cornwall [*IO*].
Reskemmer Courtenay   of Lanivet, Cornwall (also listed under Sir William Courtenay) [*IO*; and *CCAM*].
George Kempson   of Cornwall [*IO*].
William Pendarvis   of Roscrowe, Cornwall [*CCC*].
Sampson Zacherley   of Cornwall [*IO*].
Lieutenants
John Hallamore   of Cornwall [*IO*].
John Hittson   of Cornwall [*IO*].
Joseph Jewell   of Cornwall [*IO*].
Richard Lyne   of Cornwall [*IO*].
William Nance   of Cornwall [*IO*].

Thomas Simons	of Cornwall [*IO*].
Francis Twiggs	of Cornwall [*IO*].
Samuel Whare	of Cornwall [*IO*].
Ensigns	
William Bawden	of Cornwall [*IO*].
Thomas Chegwin	of Cornwall [*IO*].
Edward Edwards	of Cornwall [*IO*].
William Maine	of Cornwall [*IO*].
John Pierce	of Cornwall (Lt. Col. Robinson's Company) [*IO*].
John Sands	of Cornwall [*IO*].
Richard Sands	of Cornwall [*IO*].
Matthew Treglawne	of Cornwall [*IO*].

2. Colonel Richard Arundell's Foot

New Cornish regiment, of Sir Richard Grenville's Army. The regiment may have initially been raised by Colonel William Arundell [q.v.] in 1643, but by summer 1644 it was under his brother Richard's command. The unit served at the sieges of Plymouth (1644–5) and Taunton (1645), and took part in the battle of Langport. It was merged with the regiment of Colonel Lewis Tremaine [q.v.] in late 1645.

Colonel	
Richard Arundell	of Trerice, Cornwall [*RO*, p. 7].
Captains	
John Blight	of Cornwall [*IO*].
Peter Courtenay	of Penkevill, Cornwall [*IO*; and CRO, DDT, 1755].
Francis Gully	of Cornwall [*IO*].
John Spry	residence unknown (also listed under Colonels William Arundell and John Trevanion) [DRO, MSP 128/103/1].
Lieutenants	
Nathaniel Cooke	of Tregony, Cornwall [*IO*; and CRO, DDT, 1755].
??? Forman	residence unknown; captured at Langport, 1645 [E. 293 (17)].
Ralph Keat	of Cornwall [*IO*].
Thomas Kestell	of Cornwall [*IO*].
Nicholas Pettegrew	of Cornwall [*IO*].
Peter Polsue	of St Goran, Cornwall [*IO*; and CRO, DDT, 1755].
??? Watkins	residence unknown; captured at Langport, 1645 [E. 293 (17)].
Thomas Wyat	of Cornwall [*IO*].
Ensigns	
Thomas Carne	of Cornwall [*IO*].
William Dunkin	of Cornwall [*IO*].

Richard Pierce	of Cornwall [*IO*].
Joseph Tucker	of Cornwall [*IO*].
George Williams	of Feock, Cornwall [*IO*; and CRO, DDT, 1755].

3. Colonel William Arundell's Foot

An obscure regiment, apparently raised in April–May 1643. William Arundell died before Plymouth in December 1643. Command of the regiment may then have devolved upon his brother, Richard [q.v.].

Colonel

William Arundell	of Trerice, Cornwall [*RO*, p. 7].

Majors

Phillip Dart	residence unknown [mentioned in *IO*].
John Spry	residence unknown (also listed under Colonels Richard Arundell and John Trevanion) [mentioned in *IO*].

Lieutenant

John Spry	of Cornwall (Dart's Company) [*IO*].

Ensign

Gilbert Ford	of Devon (Major Spry's Company) [*IO*].

4. Sir William Coryton's Foot

Trained band regiment based in the Hundred of East (see Map 8). It performed local defence duties throughout the war, and surrendered at Millbrook in March 1646.

Colonel

Sir William Coryton	of Newton Ferrers, St Mellion, Cornwall [*CCC*].

Captains

John Battersby	of Calstock, Cornwall [*CCC*].
Nevill Blight	of Carnedon, Cornwall [mentioned in *IO*; and *CCC*].
Ambrose Manning	residence unknown [mentioned in *IO*].
Arthur Piper	of Launceston, Cornwall [mentioned in *IO*; and CRO, B/LAUS/179/2/3].
Robert Smyth	of Southill, Cornwall [*IO*].
Henry Spoare	of Northill, Cornwall [*CCC*].

Captain-Lieutenant

Edward Wilcock	of St Ive, Cornwall [*CCC*].

Lieutenants

John Adams	of Cornwall [*IO*].
William Haughton	of Devon (Manning's Company) [*IO*].

William Hooper	of Linkinhorne, Cornwall [CCC].
Edward Kneebone	of Linkinhorne, Cornwall [CCC].
Goyen Moore	of Cornwall [IO].

Ensigns

Nicholas Geddy	6f Cornwall (Blight's Company) [IO].
John Haughton	of Cornwall [IO].
George Jackson	of Launceston, Cornwall (Piper's Company) [CRO, B/LAUS/179/2/3].
Arthur Piper	of Cornwall (Piper's Company) [IO].

5. Sir Peter Courtenay's Foot

Volunteer regiment, which Courtenay was commissioned to raise in September 1643. The subsequent history of the unit is very obscure and it does not seem to have endured for long.

Colonel

| Sir Peter Courtenay | of Trethurfe, Cornwall [RO, p. 88]. |

Captains

| Roger Tallant | of Devon [IO]. |
| John Lavers | of Cornwall [IO]. |

Lieutenant

| John Vigors | of Cornwall [IO]. |

Ensign

| John Penwarden | of Cornwall [IO]. |

6. Sir William Courtenay's Foot

Volunteer regiment, apparently raised in Cornwall in mid-1643. It took part in the sieges of Exeter and Dartmouth later that year and formed part of Grenville's 'Army for the [defence of the] County of Cornwall' in July 1644. The regiment may later have been subsumed within the New Cornish Tertia.

Colonel

| Sir William Courtenay | of Saltash, Cornwall [RO, p. 88]. |

Captains

Charles Dart	of Devon [IO].
Thomas Hanse	of Devon [IO].
Reskemer Courtenay	of Cornwall (also listed under Colonel Jonathan Arundell) [CRO, DDT, 1616].

Lieutenants

| Edward Colmer | of Cornwall [IO]. |
| William Penny | of Cornwall [IO]. |

7. Colonel Piers Edgcumbe's Foot

Trained band regiment based in the Hundred of East (see Map 8). It guarded the west bank of the Tamar throughout the war, and took part in the Lostwithiel campaign of 1644. The regiment surrendered at Millbrook in March 1646.

Colonel

Piers Edgcumbe	of Mount Edgcumbe, Cornwall [*CCC*].

Lieutenant-Colonel

William Scawen	of Molenick, St Germans, Cornwall [*CCC*].

Major

Richard Edgcumbe	of Bodregan, Cornwall [*CCC*; and mentioned in *IO*].

Captains

William Grills	of Cornwall [*IO*].
John Scawen	of Cornwall [*IO*].
Thomas Scawen	of Cornwall [*IO*].

Lieutenants

John Arundell	of Cornwall [*IO*].
Robert Avery	of Cornwall (Lt. Col. Scawen's Company) [*IO*].
James Burrell	of Cornwall [*IO*].
Richard Cudlip	of Cornwall [*IO*].
William Killyow	of Cornwall [*IO*].
Lyney Poppleston	of Cornwall (Grills' Company) [*IO*].

Ensigns

John Curbyn	of Cornwall [*IO*].
Hanniball Grills	of Cornwall [*IO*].
Matthew Hore	of Cornwall (Major Edgcumbe's Company) [*IO*].
Paul Lavers	of Cornwall [*IO*].
Alexander Moon	of Cornwall [*IO*].
John Pope	of Cornwall [*IO*].
Ferdinando Poppleton	of Cornwall [*IO*].
Thomas Skelton	of Cornwall [*IO*].

8. Colonel William Godolphin's Foot

Old Cornish regiment, of the original Cornish Army. The unit was raised in November 1642 and took part in all the western campaigns of 1642–5. Sent into Exeter in December 1645 in order to reinforce the garrison there, it remained in Exeter until the city surrendered in April 1646. Godolphin's men then disbanded and went home. Godolphin also commanded the Western Regiment, a trained band unit based in the Hundreds of Penwith and Kerrier (see Map 8). Many of the officers listed below may well have served in both units.

Colonel
William Godolphin   of Spargor, St Mabe, Cornwall [*RO*, pp. 159–60].
Lieutenant-Colonels
??? Arundell   residence unknown [E. 16 (24)].
Thomas Robinson   òf Helston, Cornwall (previously Captain and
                                 Major in the same regiment) [E. 16 (24); and CRO,
                                 DD, BU 631 (1)].

Major
Christopher Grosse   of St Buryan, Cornwall [BL, Harleian MSS, 6804,
                                 ff.197–98; and CRO, DDB/35/44].

Captains
Francis Bleuet   of Trevarthen, Cornwall [*CCC*; and E. 16 (24)].
Francis Hutchins   of Devon [*IO*].
Petherick Jenkin   of Cornwall [*IO*].
Henry Keliow   of Cornwall [*IO*].
??? Naunce   residence unknown [E. 16 (24)].
William Orchard   of Cornwall [*IO*].
Francis Robinson   of Helston (?), Cornwall [*IO*; *CCC*; and E. 16 (24)].
Captain-Lieutenants
John Gunne   of Cornwall [*IO*].
Anthony Reskilly   of Cornwall [*IO*].
Lieutenants
Thomas Harris   of Market Jew (?), Cornwall [*IO*; and *CCC*].
John Hayme   of Cornwall [*IO*].
Richard Job   of Cornwall [*IO*].
Richard Marshal   of Cornwall [*IO*].
John Painter   of Cornwall [*IO*].
??? Robinson   residence unknown [E. 16 (24)].
Cornelius Teige   residence uncertain [*IO*].
Edward Tomkins   of Cornwall [*IO*].
Thomas Trenwith   of Cornwall [*IO*].
Ensigns
Anthony Bray   of Cornwall [*IO*].
Ralph Clyes   of Cornwall [*IO*].
Thomas Gregory   of Cornwall [*IO*].
John Luke   of Cornwall [*IO*].
William Penlease   of Cornwall [*IO*].
William Torack   of Cornwall [*IO*].
Michael Trenhick   of Cornwall [*IO*].
Quartermasters
Thomas Flemin   of Cornwall [*IO*].
John Tomkins   of Devon [*IO*].

9. Sir Bevill Grenville's Foot

Old Cornish regiment, of the original Cornish Army. It was raised in November 1642 and served in all the western campaigns of 1642–3. Following the death of Sir Bevill at Lansdown, his son John assumed command of the regiment, which subsequently served at the sieges of Plymouth (1643) and Lyme (1644) and in the Lostwithiel and Newbury campaigns (1644). The unit took part in the siege of Taunton in 1645, and probably went into Exeter with Godolphin's regiment towards the end of that year. It seems likely that Grenville's was one of the three old Cornish regiments which laid down their arms when the city surrendered in April 1646. Grenville also commanded a trained band regiment, based in the Hundreds of Stratton and Lesnewth, which was later commanded by his son (see Map 8). Many of the officers listed below may well have served in both regiments.

First Colonel
Sir Bevill Grenville   of Stowe, Cornwall [*RO*, pp. 164–5].
Second Colonel
Sir John Grenville   of Stowe, Cornwall [*RO*, p. 165].

Officers known to have served under Sir Bevill Grenville
Major
Degory Tremayne   of Poundstock, Cornwall [mentioned in *IO*; see
                                 also *CCC* and DRO, MSP, 128/82].

Captains
Andrew Cory   of Cornwall [*IO*].
Sir Peter Courtenay   of Trethurfe, Cornwall (later commanded his own
                                 regiment) [mentioned in *IO*; see also *CCC*].
Richard Hawke   of North Petherwin, Devon [*IO*; and *CCC*].
Hugh Piper   of Launceston, Cornwall [see monument in
                                 Launceston Church; and *CCC*].
Richard Porter   of Lansallos, Cornwall [mentioned in *IO*; and
                                 CCC].
Jonathan Trelawny   of Trelawne, Cornwall (later commanded his own
                                 regiment) [W.D.Cooper (ed.), *Camden Miscellany, II*
                                 (Old Series, 55, 1953), p. 10].

Lieutenants
Nicholas Berry   of Cornwall [*IO*].
William Butt   of Cornwall (Hawke's Company) [*IO*].
John Crabbe   of Cornwall (Courtney's Company) [*IO*].
John Ferris   of Ladock, Cornwall [*IO*; and CRO, DDT, 1755].
George Harwell   of Devon (Taverner's Company) [*IO*].
John Holman   of Cornwall (Grenville's Company) [*IO*].
Thomas Hutchins   of Cornwall [*IO*].
William Mursill   of Cornwall (Porter's Company) [*IO*].

Aneas Reardan   residence uncertain [*IO*].

Ensigns

William Canne	of Cornwall [*IO*].
Philip Charsell	of Cornwall (Tremayne's Company) [*IO*].
John Hay	óf Cornwall (Hawke's Company) [*IO*].
Zachery Kendall	of Devon [*IO*].
Henry Roberts	of Cornwall [*IO*].
Henry Row	of Veryan, Cornwall [*IO*; and CRO, DDT, 1755].
Henry Spour	of North Hill (?), Cornwall [*IO*; and *CCC*].
Lewis Tremaine	of Heligan, Cornwall (later commanded his own regiment) [Bod., Wood Pamphlets, 376, *Sergeant Major James Chudleigh: His Declaration to his Countrymen* (1643)].

Officers known to have served under Sir John Grenville

Lieutenant-Colonels

Richard Pomeroy	of Tregony, Cornwall [mentioned in *IO*].
Charles Roscarrock	of St Neot, Trevennot, Cornwall [mentioned in *IO*; and *CCC*].

Captains

Chamon Greenvile	of Poughill, Cornwall [*IO*; and *CCC*].
John Hore	of Netherbury (?), Dorset [*IO*].
John Plumly	of St Mabyn (?), Cornwall [*IO*].
John Taverner	of Bradstone, Devon (?) [mentioned in *IO*; and *CCAM*].
John Vacey	of Tamerton, Cornwall [E. 47 (2); and *CCC*].

Lieutenants

Tristram Bissett	of Cornwall and Devon [*IO*].
Thomas Hugh	of Cornwall (Pomeroy's Company) [*IO*].
Hugh Leatherden	of Cornwall [*IO*].
Thomas Lower	of Cornwall [*IO*].
John Matthew	of Cornwall (Roscarrock's Company) [*IO*].
Mark Tucker	of Cornwall [*IO*].
Wilden Tyack	of Cornwall [*IO*].
James Winslade	of Cornwall [*IO*].

Ensigns

John Clark	of Cornwall [*IO*].
John Eedy	of Cornwall [*IO*].
John Elliot	of Cornwall [*IO*].
Edmund Heddon	of Cornwall [*IO*].
Peter Hodge	of Cornwall [*IO*].
Thomas Hoskins	of Cornwall [*IO*].
John Pethick	of Cornwall [*IO*].

Quartermaster

Richard Olyvy   of Cornwall [*IO*].

10. Sir Richard Grenville's Foot

New Cornish regiment, of Sir Richard Grenville's Army. Apparently raised in September 1644, Grenville's regiment subsequently took part in the sieges of Plymouth (1644–5) and Taunton (1645), and was engaged at the battle of Langport. Following Grenville's dismissal from command in January 1646, his regiment was led by Lieutenant-Colonel George Collins. Having taken part in the battle of Torrington, the regiment finally surrendered at the Mount in April 1646. Grenville also commanded a trained band regiment—many of the officers listed below may well have served in both units.

Colonel

Sir Richard Grenville   of Stowe, Cornwall [*RO*, pp. 165–6].

Lieutenant-Colonel

George Collins   of Helston, Cornwall (also listed under Colonel
                                Jonathan Arundell) [mentioned in *IO*; and *RO*,
                                p. 77].

Majors

John Carnock   of Treworgy, Cornwall (?) [mentioned in *IO*; and
                                RO, p. 78].

Martin Maddren   of Penzance, Cornwall [G. Granville, *The Genuine
                                Works* (3 vols, 1736), II, p. 227].

Captains

William Coyesgarne   of Calstock, Cornwall [*IO*; and *CCC*].

Henry Ellis   residence unknown [mentioned in *IO*].

Francis Gilbert   of Boconnoc, Cornwall [*IO*; and *CCC*].

Edward Greenwood   of Bradstone, Devon [*IO*; and *CCC*].

Charles Hawke   of North Petherwin, Devon (?) [*IO* and *CCC*].

??? Maderne   of Cornwall [E. 16 (24)].

Thomas Sturton   residence uncertain [*IO*].

Peter Thomas   of Cornwall [*IO*].

Richard Weeks   residence unknown [*IO*].

Lieutenants

Thomas Evans   residence uncertain (Collins' Company) [*IO*].

Christopher Ford   of Cornwall [*IO*].

Edward Hawkin   of St Allen, Cornwall [*IO*; and CRO, DDT, 1755].

??? Mallard   residence unknown; captured at Langport, 1645
                                [E. 293 (17)].

??? Sacerly   of Cornwall [E. 16 (24)].

John Taprell   of Cornwall (Hawke's Company) [*IO*].

??? Trisilean	of Cornwall [E. 16 (24)].
John Wayte	of Cornwall [*IO*].
William Weeks	of Devon (Carnock's Company) [*IO*].
Ensigns	
Simon Beare	òf Devon (Weeks' Company) [*IO*].
John Cock	of Cornwall [*IO*].
??? Courtney	of Cornwall [E. 16 (24)].
Thomas Dewen	of Cornwall [*IO*].
Nevill Hawke	of Cornwall (Hawke's Company) [*IO*].
Philip Holditch	of Devon (Ellis's Company) [*IO*].
John Jenkin	of Cornwall [*IO*].
William Matthew	residence uncertain [*IO*].
William Sheere	of Cornwall [*IO*].
William Wise	of Cornwall (Collins' Company) [*IO*].

11. Lord Mohun's Foot

Old Cornish regiment, of the original Cornish Army. It was raised in November 1642 and served in all the western campaigns of 1642–3. Lord Mohun appears to have handed over command of the regiment to his brother, Sir Charles, during the late summer of 1643. Sir Charles was subsequently killed during the Royalist attack on Dartmouth, in October, and command of the regiment devolved upon John Digby, who led it in the siege of Plymouth during October–December 1643. When the other regiments of the Cornish Army marched off to Lyme in early 1644, Digby's regiment remained behind, at Plymouth. It later rejoined the other four regiments, however, and took part in the Lostwithiel and Newbury campaigns (1644), the siege of Taunton (1645) and the battle of Langport. The regiment then appears to have returned to assist in the siege of Plymouth. It was present at the battle of Torrington in February 1646, where Digby was wounded. Sir Chichester Wray may possibly have taken command of the regiment immediately after this. The location at which the unit finally lay down its arms is unknown. Mohun may also have commanded the trained band regiment of the Hundred of West (see Map 8).

First Colonel	
Warwick, Lord Mohun	of Bocconoc, Cornwall [*RO*, p. 257].
Second Colonel	
Sir Charles Mohun	of Bocconoc, Cornwall [J.L. Vivian, *The Visitations of Cornwall* (Exeter, 1887), p. 326.
Third Colonel	
John Digby	residence unknown [*RO*, p. 109].
Fourth Colonel	
Sir Chichester Wray	of Trebigh, St Ive, Cornwall [*CCC*].

Officers known to have served under Lord Warwick Mohun

Lieutenant-Colonel

Sir Walter Slingsby — of Bifrons, Kent [*RO*, p. 347].

Major

William Trevisa — of St Mellion, Cornwall [DRO, MSP, 128/83/1; and *CCC*].

Captains

James Basset — residence unknown; killed at Launceston 1643 [mentioned in *IO*; and C.E.M. Chadwyck-Healey (ed.), *Bellum Civile: Hopton's Narrative of His Campaign in the West* (Somerset Record Society, 18, 1902), p. 37].

??? Bluett — residence unknown; wounded at Devizes 1643 [Chadwyck-Healey, *Bellum Civile*, p. 97].

Sampson Mannaton — of Cornwall [*IO*].

Henry Maynard — of Cornwall [*IO*].

Lieutenants

Nicholas Gilbert — of Cornwall [*IO*].

??? May — residence unknown [Chadwyck-Healey, *Bellum Civile*, p. 97].

John Maynard — of Cornwall (Maynard's Company) [*IO*].

John Vashmond — of Cornwall [*IO*].

Ensigns

Christopher Collier — of Cornwall [*IO*].

Stephen Jay — of St Pinnock (?), Cornwall [*IO*; and *CCC*].

John Sleepe — of Cornwall (Maynard's Company) [*IO*].

Nicholas Typper — of Cornwall (Bassett's Company) [*IO*].

Thomas Vosper — of Cornwall [*IO*].

Quartermaster

Thomas Adams — residence uncertain [*IO*].

Officers known to have served under Colonel John Digby

Major

John Coswarth — residence unknown [mentioned in *IO*].

Captains

John Battersby — of Rame, Calstock, Cornwall [*IO*; and *CCC*].

John Bishop — of Northam (?), Devon [*IO*; and *CCC*].

Thomas Coffine — of Parkham, Devon (?); captured at Langport, 1645 [E. 293 (17)].

Robert Hammond — of Dorset [*IO*].

John Marshall — of Cornwall [*IO*].

Edward Pyne — of East Down, Devon [*CCC*].

Captain-Lieutenant
Nicholas Smith   of Cornwall [*IO*].
Lieutenants
Richard Abraham   of Cornwall; captured at Langport, 1645 [*IO*; and
                        E. 293 (17)].
Richard Bennet   of Northam (?), Devon [*IO*; and *CCC*].
Ensigns
Richard Couch   of Cornwall [*IO*].
Ralph Davy   of Cornwall [*IO*].
Nicholas Howell   of Cornwall [*IO*].
Roger Marten   of Cornwall (Coswarth's Company) [*IO*].
Reynolds Stacy   of Cornwall [*IO*].

Officers known to have served under Sir Chichester Wray
Captains
??? Goysgarne   residence unknown [mentioned in *IO*].
Charles Hammond   of London [*IO*].
Nicholas Jolly   of Lanivet, Cornwall [*IO*; and *CCC*].
Simon Thurloe   residence uncertain [*IO*].
William Wray   of Cornwall [*IO*].
Lieutenants
Ezekiel Dymond   of Cornwall [*IO*].
John Stephens   of Cornwall (Goysgarne's Company) [*IO*].
Ensign
John Perkins   of Cornwall [*IO*].
Quartermasters
Christopher Owston   of York [*IO*].
William Tozer   of Cornwall [*IO*].

12. Sir Nicholas Slanning's Foot ('The Tinners')

Old Cornish regiment, of the original Cornish Army. It was raised in November 1642, and served throughout the western campaigns of 1642–3. Following Slanning's death at Bristol, Sir Thomas Basset took command of the regiment which then served in the sieges of Plymouth (1643) and Lyme (1644) and in the Lostwithiel and Newbury campaigns (1644). Briefly under the command of Sir John Acland, the Tinners were chosen to form the nucleus of the Prince of Wales' Lifeguard of Foot in early 1645. They served at the siege of Plymouth (1645) and at the battle of Torrington (1646) under Lord Capel. The unit finally surrendered at Pendennis in August 1646.

First Colonel
Sir Nicholas Slanning   of Marystowe, Devon [*RO*, pp. 343–4].

Second Colonel
Sir Thomas Bassett — of Tehidy, Cornwall [*RO*, p. 19].
Third Colonel
Sir John Acland — of Culm John, Devon [DRO, MSP, 94/1].
Fourth Colonel
Lord Arthur Capel — of Hadham, Hertfordshire [*RO*, pp. 58–59].

Officers known to have served under Sir Nicholas Slanning
Major
??? Tremaine — residence unknown [DRO, MSP, 128/83/2].
Captains
Henry Bidlake — of Bridestowe, Devon [mentioned in *IO*; and DRO, MSP, 128/16].
George Cutteforde — of Whitchurch, Devon [DRO, MSP, 128/134; and 128/121/5].
Bartholomew Gidley — of Gidleigh, Devon [DRO, MSP, 128/94/1].
William Howells — of Plympton St Mary, Devon [DRO, MSP, 128/83/2; and PRO, SP 23, 152, f.447].

Lieutenants
James Carnsew — of Cornwall [*IO*].
Richard Franklin — of Tavistock, Devon (Bidlake's Company) [*IO*; and BL, Add. MSS, 34012].

Ensigns
Teage Mohun — of Cornwall [*IO*].
John Wall — of Cornwall [*IO*].

Officers known to have served under Sir Thomas Basset
Major
John Rossiter — of Old Cleeve, Somerset [*IO*; and *RO*, p. 319].
Captains
William Bond — of Holwood, Cornwall [*IO*; and *CCC*].
Patrick Jenkin — of Cornwall [*IO*].
Reginald Tregone — of Cornwall [*IO*].
Captain-Lieutenant
Alexander Stuart — of Durham [*IO*].
Lieutenants
William Giddy — of Cornwall [*IO*].
William Rossiter — residence uncertain but probably Somerset (Major Rossiter's Company) [*IO*].

Ensigns
Tobias Bawden — of Cornwall [*IO*].
Philip Hele — of Essex (Bidlake's Company) [*IO*].

Lieutenant-Colonel
George Yeo — of Huish, Devon [DRO, MSP, 117/3; and *CCC*].
Major
John Frayne — of Langtree, Devon (killed at Torrington, 1646) [R.W. Cotton, *Barnstaple and the Northern Part of Devonshire during the Great Civil War* (London, 1889), p. 490, note 1].

Captains
Simon Cottle — of Morwenstow, Cornwall [mentioned in *IO*; and *CCC*].
Oliver Dynham — of Cornwall [*IO*].
John Prideaux — of Lanlivery, Cornwall [CRO, DDT, 1755].
Walter Rous — of Devon [*IO*].
Thomas Speccot — of Clawton, Devon [*IO*; and DRO, MSP, 128/33].
Philip Tremayne — of Cornwall [*IO*; and CRO, DDT, 1755].
Captain-Lieutenant
Robert Robins — of Cornwall [*IO*; and CRO, DDT, 1755].
Lieutenants
Leonard Frayne — of Frithelstock (?), Devon [*IO*].
William Kessell — of Cornwall (Prideaux's Company) [*IO*].
Thomas Lower — residence unknown [CRO, DDT, 1621].
Hugh Moores — of Cornwall (Dynham's Company) [*IO*].
John Penbertha — of Cornwall [*IO*].
Warne Remphry — of Guindren (?), Cornwall [*IO*; and CRO, DDT, 1755].

Ensigns
Sampson Cole — residence unknown [CRO, DDT, 1621].
William Matthews — of St Keverne, Cornwall [*IO*; and CRO, DDT, 1755].
John Merryfield — of Tavistock, Devon (Speccot's Company) [*IO*; and DRO, MSP, 128/121/3].
John Norman — of Tavistock, Devon (Rous' Company) [*IO*; and DRO, MSP, 128/121/17].
Stephen Pardow — of Grampound, Cornwall (Tremayne's Company) [*IO*; and CRO, DDT, 1755].
Thomas Pierce — of St Ive, Cornwall [*IO*; and CRO, DDT, 1755].
Francis Rowe — of Devon (Cottle's Company) [*IO*].
Quartermaster
Hugh Morrice — residence unknown [CRO, DDT, 1621].

15. Sir Charles Trevanion's Foot

Trained band regiment, based in the Hundred of Powder (see Map 8), which performed local defence duties throughout the war. Many of Trevanion's officers and men were captured at St Budeaux Church, near Plymouth, in December 1645. The regiment subsequently took part in the battle of Torrington, and Trevanion and the remains of his regiment surrendered at Penryn in March 1646.

Colonel
Sir Charles Trevanion   of Caerhayes, Cornwall [*CCC*].
Lieutenant-Colonel
??? Tremayne   of Cornwall [mentioned in *IO*; and E. 16 (24)].
Major
Robert Saule   of Penrice, Cornwall [*CCC*; and E. 16 (24)].
Captains
John Catcher   of Truro, Cornwall (also listed under Sir John Acland) [*IO*; and *CCC*].
Hugh Edmonds   of Cornwall [*IO*].
John Edwards   of Cornwall [*IO*].
Thomas Oliver   of Mevagissey (?), Cornwall [*IO*; and *CCC*].
Lieutenants
Richard Davy   of Cornwall [*IO*].
Henry Hicks   of Cornwall [*IO*].
William Honeywell   of Cornwall [*IO*].
Amethyst Hooker   of Cornwall (Tremayne's Company) [*IO*].
Richard Weeks   of Cornwall [*IO*].
Ensigns
John Caleb   of Cornwall [*IO*].
John Oliver   of Cornwall [*IO*].
Francis Osgood   of Cornwall (Catcher's Company) [*IO*].
Nicholas Rowe   of Cornwall [*IO*].
John Thomas   of Cornwall [*IO*].
Andrew Tregonner   of Cornwall [*IO*].
Richard White   of Cornwall [*IO*].
Quartermaster
Richard Davy   of Cornwall [*IO*].

16. Colonel John Trevanion's Foot

Old Cornish regiment, of the original Cornish Army. It was raised in November 1642 and took part in all the western campaigns of 1642–3. Following Trevanion's death at Bristol, St Aubyn assumed command of the regiment, and led it at the siege of Plymouth (1643), the siege of Lyme (1644) and in the Lostwithiel campaign. The regiment probably took part in the Newbury campaign and the siege of

Taunton and ended the war in the garrison of Exeter.

First Colonel

John Trevanion   of Caerhayes, Cornwall [*RO*, p. 378].

Second Colonel

Thomas St Aubyn   of Clowance, Cornwall (see Plate 4) [*RO*, p. 323].

Officers known to have served under John Trevanion

Lieutenant-Colonel

Walter Kendall   of Pelyn, Lanlivery, Cornwall [mentioned in *IO*; and *CCC*].

Majors

Nicholas Kendall   of Pelyn, Lanlivery, Cornwall [Vivian, *Visitations*, p.259].

John Sprye   residence unknown (also listed under Colonels Richard and William Arundell) [DRO, MSP, 100].

Captains

Edward Cooke   residence unknown [mentioned in *IO*].

Thomas Nicholson   of St Just, Cornwall [*IO*; and CRO, DDT, 1755; and *CCC*].

Jonathan (?) Rashley   of Menabilly (?), Cornwall [mentioned in *IO*; and *CCC*].

??? Samuell   residence unknown [DRO, MSP, 128/28/6].

Francis Saul   of Cornwall [*IO*].

William Williams   of Probus, Cornwall [*IO*; and *CCC*].

Lieutenants

Degory Baker   of Cornwall [*IO*].

Francis Colquit   of Cornwall (Cooke's Company) [*IO*].

George Slee   of Devon [*IO*].

John Vivian   of Cornwall [*IO*].

Ensigns

Francis Hawky   of Cornwall [*IO*].

Randal Hicks   of Cornwall (Rashly's Company) [*IO*].

John Howes   of Cornwall (Nicholson's Company) [*IO*].

Richard Leane   of Cornwall (Kendall's Company) [*IO*; and CRO, DDT, 1755].

John Pullen   of Cornwall [*IO*].

Officers known to have served under Colonel Thomas St Aubyn

Major

Matthias Floyd   of Shropshire [*IO*].

Captains

Thomas Arnold   of Cornwall [*IO*].

John Arundell	of Somerset [*IO*].
John King	residence uncertain [*IO*].
??? Munday	residence unknown [mentioned in *IO*].
Lieutenants	
Maugan Cock	of Cornwall (Munday's Company) [*IO*].
Stephen Colliver	of Cornwall [*IO*].
Michael Hodden	of Cornwall [*IO*].
John Munday	of Cornwall [*IO*].
Ensigns	
George Dingle	of Cornwall [*IO*].
William Hutchins	of Cornwall [*IO*].
John Lobbe	of Cornwall [*IO*].
Francis Prideaux	of Cornwall [*IO*].
George Trenhale	of Cornwall [*IO*].

17. Sir Richard Vivian's Foot

Trained band regiment, based in the Hundred of Powder (see Map 8), elements of
which appear to have crossed into Devon to join Prince Maurice's army in 1644.

Colonel	
Sir Richard Vivian	of Trelowarren, Mawgan-in-Meneage, Cornwall [*CCC*].
Captain	
John Allen	of Cornwall [*IO*].
Ensigns	
Philip Cock	of Cornwall (Allen's Company) [*IO*].
Nicholas Jewell	of Cornwall [*IO*].
George Moyser	of St Mawes, Cornwall [*IO*; and CRO, DDT, 1755].

Notes

Introduction

1   See A. Duffin, *Faction and Faith: Politics and Religion of the Cornish Gentry before the Civil War* (Exeter, 1996), pp. 30–1.

2   W.D. Christie (ed.), *Memoirs, Letters and Speeches of Anthony Ashley Cooper* (London, 1859), p. 16.

3   J. Hickes, *A True and Faithful Narrative of the Unjust and Illegal Sufferings . . . of Many Christians . . . Injudiciously Called Fanaticks* (1671). For similar comments made by another Devonian in *c.*1630, see T. Risdon, *The Chorographical Description or Survey of the County of Devon* (Barnstaple, 1970 edn), p. 4.

4   M. Stoyle, 'Divisions within the Devonshire "County Community", *c.*1600–1646', (D.Phil. thesis, Oxford, 1992).

5   For some important recent remarks on this subject, see A. Wood, 'Beyond Post-Revisionism?: The Civil War Allegiance of the Miners of the Derbyshire "Peak Country"', *HJ*, 40 (1997), especially pp. 26, 31–3, 40; and R. Hutton, *The Royalist War Effort* (2nd edn, London, 1999), pp. xiii–xv.

6   S.R. Gardiner, *History of the Great Civil War, 1642–49* (4 vols, London, 1893), I, p. 69; and M. Coate, *Cornwall in the Great Civil War and Interregnum, 1642–60* (Truro, 1963 edn), pp. 1, 139.

7   M. Stoyle, *Loyalty and Locality: Popular Allegiance in Devon during the English Civil War* (Exeter, 1994), pp. 232–41.

8   See, for example, A. Grant and K. Stringer (eds), *Uniting the Kingdom: The Enigma of British History* (London, 1995); and S.G. Ellis and S. Barber (eds), *Conquest and Union: Fashioning a British State, 1485–1720* (London, 1995).

9   See, for example, H.F. Kearney, *The British Isles: A History of Four Nations* (London, 1995), p. 138; and J. Pocock, 'The Atlantic Archipelago and the War of the Three Kingdoms', in B. Bradshaw and J. Morrill (eds), *The British Problem, circa 1534–1707: State Formation in the Atlantic Archipelago* (London, 1996), p. 181.

10   M. Hechter, *Internal Colonialism: The Celtic Fringe in British National Development* (London, 1975), p. 64.

11   A. Hastings, *The Construction of Nationhood: Ethnicity, Religion and Nationalism* (Cambridge, 1997), pp. 45, 66–7.

12 T.Q. Couch, 'Cornish Language', *JRIC*, I (2) (1864–65), p. 76; A.L. Rowse, *Tudor Cornwall* (New York, 1969 edn), especially pp. 10, 20–30; and P. Payton, *The Making of Modern Cornwall* (Redruth, 1992), pp. 54–63.

13 Though see P. Payton, 'The Cornish Rebellions', *Cornish Nation* (1973), p. 81; Payton, *Making of Modern Cornwall*, p. 63; and P. Payton, *Cornwall* (Fowey, 1996), pp. 150–75.

14 S.G. Ellis, 'The Concept of British History' in Ellis and Barber, *Conquest and Union*, p. 4, note 3.

15 For an early seventeenth-century English translation of Camden's original, Latin text, see W. Camden, *Britain: Or a Chorographical Description of . . . England, Scotland and Ireland* (London, 1637). On page 183 of this work it is noted that 'Cornwall is inhabited by that remnant of Britans which Marianus Scotus calleth *Occidentales Britones*, that is, Britaines of the west parts'. For a late seventeenth-century rendition of this latter phrase as 'Western Britaines', see E. Gibson, *Camden's Brittania: Newly Transcribed into English, With Large Additions* (London, 1695), pp. 1–2.

16 *The West Briton* commenced publication in 1810, see A. Toase (ed.), *Bibliography of British Newspapers* (London, 1991), p. 36.

1 'The Dissidence of Despair': Rebellion and Identity in Early Modern Cornwall

1 E. 445 (28), *A Letter from the Isle of Wight* (June 1648), p. 6; and M. Coate, *Cornwall in the Great Civil War and Interregnum, 1642–60: A Social and Political Study* (Oxford, 1933), p. 240.

2 For some honourable exceptions (at least as far as the Tudor revolts are concerned) see A.L. Rowse, *Tudor Cornwall* (London, 1969), pp. 20, 22; P. Berresford-Ellis, *The Cornish Language and its Literature* (London, 1974), p. 52; J. Cornwall, *Revolt of the Peasantry, 1549* (London, 1977), pp. 41–2ff.; and P. Payton, *The Making of Modern Cornwall* (Redruth, 1992), pp. 58–62. Most recently, see M. Stoyle, 'Pagans or Paragons?: Images of the Cornish during the English Civil War', *EHR*, CXI, 441 (April 1996) pp. 321–23 (Chapter 4, below); and P. Payton, *Cornwall* (Fowey, 1996), chapters 6–7.

3 J. Sprigg, *Anglia Rediviva: England's Recovery* (London, 1647), p. 230.

4 See M. Todd, *The South-west to AD 1000* (London, 1987), pp. 273–5.

5 For the earliest explicit statement of what might be termed the 'Kernowsceptic' view, see D.C. Fowler, *Authors of the Middle Ages: 2. John Trevisa* (Aldershot, 1993), p. 1. For the latest, see J. Chynoweth, 'The Gentry of Tudor Cornwall' (unpublished Ph.D. thesis, University of Exeter, 1994), especially pp. 17–28.

6 The first Cornish scholar to attack the Anglocentric view of Cornwall's past was William Scawen, whose *Antiquities Cornu-Brittanic* was written in the 1670s and 1680s (see BL Add. MSS 33,420, ff.108–125r). The latest is Philip Payton, whose *Cornwall* provides a radical rejection of the dominant paradigm.

7 See S. Ellis, 'Not Mere English: The British Perspective, 1400–1650', *HT*,

38, 12 (December 1988) pp. 43, 46; H. Kearney, *The British Isles: A History of Four Nations* (London, 1995 edn), p. 138; and S. Ellis, 'Tudor State Formation and the Shaping of the British Isles', in S.G. Ellis and S. Barber (eds), *Conquest and Union: Fashioning a British State, 1485–1725* (London, 1995), p. 58.

8 J. Morrill, 'The British Problem', in B. Bradshaw and J. Morrill (eds), *The British Problem, 1534–1707: State Formation in the Atlantic Archipelago* (London, 1996), p. 1.

9 See H. Jenner, 'Cornwall a Celtic Nation', *Celtic Review*, I (1905) pp. 234–46.

10 B. Anderson, *Imagined Communities: Reflections on the Spread of Nationalism* (London, 1995), especially chapters 2–3; E. Gellner, *Thought and Change* (London, 1964), pp. 147–78; E. Gellner, *Nations and Nationalism* (London, 1983), especially pp. 6, 49, 55. See also L. Colley, *Britons: Forging the Nation, 1707–1837* (London, 1992), especially pp. 5–9.

11 A.D. Smith, *The Ethnic Origin of Nations* (London, 1994 edn), p. 11.

12 Ibid., especially pp. 13–14.

13 R.R. Davies, 'The Peoples of Britain and Ireland, 1100–1400: 1. Identities', *TRHS*, 6th Series, IV (1994) pp. 1–20, especially 2.

14 Ibid., pp. 18, 16.

15 Ibid., pp. 6, 11, 4, 9.

16 L. Thorpe (ed.), *Geoffrey of Monmouth: The History of the Kings of Britain* (London, 1988), pp. 71–5.

17 See, for example, Morrill, 'The Fashioning of Britain', in Ellis and Barber, *Conquest and Union*, p. 15; and R.R. Davies, 'The Peoples of Britain and Ireland, 1100–1400: II Names, Boundaries and Regnal Solidarities', *TRHS*, 6th Series, V (1995) p. 1.

18 Thorpe, *Geoffrey of Monmouth*, pp. 66, 72.

19 Admittedly, Geoffrey possessed strong links with Cornwall and may therefore have been particularly keen to stress its importance, see O.J. Padel, 'Geoffrey of Monmouth and Cornwall', *Cambridge Medieval Celtic Studies*, 8 (1984) pp. 8–9.

20 R. Gough (ed.), *Brittania: Or a Chorographical Description of the Flourishing Kingdoms of England, Scotland and Ireland* (4 vols, London, 1806), I, p. 12.

21 J. Norden, *Speculi Britanniae Pars: A Topographical and Historical Description of Cornwall* (London, 1728), p. 7. See also F.E. Halliday (ed.), *Richard Carew of Anthony: The Survey of Cornwall* (New York, 1969), p. 151.

22 CRO, F2/39 (William Scawen's Cornish Manuscript), ff.43–47; Davies, 'Identities', pp. 6–7.

23 CRO, F2/39, title-page.

24 The best introduction to the history of the Cornish language is M.F. Wakelin, *Language and History in Cornwall* (Leicester, 1975).

25 Ibid., p. 22. The tradition continues, see maps in Ellis, 'Not Mere English', p. 41; Ellis and Barber, *Conquest and Union*, p. 317; and J.S. Morrill (ed.), *The Oxford Illustrated History of Tudor and Stuart Britain* (Oxford, 1996), p. 463.

26 Wakelin, *Language and History*, p. 67.

27 On 'the retreat of Cornish', see Wakelin, *Language and History*, pp. 93–7; and, more recently, K.J. George, 'How Many People Spoke Cornish

Traditionally?', *CS*, Old Series 14 (1986) pp. 67–70. George posits a slower rate of retreat than Wakelin: the truth probably lies somewhere in between.

28 Chynoweth notes that 'many of the Western gentry' continued to speak Cornish until well into the 1500s ('Gentry', p. 193). On Cornish-speaking clergy, see Wakelin, *Language and History*, pp. 83, 88–9; and T.C. Peter, *The History of Glasney Collegiate Church* (Camborne, 1903), p. 117.

29 Halliday, *Survey*, p. 154; Gough, *Brittania*, I, p. 3; and T. Fuller, *The History of the Worthies of England* (2 vols, London, 1811 edn), I, p. 214.

30 See T. Middleton and W. Rowley, *A Faire Quarrel* (G.R. Price, ed., London, 1977), p. 41. Cornishmen clearly had gone bare-legged during the 1500s, though by 1617 this may no longer have been the case, see Halliday, *Survey*, p. 138.

31 See Chapter 4. The two pastimes had long been associated with Cornwall, see Thorpe, *Geoffrey of Monmouth*, pp. 72–3; and Chynoweth, 'Gentry', p. 107.

32 Norden, *Speculi*, p. 26. For the most recent discussion of the 'Cornish acre', see D. Harvey, 'The Tithing Framework of West Cornwall', *CS*, 5 (1997) pp. 38–47.

33 G.R. Lewis, *The Stannaries: A Study of the Medieval Tin-Miners of Devon and Cornwall* (Truro, 1965), especially pp. 107–8.

34 Halliday, *Survey*, p. 125; Chynoweth, 'Gentry', pp. 54–6; and W. Camden, *Remains Concerning Britain* (M.A. Lower, ed., London, 1870), p. 143.

35 D.H. Cullum, 'Society and Economy in West Cornwall' (unpublished Ph.D. thesis, Exeter, 1994), p. 288.

36 See H.M. Speight, 'Local Government and Politics in Devon and Cornwall, 1509–49' (Sussex University, Ph.D. thesis, 1991), p. 16—citing comments made in a mid-sixteenth-century manorial survey.

37 See T. Stoate (ed.), *The Cornwall Military Survey: 1522* (Bristol, 1987); and H.L. Douch (ed.), *The Cornwall Muster Roll for 1569* (Bristol, 1984). These two sources reveal that the use of slings in Cornwall receded westwards over time during the 1500s, just as the language did. Bearing this in mind, the fact that the community which boasted the highest number of sling-owners in 1569 was the notoriously rebellious parish of St Keverne (Douch, p. iii) seems unlikely to be mere coincidence. There are hints of a rich complex of interconnections here.

38 Halliday, *Survey*, p. 138.

39 Davies, 'Identities', p. 11.

40 Fuller, *Worthies*, p. 209; and Norden, *Speculi*, p. 29.

41 Halliday, *Survey*, p. 147. See also Norden, *Speculi*, p. 29.

42 E. Smirke, 'Report', *JRIC*, 6 (1866) pp. vii–viii; and B. Murdoch, *Cornish Literature* (Cambridge, 1993), pp. 134–5.

43 E.H. Pedler, 'Notes on the Names of Places', in E. Norris (ed.), *The Ancient Cornish Drama* (2 vols, London, 1859), II, pp. 507–14.

44 Peter, *Glasney Collegiate Church*, p. 102.

45 Halliday, *Survey*, pp. 127, 138–9.

46 R.N. Worth, *The Buller Papers* (privately printed, 1895), p. 103.

47 C. Hill, *The English Bible and the Seventeenth-Century Revolution* (London, 1994),

Post, 12 November 1644.

63 P. Berresford-Ellis, *The Cornish Language and its Literature* (London, 1974), p. 66. See also Jenner, *Handbook of the Cornish Language*, p. 12; M.F. Wakelin, *Language and History in Cornwall* (Leicester, 1975), pp. 98–9; C. Fudge, *The Life of Cornish* (Redruth, 1982), p. 25; and B. Murdoch, *Cornish Literature* (Cambridge, 1993), p. 15.

64 Hastings, *Construction of Nationhood*, pp. 66–7.

65 N. Pocock (ed.), *Troubles Connected with the Prayer Book of 1549* (Camden Society, New Series, 37, 1884), p. 171. For Nichols's authorship, see G. Scheurweghs, 'On an Answer to the Articles of the Rebels of Cornwall and Devonshire (Royal MS, 18, B.XI)', *British Museum Quarterly*, 8 (1933–4), pp. 24–5.

66 Jenner, *Handbook of the Cornish Language*, p. 13.

67 Halliday, *Richard Carew*, p. 56; W. Hals, *The Compleat History of Cornwall, Volume II* (Exeter, 1750), p. 133; and D. Gilbert, *The Parochial History of Cornwall* (4 vols, 1838), IV, pp. 205, 216.

68 CRO, F2/39, f.49. It is interesting to note that, in a later revision of his manuscript, Scawen added the comment that the Cornish had 'not out of true judgement desired it [i.e. the English Liturgy]'. See CRO, F2/39, f.49.

69 See, for example, Gibson, *Camden's Britannia*, p. 18; and Borlase, *Natural History*, p. 315.

70 See, for example, A.S.D. Smith, *The Story of the Cornish Language* (Camborne, 1969); A.K. Hamilton-Jenkin, *Cornwall and its People* (1970), p. 167; P. Berresford-Ellis, *The Story of the Cornish Language* (Truro, n.d.), p. 15; and J. Whitaker, *The Ancient Cathedral of Cornwall* (2 vols, London, 1804), II, p. 37.

71 Though see the sensible comments made in Jenner, *Handbook of the Cornish Language*, p. 12; and in F.W.P. Jago, *The Ancient Language and the Dialect of Cornwall* (Truro, 1882), pp. 14–15.

72 J. Gwynfor-Jones, *Early Modern Wales, 1525–1640* (London, 1994), pp. 148–50.

73 Rose-Troup, *Western Rebellion*, p. 435.

74 On the concept of the 'stigmatised identity', see T.H. Eriksen, *Ethnicity and Nationalism: Anthropological Perspectives* (London, 1993), pp. 28–30.

3 'England No England, but Babel': English 'Nationalism', Welsh and Cornish Particularism and the English Civil War

1 For classic statements of the 'modernist' position, see E.J. Hobsbawm, *Nations and Nationalism since 1780: Programme, Myth and Reality* (Cambridge, 1992), especially pp. 3, 5, 9–10, 14–45; B. Anderson, *Imagined Communities: Reflections on the Origins and Spread of Nationalism* (London, 1995), pp. 4–5, 11–12, 90; and E. Gellner, *Nations and Nationalism* (Oxford, 1983), pp. 34–5, 38, 138.

2 See, for example, M.T. Clanchy, *England and its Rulers 1066–1272: Foreign Lordship and National Identity* (London, 1983), especially pp. 240–62; L. Greenfeld, *Nationalism: Five Roads to Modernity* (London, 1993), especially pp. 6–7, 14 and 29–87; P. Wormald, 'Enga-Lond: The Making of an Allegiance',

Journal of Historical Sociology, 7 (1994), pp. 1–24; J. Campbell, 'The United Kingdom of England: The Anglo-Saxon Achievement', in A. Grant and K. Stringer (eds), *Uniting the Kingdom? The Making of British History* (London, 1995), *passim*; and A. Hastings, *The Construction of Nationhood: Ethnicity, Religion and Nationalism* (Cambridge, 1997) *passim*, especially pp. 4–5.

3 R. Cust and A. Hughes, 'Introduction', in R. Cust and A. Hughes (eds), *The English Civil War* (London, 1997), pp. 7, 22.

4 Conrad Russell's description of the English Civil War as merely 'the fourth round in a ten-round battle'—*The Causes of the English Civil War* (Oxford, 1990), p. 218—has proved enormously influential. For a recent attempt to reassert the primacy of the conflict in England, see J. Adamson, 'The English Context of the British Civil Wars', *HT*, 48 (11) (November 1998), pp. 23–9.

5 N. Canny, 'The Attempted Anglicization of Ireland in the Seventeenth Century: An Exemplar of British History', in J.F. Merritt (ed.), *The Political World of Thomas Wentworth, Earl of Strafford, 1621–41* (Cambridge, 1996), p. 158; Cust and Hughes, 'Introduction', pp. 10–11; and R. Samuel, *Island Stories: Unravelling Britain, Theatres of Memory, Volume II* (London, 1998), p. 33.

6 For some honourable exceptions, see K.J. Lindley, 'The Impact of the 1641 Rebellion upon England and Wales, 1641–45', *Irish Historical Studies*, 18(70) (1972), pp. 143–76; J.L. Malcolm, 'All the King's Men', *Irish Historical Studies*, 21(83) (March 1979), pp. 239–64; Cust and Hughes, 'Introduction', pp. 8–10; and E.H. Shagan, 'Constructing Discord; Ideology, Propaganda and English Responses to the Irish Rebellion of 1641', *JBS*, 36(1) (January 1997), pp. 4–34.

7 For some cautionary remarks on this subject, see J.G.A. Pocock, 'The Atlantic Archipelago and the War of the Three Kingdoms', in J. Morrill and B. Bradshaw (eds), *The British Problem, 1534–1707: State Formation in the Atlantic Archipelago* (London, 1996), pp. 180–1, 183–4.

8 For previous suggestions that the behaviour of the Welsh and Cornish might merit closer consideration, see M. Stoyle, *Loyalty and Locality: Popular Allegiance in Devon during the English Civil War* (Exeter, 1994), pp. 232–41; and Pocock, 'The War of the Three Kingdoms', pp. 181, 184.

9 M. Todd, *The South West to AD 1000* (London, 1987), pp. 273–4; J. Gwynfor Jones, *Early Modern Wales, 1525–1640* (London, 1994), pp. 75–90; S.G. Ellis, *Ireland in the Age of the Tudors, 1447–1603: English Expansion and the End of Gaelic Rule* (Harlow, 1998), pp. 150–2.

10 Adamson, 'The English Context of the British Civil Wars', p. 27.

11 Lindley, '1641 Rebellion', pp. 151–5, 159–62; B. Manning, *The English People and the English Revolution* (London, 1991), pp. 68, 77–9, A. Fletcher, *The Outbreak of the English Civil War* (London, 1981), pp. 138, 200–3, 214–15.

12 R. Clifton. 'The Popular Fear of Catholics during the English Revolution', *P & P*, 52 (August 1971), pp. 34–43, 54; P. Lake, 'Anti-Popery: The Structure of a Prejudice', in R. Cust and A. Hughes (eds), *Conflict in Early Stuart England: Studies in Religion and Politics, 1603–42* (London, 1989), pp. 92–5; and Shagan, 'Constructing Discord', *passim.*

13 C. Hibbard, *Charles I and the Popish Plot* (Chapel Hill, North Carolina, 1983), *passim*; and Clifton, 'Popular Fear of Catholics', pp. 29–31, 39–41.

14   For rumours of Danish invasion, see *CJ*, II (1640–2), pp. 487, 535; Fletcher, *Outbreak*, p. 234; DRO, Book 73/1 (James White's Chronicle), f.111; and BL, E. 141 (9), *The Danes Plot Discovered against this Kingdom*, 23 March 1642.

15   Lindley, '1641 Rebellion', p. 161; M. Stoyle, *From Deliverance to Destruction: Rebellion and Civil War in an English City* (Exeter, 1996), p. 170; Fletcher, *Outbreak*, pp. 201–3, 214–15, 233–4. As Professor Fletcher observes (p. 223), most 'were preparing not for Civil War, but for a national state of emergency'.

16   M. Sylvester (ed.), *Reliquiae Baxterianae, or Mr Richard Baxter's Narrative of the Most Memorable Passages of his Life and Times* (London, 1696), p. 39.

17   S.R. Gardiner, *History of the Great Civil War, 1642–49* (4 vols, London, 1893), II, p. 202.

18   C. Russell, 'The Nature of a Parliament in Early Stuart England' in H. Tomlinson (ed.), *Before the English Civil War: Essays on Early Stuart Politics and Government* (London, 1983), p. 133.

19   Greenfeld, *Nationalism*, pp. 38–9, 44–5, 50–1; and R. Cust and P. Lake, 'Sir Richard Grosvenor and the Rhetoric of Magistracy', *BIHR*, 54 (1981), pp. 40–53, especially p. 52.

20   See R. Cust (ed.), *The Papers of Sir Richard Grosvenor, 1st Bart., 1585–1645* (Record Society of Lancashire and Cheshire, 134, 1996), pp. xx, xxvii; and R. Cust, 'Politics and the Electorate in the 1620s', in Cust and Hughes (eds), *Conflict in Early Stuart England*, pp. 134–67, especially pp. 145, 150, 155.

21   Roundhead military commanders, extolled as 'patriots' by their supporters from the moment the conflict began, were being fêted with such titles as 'England's Worthies' and 'England's Champions' by 1645–6. See, for example, E. 118 (27), *A True Character of Worcesters Late Hurly Burly*, 22 September 1642; and E. 293 (12), *The Scottish Dove*, 11–18 July 1645.

22   C.H. Firth (ed.), *The Memoirs of Edmund Ludlow* (2 vols, Oxford, 1894), I, p. 38; C. Holmes (ed.), *The Suffolk Committees for Scandalous Ministers* (Suffolk Records Society, 13, Ipswich, 1970), p. 47.

23   See, for example, G.M. Trevelyan, *England Under the Stuarts* (London, 1925; 1954 edn), pp. 162–3; and, more generally, R.C. Richardson, *The Debate on the English Revolution* (Manchester, 1998 edn), pp. 44–7, 58, 69, 81, 95–6. The 'patriotic' interpretation of the Civil War has never been more cogently advanced than in the work of S.R. Gardiner, see *History*, I, especially pp. 18, 153, 204; II, especially pp. 171, 177, 202, 258; and III, especially 69 and 80–1. Like every other historian of the period, I am heavily in Gardiner's debt.

24   See Richardson, *Debate on the English Revolution*, pp. 110–11.

25   There are only three book-length surveys of the conflict in Wales, see J.R. Phillips, *Memoirs of the Civil War in Wales and the Marches* (2 vols, London, 1874); R. Hutton, *The Royalist War Effort, 1642–46* (London, 1982); and P. Gaunt, *A Nation Under Siege: The Civil War in Wales, 1642–48* (London, 1991).

26   This is true of even the most perceptive historians of the period, see, for example, J. Morrill, 'The British Problem, circa 1534–1707', in Morrill and Bradshaw (eds), *The British Problem*, p. 6; and P. Gaunt, *The British Wars, 1637–51* (London, 1997), p. 8.

27   Gwynfor Jones, *Early Modern Wales*, pp. 31–5.

28   A.H. Dodd, *A Short History of Stuart Wales* (London, 1977), p. 87; Gaunt, *A Nation Under Siege*, p. 8.

29   Gwynfor Jones, *Early Modern Wales*, pp. 8–9, 12–14; and P. Williams, 'The Welsh Borderland under Queen Elizabeth', *Welsh History Review* 1 (1960), pp. 34–5.

30   J. Gwynfor-Jones, *Wales and the Tudor State: Government, Religious Change and the Social Order, 1534–1603* (London, 1989), p. 78; Gwynfor Jones, *Early Modern Wales*, pp. 1–2, 85–6; and P.R. Roberts, 'The Union with England and the Identity of "Anglican" Wales', *TRHS* fifth series, 22 (1972), pp. 49, 58.

31   P. Roberts, 'The English Crown, The Principality of Wales and the Council in the Marches, 1534–1641', in Morrill and Bradshaw (eds), *The British Problem*, pp. 118–47, especially p. 128.

32   Dodd, *A Short History of Stuart Wales*, p. 84; and B. Bradshaw, 'The Tudor Reformation and Revolution in Wales and Ireland: The Origins of the British Problem', in Morrill and Bradshaw (eds), *The British Problem*, pp. 39–65, especially pp. 52–3.

33   Ibid., pp. 45–6.

34   G. Williams, *Recovery, Reorientation and Reformation, Wales 1415–1642* (Oxford, 1987), p. 460; Roberts, 'Anglican Wales', pp. 66–9; Gwynfor-Jones, *Wales and the Tudor State*, pp. 93–7.

35   Roberts, 'Anglican Wales', p. 67.

36   Dodd, *A Short History of Stuart Wales*, p. 68; Gwynfor-Jones, *Wales and the Tudor State*, pp. 96–7; Williams, *Recovery, Reorientation and Reformation*, pp. 476, 482; G.H. Jenkins, *Protestant Dissenters in Wales, 1639–88* (Cardiff, 1992), p. 9.

37   Williams, *Recovery, Reorientation and Reformation*, pp. 473–5, 479–80.

38   Dodd, *A Short History of Stuart Wales*, p. 87; A.H. Dodd, *Studies in Stuart Wales* (Cardiff, 1952), p. 59.

39   For the early Stuart view of Wales as 'a Catholic heartland', see P. Jenkins, *A History of Early Modern Wales, 1536–1990* (London, 1992), p. 111.

40   Williams, *Recovery, Reorientation and Reformation*, p. 485; Dodd, *A Short History of Stuart Wales*, p. 90.

41   *CJ*, II, pp. 317–18; R. Webb (ed.), *Nehemiah Wallington: Historical Notices of Events Occurring Chiefly in the Reign of Charles I* (2 vols, London, 1869), II, p. 45; E. 176 (13), *A Great Discovery of a Damnable Plot at Rugland Castle in Monmouthshire*, 12 November 1641; and E. 176 (12), *A Plot by the Earle of Worcester in Wales*, 15 November 1641.

42   In 1601 there were just 29 Welsh MPs in a House of Commons with 462 members, see S.G. Ellis, 'Tudor State Formation and the Shaping of the British Isles', in S.G. Ellis and S. Barber (eds), *Conquest and Union: Fashioning a British State, 1485–1725* (London, 1995), p. 62.

43   See P. Williams, 'The Attack on the Council in the Marches, 1603–42', *Transactions of the Honourable Society of Cymmrodorion*, (1961), pp. 18–22; and Roberts, 'Council in the Marches', in Morrill and Bradshaw (eds), *The British Problem*, pp. 145–7.

44   NLW, Wb. 7844, *The Humble Petition of Many Hundred Thousands, inhabiting within the Thirteene Shires of Wales*, 12 February 1642.

45   E. 147 (4), *Newes from Wales: Or the Prittish Parliament*, May 1642. See also M. Stoyle, 'Caricaturing Cymru: Images of the Welsh in the London Press, 1642–46', in D. Dunn (ed.), *War and Society in Medieval and Early Modern Britain* (Liverpool, 2000), pp. 162–79.

46   See E. 109 (27), *Two Petitions Presented to the King . . . at York*, 8 August 1642, in which the Welsh petitioners begged for 'protection' from the King.

47   Stoyle, 'Caricaturing Cymru', *passim*.

48   E. 118 (4), *The Welchmans Declaration*, 17 September 1642 (*sic*, actually 1643); J. Washbourn (ed.), *Bibliotheca Gloucestrensis: A Collection of Scarce and Curious Tracts Relating to . . .Gloucester* (3 vols, Gloucester, 1823), I, p. 119.

49   See Chapter 1.

50   D. Nicholas, *Medieval Flanders* (London, 1992), p. 89. I owe this reference to Alastair Duke. See also *CSPV*, I (1202–1509), pp. 266, 311–12, 314; *CSPV*, IV (1527–33), p. 294.

51   See Chapter 1; and M. Stoyle, 'Cornish Rebellions, 1497–1648', *HT*, 47(5) (May 1997), pp. 22–8.

52   For the Stannaries, see G.R. Lewis, *The Stannaries: A Study of the Medieval Tin Miners of Devon and Cornwall* (Truro, 1965 edn), especially pp. 35–7, 39–41, 86–7, 107, 157.

53   It has been calculated that 86 per cent of the Cornish burgesses were 'outsiders' in 1601, and that 'the proportion of outsiders returned by Cornish boroughs was twice as great as it was in boroughs elsewhere in England and Wales', see J. Chynoweth, 'The Gentry of Tudor Cornwall' (Ph.D. thesis, Exeter University, 1994), pp. 185–6.

54   For the attacks launched on the Stannary jurisdiction in the Long Parliament, see A. Duffin, *Faction and Faith: Politics and Religion of the Cornish Gentry Before the Civil War* (Exeter, 1996), p. 177.

55   E. 669, f.4, 64, 'The Petition of the County of Cornwall' (February 1642); *CSPV*, 1642–3, pp. 17, 101–2; and R.N. Worth (ed.), *The Buller Papers* (Plymouth, 1895), pp. 49–51.

56   Bod., Tanner MSS, 63, ff.21–22; *LJ*, IV (1628–42), p. 275.

57   M. Coate, *Cornwall in the Great Civil War and Interregnum: A Social and Political Study (Truro, 1963)*, p. 32; Duffin, *Faction and Faith*, especially pp. 186–96.

58   Stoyle, *Loyalty and Locality*, pp. 232–6; Chapter 4, below; J. Stucley, *Sir Bevill Grenville, 1596–1643* (Chichester, 1983) p. 115.

59   See Chapter 4.

60   T. Carte (ed.), *A Collection of Original Letters . . . found among the Duke of Ormonde's Papers* (2 vols, London, 1739), I, p. 52.

61   See Chapter 4; and E. 12 (15), *England's Troubles Anatomised*, 11 October 1644.

62   E. 294 (26), *Mercurius Veridicus*, 26 July to 4 August 1645; J. Vicars, *The Burning Bush Not Consumed: England's Parliamentarie Chronicle* (London, 1646), pp. 375–9.

63   J. Morrill, 'The British Problem', p. 6; and Williams, *Recovery, Reorientation and Reformation*, p. 464.

64   References to such men are legion. See, for example, *CSPD*, 1641–3, pp. 367, 401; *CJ*, II, pp. 855, 890, 939, 941, 978, 993; and R. Bell (ed.), *Memorials of the*

Civil War, Comprising the Correspondence of the Fairfax Family (2 vols, London, 1849), I, p. 29.

65 Exhaustive research has identified a total of thirty Scottish field officers who served in the King's army, see P.R. Newman, 'The Royalist Officer Corps, 1642–60: Army Command as a Reflexion of the Social Structure', *HJ*, 26(4) (1983), p. 953.

66 J. Kenyon, *The Civil Wars of England* (London, 1998), p. 45; and J. Adair, *Roundhead General: The Campaigns of Sir William Waller* (Stroud, 1997), p. 116.

67 For this affair, see *CJ*, III (1642–4), pp. 3, 5, 13, 22, 25; and BL, Additional MSS, 31,116, Whitaker's Diary, f.33r. Parliament took the incident seriously enough to issue a declaration forbidding such quarrels, see E. 94 (4), *A Declaration of Parliament Concerning a Late Difference between Officers of the English and Scottish Nation*, 23 March 1643.

68 For the King's foreign soldiers, see I. Roy, 'The Royalist Army in the First Civil War', (Oxford University D.Phil. thesis, 1963), especially pp. 106, 143–6; I. Roy, *The Royalist Ordnance Papers, 1642–46* (Volumes I and II, Oxford Record Society, 43 and 49, 1963 and 1975), *passim*; Newman, 'The Royalist Officer Corps', pp. 945, 953; P.R. Newman, 'The 1663 List of Indigent Officers Considered as a Primary Source', *HJ*, 30 (1987), especially pp. 892–3; and J.L. Malcolm, *Caesar's Due: Loyalty and Charles, 1642–46* (London, 1983), pp. 91–3, 112–13. For the most recent account of Rupert, see F. Kitson, *Prince Rupert: Portrait of a Soldier* (London, 1996).

69 I. Roy, 'England Turned Germany?: The Aftermath of the Civil War in its European Context', *TRHS*, 28 (1978), pp. 131–2.

70 E. 117 (3), *The List of the Army . . . under the . . . Earle of Essex*, 14 September 1642; and *CJ*, II, p. 939.

71 P. Tennant, *The Civil War in Stratford-Upon-Avon: Conflict and Community in South Warwickshire, 1642–46* (Stroud, 1996), pp. 82–4; Adair, *Roundhead General*, pp. 149–50, 207; *CSPD*, 1644, pp. 89–91, 97.

72 Malcolm, *Caesar's Due*, p. 92.

73 E. 122 (2), *An Encouragement to Warr*, 13 October 1642.

74 Charles I's 'Irish troops' still make regular appearances in histories of the conflict, see, for example, Malcolm, *Caesar's Due*, pp. 113–21; and M. Bennett, *The Civil Wars in Britain and Ireland, 1638–51* (Oxford, 1997), pp. 205–6, 234.

75 J. Barratt, 'Native Irishmen', *HT*, 49(1) (January 1999), p. 61.

76 Even some Royalists believed this, see Lindley, '1641 Rebellion', pp. 170–5.

77 Kenyon, *Civil Wars of England*, p. 16.

78 C. Russell, 'The British Problem and the English Civil War', reprinted in Cust and Hughes (eds), *The English Civil War*, pp. 121–8; Russell, *The Causes of the English Civil War*, pp. 15–16, 38, 122, 125, 187.

79 J.F. Larkin (ed.), *Stuart Royal Proclamations, Volume II, 1625–46* (Oxford, 1983), pp. 987–9. See also Gardiner, *History*, I, pp. 259–60, 299.

80 See, for example *CSPD*, 1644, p.14; E. Walker, *Historical Discourses upon Several Occasions* (London, 1705), pp. 43, 53, 96; and BL, Harleian MSS, 6804, f.53.

81 R. Sherwood, *The Civil War in the Midlands, 1642–51* (Stroud, 1992), pp. 147–8;

Tennant, *The Civil War in Stratford-Upon-Avon*, pp. 127–33.

82 J. and T.W. Webb, *Memorials of the Civil War . . . as it affected Herefordshire* (2 vols, London, 1879), II, p. 396.

83 Clarendon termed Charles I 'an immoderate lover of the Scottish nation', see Richardson, *The Debate on the English Revolution*, p. 35.

84 K.M. Brown, 'Courtiers and Cavaliers: Service, Anglicisation and Loyalty among the Royalist Nobility', in J. Morrill (ed.), *The Scottish National Covenant in its British Context* (Edinburgh, 1990), pp. 157, 162, 166, 167, 171, 175.

85 In late 1645 'most' of the officers in the King's Lifeguard were reported to be Scots, see C.E. Long and I. Roy (eds), *Richard Symonds' Diary of the Marches of the Royal Army* (Cambridge, 1997 edn), p. 242. For a Royalist commission of March 1645 authorizing Colonel George Maxwell to recruit 'all such officers and souldiers of the Scottish Nation who will . . . put themselves under his commaund', see Bod., Rawlinson MSS, classis C, 125, f.108.

86 In May 1645, for example, see E. Warburton, *Memoirs of Prince Rupert and the Cavaliers* (3 vols, London, 1849), III, p. 98.

87 See, for example, *CSPD*, 1644–5, pp. 98, 103, 104–5, 120–1, 162–3, 174; and, more generally, Sylvester, *Reliquiae Baxterianae*, p. 49.

88 See, for example, *CSPD*, 1644, pp. 89–91, 97, 155, 161–2, 487, 491, 494–5, 524; and Gardiner, *History*, I, pp. 368–70; II, pp. 2–3, 23.

89 W.C. Abbott, *The Writings and Speeches of Oliver Cromwell* (2 vols, Cambridge, 1937), I, pp. 314–15. The 'nationalist' implications of the military reorganization of 1644–5 have gone largely unnoticed by previous historians of the New Model Army, see, for example, I. Gentles, *The New Model Army in England, Ireland and Scotland, 1645–53* (Oxford, 1994); and M. Kishlansky, *The Rise of the New Model Army* (Cambridge, 1979).

90 Sylvester, *Reliquiae Baxterianae*, p. 48; R.K.G. Temple, 'The Original Officer List of the New Model Army', *BIHR*, 59, 139 (1986), pp. 54–70, especially p. 55, n.33 and n.35; p. 56, n.41; p. 60, n.72; p. 62, n.105; p. 64, n.123; p. 68, n.150; and Gentles, *The New Model Army*, p. 21.

91 This trend reached its climax in the 'official' account of the New Model Army's wartime campaigns—J. Sprigge, *Anglia Rediviva: England's Recovery* (London, 1647)—a work which is dedicated to 'All True English-men', and suffused with English nationalist imagery.

92 E. 293 (12), *The Scottish Dove*, 11–18 July 1645.

93 See *CJ*, IV (1644–6), pp. 194, 220, 264, 273, 283, 298, 301, 305, 339; *CSPD*, 1645–7, pp. 105, 114–16, 149, 177–9, 200–1, 215; Warburton, *Memoirs*, III, p. 62. The New Model Army's grievances against the Scots are well chronicled, albeit retrospectively, in Sprigge, *Anglia Rediviva*, pp. 20, 23, 25–6, 28, 30, 92, 96–7, 179, 257, 280.

94 In August and November 1645, for example, see Gardiner, *History*, II, p. 285; and III, pp. 1–5, 45.

95 For a scheme to set up a semi-independent statelet in Cornwall in 1645, see Chapter 5.

96 R.N. Dore (ed.), *The Letter Book of Sir William Brereton, Volume I* (Record Society of Lancashire and Cheshire, 123, 1984), pp. 21–3, 248–9, 259, 294–8,

320.

97   For Parliamentarian attempts to win over the Welsh, see Malcolm, *Caesar's Due*, pp. 196–7; Stoyle, *Loyalty and Locality*, pp. 238–9; *CSPD*, 1645–7, p. 341; *CJ*, IV, pp. 242, 264–7; and NLW, Civil War Tracts, 204, *A Declaration of the Lords and Commons*, 8 September 1645. For similar attempts to win over the Cornish, see Chapter 4, below; Bell, *Memorials of the Civil War*, I, p. 286; and Abbott, *The Writings and Speeches of Oliver Cromwell*, pp. 372–3.

4 'Pagans or Paragons?': Images of the Cornish during the English Civil War

1   A. Gibson (ed.), *Early Tours in Devon and Cornwall* (Newton Abbot, 1967), p. 91.

2   F.E. Halliday, (ed.), *Richard Carew of Antony: The Survey of Cornwall* (New York, 1969), pp. 82–3.

3   For Cornwall's population between 1600 and 1650, see K.J. George, 'How Many People Spoke Cornish Traditionally?', *CS*, 14 (1986), p. 70.

4   For the most recent attempt to refute the notion of Cornish distinctiveness, see J. Chynoweth, 'The Gentry of Tudor Cornwall' (unpublished Ph.D. thesis, University of Exeter, 1994), pp.17–29.

5   D.C. Fowler, *Authors of the Middle Ages: 2, John Trevisa* (Aldershot, 1993), p. 1.

6   For 'the retreat of Cornish', see George, 'How Many People Spoke Cornish Traditionally?', *passim*.

7   Halliday, *Carew of Antony*, p. 125.

8   Ibid., p. 147.

9   Ibid., p. 125 and H.M. Speight, 'Local Government and Politics in Devon and Cornwall, 1509–49' (unpublished Ph.D. thesis, University of Sussex, 1991), p. 16.

10   For further discussion of the tinners' distinctiveness, see M. Stoyle, *Loyalty and Locality: Popular Allegiance in Devon during the English Civil War* (Exeter, 1994), pp. 16–18.

11   Halliday, *Carew of Antony*, p. 136.

12   See Chynoweth, 'Gentry of Tudor Cornwall', p. 91; and A. Duffin, 'The Political Allegiances of the Cornish Gentry, 1600–42' (Ph.D. thesis, University of Exeter, 1989), p. 72.

13   D.H. Cullum, 'Society and Economy in West Cornwall, 1588–1750' (unpublished Ph.D. thesis, University of Exeter, 1994), pp. 39, 273–4.

14   Duffin, 'Political Allegiance', pp. 72–3.

15   Ibid., *passim*; and Chynoweth, 'Gentry of Tudor Cornwall', *passim*, especially p. 29.

16   See, for example, R. Buller, *The Buller Papers* (privately printed, 1895), p. 103; and, more generally, Chapter 1, above.

17   On the puritan gentry network in East Cornwall, see Duffin, 'Political Allegiance', pp. 85–7, 232–46.

18   C.E.H. Chadwycke Healey (ed.), *Bellum Civile: Hopton's Narrative of his Campaign in the West, 1642–46* (Somerset Record Society, 18, 1902), p. 20.

19   E. 124 (20), *New News from Cornwall* (27 October 1642).

20 Ibid., and BL, Add MSS, 11,314, f.13.

21 CRO; DDT 1767. For Arundell's pivotal role, see also E. 124 (29), *A Remonstrance or Declaration* (29 October 1642).

22 CRO, DDT 1767.

23 For the strength of Buller's forces, see E. 124 (20).

24 See E. 102 (17), *A True Relation of the Proceedings of the Cornish Forces* (19 May 1643); E. 124 (29); E. 240 (48), *A Perfect Diurnal* (24–31 October 1642); and E. 240 (49), *England's Memorable Accidents* (24–31 October 1642).

25 For 1497, see A.L. Rowse, *Tudor Cornwall* (1941), pp. 114–40; I. Arthurson, 'The Rising of 1497: A Revolt of the Peasantry?' in J. Rosenthal and C. Richardson (eds), *People, Politics and Community in the Later Middle Ages* (Gloucester, 1987); and I. Arthurson, *The Perkin Warbeck Conspiracy, 1491–99* (1994), pp. 162–88. For 1549, see J. Cornwall, *Revolt of the Peasantry, 1549* (1977); F. Rose-Troup, *The Western Rebellion of 1549* (1913); Rowse, *Tudor Cornwall*, pp. 253–90; J. Sturt, *Revolt in the West* (Exeter, 1987); and J. Youings, 'The South-Western Rebellion of 1549', *SH*, I, (1979).

26 E. 124 (20). See also E. 17 (17), *England's Antidote* (22 October 1644).

27 E. 125 (5); and E. 124 (14).

28 For the continued use of this term, see E. 93 (4), *Certaine Informations* (6–13 March 1643); E. 100 (20), *A Full Relation of the Defeat given to the Cornish Cavaliers* (3 May 1643); and E. 65 (24), *Certaine Informations* (14–21 August 1643). Although the pamphleteers generally encouraged the myth of a completely homogeneous Cornish Royalism, they did not always do so. See E. 99 (24), *A Continuation of Certain Speciall . . . Passages* (20–27 April 1643) for a report that 300 Cornish freeholders were serving in the Parliamentary army in Devon.

29 *CSPV*, 1642–3, p. 189.

30 For the events of November 1642 to April 1643, see E.A. Andriette, *Devon and Exeter in the Civil War* (Newton Abbot, 1971), pp. 73–84.

31 Halliday, *Carew of Antony*, p. 139.

32 On the frequency with which Cornish vagrants were arrested in Devon during the 1630s, see A.L. Beier, *Masterless Men: The Vagrancy Problem in England, 1560–1640* (1985), p. 34.

33 See M.A. Courtenay, *Folklore and Legends of Cornwall* (Exeter, 1989 edn), pp. 200–3.

34 E. 128 (11), *True and Joyful News from Exeter* (25 November 1642); and E. 8 (29), *The Weekly Account* (4–11 September 1644).

35 E. 100 (20); and E. 126 (35), *True and Remarkable Passages* (9 November 1642).

36 W.C and C.E. Trevelyan (eds), *Trevelyan Papers*, Volume III, (Camden Society, Old Series 105, 1872), p. 230; and E. 84 (36), *Special Passages* (5–12 January 1643).

37 E. 92 (8), *Special Passages* (28 February to 7 March 1643).

38 E. 126 (35).

39 E. 86 (3), *Special Passages* (17–24 January 1643).

40 E. 128 (11).

41 For a Roundhead jibe that Hopton's men had fled to their 'lurking holes in

Cornwall', see Andriette, *Devon in the Civil War*, p. 75.

42   Bod., Wood Pamphlets, 376, No. 6. See also *HMC*, Portland MSS, p. 111; and E. 100 (6), *A Most Miraculous and Happy Victory* (29 April 1643).

43   Rowse, *Tudor Cornwall*, p. 62; and *CSPV*, 1642–3, p. 101.

44   E. 126 (35).

45   DRO; EQSOB, 64 (1642–60), f.22.

46   N. Tucker and P. Young (eds), *Military Memoirs: The Civil War* (Hamden, Connecticut, 1968), p. 12.

47   Bod., Tanner MSS, 62, f.164.

48   For the disreputable associations of hedges during the early modern period, see *OED*.

49   See A.R. Bayley, *The Great Civil War in Dorset* (Taunton, 1910), p. 139.

50   E. 258 (28), *Perfect Occurrences* (21–28 February 1645). I cannot resist observing that the Royalist 'Captain Stoyle and his man' were also captured on this occasion.

51   G. Chapman, *The Siege of Lyme Regis* (Lyme Regis, 1982), p. 32.

52   E. 4 (30).

53   C.E. Long (ed.), *Diary of the Marches of the Royal Army During the Great Civil War, Kept by Richard Symonds* (Camden Society, Old Series, 74, 1859), p. 67.

54   M. Coate, *Cornwall in the Great Civil War and Interregnum* (1963 edn), pp. 140, 147.

55   E. 8 (12), *Mercurius Civicus* (29 August to 5 September 1644).

56   E. Walker, *Historical Discourses on Several Occasions* (1705), p. 51.

57   E. 6 (16), *The Parliament's Scout* (8–15 August 1644). See also *CSPV*, 1643–7, p. 137.

58   BL, Add MSS, 35,297, (John Syms' Day Book), f.41.

59   E. 12 (12), *The Parliament's Scout* (3–10 October 1644).

60   Coate, *Cornwall*, p. 151.

61   Long, *Diary*, p. 67.

62   BL, Add MSS, 35,331, f.241.

63   Clarendon, *History*, III, p. 405.

64   Walker, *Historical Discourses*, p. 80.

65   E. 13 (14), *Mercurius Aulicus* (22–28 September 1644); and Coate, *Cornwall*, p. 152

66   See E. 13 (20), *The Weekly Account* (16–23 October 1644); E. 9 (1), *The Court Mercury* (7–14 September 1644); E. 8 (4); and E. 12 (23), *The Kingdom's Weekly Intelligencer* (8–15 October 1644).

67   E. 8 (34), *The Parliament's Scout* (5–13 September 1644).

68   E. 10 (7), *A True Relation of the Sad Passages . . . in the West* (2 October 1644).

69   A contemporary illustration of a massacre committed on a bridge in Ireland is reproduced in J. Morrill (ed.), *The Impact of the English Civil War* (1991), p. 12.

70   E. 10 (7).

71   See, for example, E. 8 (34); E. 10 (7); E. 12 (4), *The Kingdom's Weekly Intelligencer* (1–8 October 1644); E. 12 (23); and E. 13 (12), *The True Informer* (12–19 October 1644).

72   E. 12 (5), *The London Post* (8 October 1644).
73   E. 13 (20).
74   E. 13 (15), *Mercurius Britanicus* (14–21 October 1644).
75   *HMC*, Portland MSS, pp. 188–9.
76   See J. Vicars, *The Burning Bush Not Consumed: England's Parliamentarie Chronicle* (1646), p. 59; and E. 14 (16), *A Letter sent to . . . William Lenthall* (29 October 1644).
77   E. 22 (5).
78   H.G. Tibbutt (ed.), *The Letter Books of Sir Samuel Luke, 1644–45* (1963), p. 71.
79   E. 16 (4), *Mercurius Britanicus* (28 October to 4 November 1644).
80   Halliday, *Carew of Anthony*, p. 121. The nickname was still current in the 1670s, see Gibson, *Early Tours*, p. 132.
81   See, for example, BL, Burney Collection, 19A, *A Perfect Diurnal*, 1–7 July 1644.
82   E. 12 (19), *Mercurius Britanicus* (7–14 October 1644); and E. 16 (4).
83   Bod., Ashm. 721, vet.A3e, 1762, (J. Vicars, *Gods Ark*), f.29.
84   For the use of the term 'cormorant' to denote 'an insatiably greedy person' during the early modern period, see *OED*. It is interesting to note that a Cornish giant called 'Cormoran' features in the contemporary ballad *Jack the Giant Killer* (see I.H. Evans (ed.), *Brewer's Dictionary of Phrase and Fable* (1991), p. 270).
85   Bod., Ashm. 1027 (3), *Mercurius Britanicus*, 10–17 February 1645.
86   E. 330 (14). Crabs, like choughs, are notorious scavengers. I owe this point to Todd Gray.
87   E. 2 (13), *A Continuation of Certain Speciall . . . Passages* (10–17 July 1644).
88   E. 49 (32).
89   E. 25 (10), *Mercurius Britanicus* (13–20 January 1645).
90   E. 91 (25), *A True Relation of the late Victory* (3 March 1643).
91   For Cornish wrestling in general, see Halliday, *Carew of Anthony*, pp. 150–1.
92   E. 69 (18), *Mercurius Aulicus* (17–24 September 1643).
93   Evans, *Brewer's Dictionary*, p. 271.
94   Bod., Hope Adds, 1133, *Mercurius Academicus*, 2–7 March 1646.
95   See E. 15 (1), *Mercurius Civicus* (24–31 October 1644); and Vicars, *Burning Bush*, p. 59.
96   Bod., Hope Adds, 1132, *The Weekly Account*, 2–9 April 1645.
97   See E. 93 (4), *Certaine Informations* (6–13 March 1643).
98   E. 35 (24).
99   See E. 13 (10), *Mercurius Britanicus* (30 September to 7 October 1644); and for the original comment in *Mercurius Aulicus* (15–21 September 1644), E. 13 (9).
100 E. 12 (23); see also E. 33 (27), *The Spie* (13–20 February 1644).
101 E. 12 (23).
102 E. 12 (16), *The Scottish Dove* (4–11 October 1644); see also E. 12 (23).
103 See E. 16 (25), *Mercurius Britanicus* (4–11 November 1644); and Vicars, *Burning Bush*, f.9.
104 See, for example, E. 13 (15) E. 16 (4); E. 18 (7), *The Scottish Dove* (15–22

November 1644); E. 19 (3), *Perfect Passages* (20–27 November 1644); and E. 128 (11).

105   Bod., Wood, 622, *A Full Answer to a Scandalous Pamphlet* (1645).

106   Walker, *Historical Discourses*, p. 49.

107   Long, *Diary*, p. 49.

108   E. Hyde, Earl of Clarendon, *The History of the Rebellion and Civil Wars in England* (W. Dunn-Macray (ed.) 6 vols, Oxford, 1888), III, p. 387.

109   Walker, *Historical Discourses*, p. 50.

110   Long, *Diary*, p. 47.

111   See E. 104 (21), *Mercurius Aulicus* (14–20 May 1643); E. 9 (5), *Mercurius Aulicus* (18–24 August 1644); E. 16 (24), *Mercurius Aulicus* (13–19 October 1644); and E. 7 (10), *Mercurius Aulicus* (28 July to 3 August 1644). See also E. 72 (1), *Mercurius Aulicus* (8–14 October 1643).

112   E. 9 (5).

113   See E. 104 (21); E. 3 (19), *Mercurius Aulicus* (7–13 July 1644); and E. 68 (4), *Mercurius Aulicus* (10–16 September 1644).

114   E. 6 (25); and E. 8 (2), *Mercurius Aulicus* (4–10 August 1644).

115   E. 8 (2).

116   For St Ives, see Coate, *Cornwall*, p. 194. For the disturbances in North-east Cornwall, see E. 266 (24), *Perfect Occurrences* (28 November to 5 December 1645) and E. 266 (27), *Perfect Occurrences* (5–12 December 1645).

117   On this subject generally, see S.C. Osborne, 'Popular Religion, Culture and Politics in the Midlands, 1638–46' (unpublished Ph.D. thesis, University of Warwick, 1993), p. 291 and *passim*.

118   BL, Add MSS, 35,297, f.82r.

119   For the strength of the Cornish Trained bands at this time, see Clarendon, *History of the Rebellion*, IV, p. 113.

120   *HMC*, Portland MSS, p. 334.

121   For Massey's attempt to win over the Welsh in 1644, see J.R. Phillips, *Memoirs of the Civil War in Wales and the Marches* (2 vols, 1874), II, p. 211.

122   P.Q. Karkeek, 'Fairfax in the West, 1645–46', *TDA*, 8, (1876), pp. 137, 140.

123   Ibid., p. 133.

124   Ibid., p. 140.

125   J. Sprigge, *Anglia Rediviva: England's Recovery* (Oxford, 1854 edn), p. 208.

126   Vicars, *Burning Bush*, p. 375, see also p. 379.

127   Sprigge, *Anglia Rediviva*, p. 208.

128   Derby Record Office, Gell Papers, 1232 m/o, 65. I owe this reference to Todd Gray.

129   Karkeek, 'Fairfax in the West', p. 144.

130   A.C. Miller, 'Joseph Jane's Account of Cornwall during the Civil War', *EHR*, 90 (1975), p. 98.

131   Karkeek, 'Fairfax in the West', p. 145.

132   See Stoyle, *Loyalty and Locality*, chapter vii, *passim*.

133   See Karkeek, 'Fairfax in the West', p. 144; and Walker, *Historical Discourses*, p. 49.

134   Bod., J. Walker MSS, IV, f.156.

135 See, for example, *HMC*, Portland MSS, p. 100; E. 101 (6), *Speciall Passages* (1–9 May 1643); and E. 240 (45), *England's Memorable Accidents* (17–24 October 1642).

136 See E. 99 (15), *Certaine Informations* (17–24 April 1643).

137 The inhabitants of Plymouth, for example, were instructed to keep clubs ready 'for times of strife' during the sixteenth century. See R.N. Worth (ed.), *Calendar of the Plymouth Municipal Records* (Plymouth, 1893), p. 55.

138 See, for example, E. 12 (15), *England's Troubles Anatomised* (11 October 1644); and E. 16 (4). See also M. Stoyle, 'Caricaturing Cymru: Images of the Welsh in the London Press, 1642–46', in D. Dunn (ed.), *War and Society in Medieval and Early Modern Britain* (Liverpool, 2000), pp. 162–79.

139 Young and Tucker, *Military Memoirs*, p. 12.

140 See E. 2 (19), *The Scottish Dove* (13–19 July 1644); E. 2 (11), *The Kingdom's Weekly Intelligencer* (9–16 July 1644); E. 2 (13); E. 2 (15); E. 2 (16), *Mercurius Civicus* (11–17 July 1644); and Sprigge, *Anglia Rediviva*, p. 66.

141 E. 79 (17), *The Weekly Account* (20–28 December 1643).

142 See P.R. Newman, 'The 1663 List of Indigent Royalist Officers Considered as a Primary Source for the Study of the Royalist Army', *HJ*, 30(4) (1987), p. 895.

143 Tibbutt, *Letter Books of Samuel Luke*, p. 71.

144 For Grenville's original proposal, see T. Carte, *A Collection of Letters and Papers Concerning the Affairs of England* (1739), pp. 102–6. For detailed discussion of this scheme, see Chapter 5, below.

145 J. Norden, *Speculi Britanniae Pars: A Topographical and Historical Description of Cornwall* (London, 1728), p. 28.

146 For a presentation of the rebellions of 1497 and 1549 in just this light, see P. Payton, *The Making of Modern Cornwall* (Redruth, 1992), pp. 58–60. I am grateful to Jonathan Barry for drawing this important work to my attention.

147 The importance of these institutions in affording 'a certain aura (and indeed reality) of territorial semi-independence' is noted by Payton (*Making of Modern Cornwall*, p. 56).

148 See Stoyle, *Loyalty and Locality*, pp. 157–8.

149 For the popular association of the Royalist cause with the 'old wayes', see E. 7 (30).

150 I owe this point to George Bernard.

151 Karkeek, 'Fairfax in the West', p. 144.

152 Worth, *Buller Papers*, p. 103.

153 The fact that the gentry of Cornwall had become almost entirely 'anglicized' during the late medieval period, while many of the common people had not, is of crucial significance. I would argue that it is this social divergence which explains why the picture of Cornwall presented in Duffin, 'Political Allegiance of the Cornish Gentry', contrasts so markedly with that which is presented above. Examined through the eyes of the local gentry, Cornwall appears as just another English county: examined through the eyes of the common people, it becomes something rather different. The two views complement, rather than contradict each other, therefore. (Dr Duffin's thesis

was published shortly after this chapter first appeared. See A. Duffin, *Faction and Faith, Politics and Religion of the Cornish Gentry Before the Civil War* (Exeter, 1996).)

154 For 1497 see Rowse, *Tudor Cornwall*, p. 121. For 1537 and 1548, see R. Whiting, *The Blind Devotion of the People: Popular Religion and the English Reformation* (Cambridge, 1991), pp. 71, 76.

155 See M.F. Wakelin, *Language and History in Cornwall* (Leicester, 1975), p. 93.

5 'The Last Refuge of a Scoundrel': Sir Richard Grenville and Cornish Particularism, 1644–1646

1 See E. Hyde, Earl of Clarendon, *The History of the Rebellion and the Civil Wars in England* (W. Dunn-Macray (ed.), 6 vols, Oxford, 1888), *passim*.

2 R. MacGillivray, *Restoration Historians and the English Civil War* (The Hague, 1974), p. 216. See also the comments made in the excellent, judicious biography, A.C. Miller, *Sir Richard Grenville of the Civil War* (1979), pp. 1–3, 163–80. For some typical comments illustrating Grenville's reputation amongst modern historians, see P. Young and W. Emberton, *The Cavalier Army: Its Organisation and Everyday Life* (1974), p. 104; J. Kenyon, *The Civil Wars of England* (1988), p. 54; and C. Hibbert, *Cavaliers and Roundheads* (1993), p. 194.

3 For Grenville's 'Narrative', see *A Collection of Original Letters and Papers . . . Found among the Duke of Ormonde's Papers* (T.E. Carte (ed.); 2 vols, 1733–9), I, 96–109; and—for another version, differing in some minor particulars—Bod., Clarendon MS 27, fos 77–80. As Miller observes, the 'Narrative' is 'extremely unreliable', for Sir Richard 'omitted a great deal that would have reflected discredit upon himself' (Miller, *Grenville*, p. 169). These comments are fully borne out by the findings of the present chapter.

4 G. Granville, *The Genuine Works* (3 vols, 1736), II, 200–48.

5 See S.R. Gardiner, *History of the Great Civil War* (4 vols, 1893), III, p. 60; M. Coate, *Cornwall in the Great Civil War and Interregnum, 1642–60: A Social and Political Study* (Oxford, 1933), p. 177; M.D.G. Wanklyn, 'The King's Armies in the West of England, 1642–46', (unpublished University of Manchester M.A. thesis, 1966), p. 123; F.T.R. Edgar, *Sir Ralph Hopton: The King's Man in the West* (Oxford, 1968), pp. 171, 179; Miller, *Grenville*, pp. 165–6, 169–71; and R. Hutton, 'Clarendon's History of the Rebellion', *EHR*, XCVII (1982), p. 85.

6 See M. Stoyle, 'Sir Richard Grenville's Creatures: The New Cornish Tertia, 1644–46', *CS*, IV (1996), pp. 26–44.

7 P.R. Newman, *The Old Service: Royalist Regimental Colonels and the Civil War* (Manchester, 1993), p. 45.

8 See R. Granville, *The King's General in the West: the Life of Sir Richard Granville* (1908), chapter 1; Miller, *Grenville*, chapters 1–4; and J. Stucley, *Sir Bevill Grenville* (1983), chapters 1–9. For an account of the Grenvilles' position in pre-war county society, see A. Duffin, *Faction and Faith: Politics and Religion of the Cornish Gentry before the Civil War* (Exeter, 1996), *passim*, especially pp. 32–37. For Sir Richard's 'bloody' behaviour in Ireland, see Miller, *Grenville*,

pp. 61–2.

9 For Bevill's military career, see J. Stucley, *Sir Bevill Grenville*, chapters 10–13.

10 Miller, *Grenville*, pp. 60–6.

11 Ibid., pp. 67–71.

12 Ibid., p. 71.

13 On Grenville's activities before Plymouth during March–July 1644, see Miller, *Grenville*, pp. 72–83; and E.A. Andriette, *Devon and Exeter in the Civil War* (Newton Abbot, 1971), pp. 123–6.

14 On the Lostwithiel campaign, see Coate, *Cornwall*, pp. 139–59; Miller, *Grenville*, pp. 83–9; KAO, U269, 'Bourchier Papers', C.289; and Chapter 4, above.

15 Granville, *King's General*, p. 100; Miller, *Grenville*, pp. 89–90.

16 Miller, *Grenville*, p. 97.

17 See, for example, Granville, *King's General*, pp. vi–vii.

18 Miller, *Grenville*, p. 168.

19 'Tavistock Parish Registers, 1614–1781', (T.L. Stoate (ed.), 1994, copy held in DRO), pp. 150–2.

20 T. Larkham, *The Wedding Supper* (1652), pp. 124–5.

21 See R.N. Worth, 'Lydford and its Castle', *TDA*, XI, (1879), pp. 288, 298.

22 R.E. St Leger Gordon, *The Witchcraft and Folklore of Dartmoor* (1965), p. 113.

23 See, for example, Miller, *Grenville*, pp. 176–7.

24 The best contemporary description of conditions at Lydford appears in J. Bond, *Occasus Occidentalis* (1645), pp. 49–50.

25 Larkham, *The Wedding Supper*, p. 124.

26 O.M. Moger (ed.), 'Devonshire Quarter Sessions Petitions, 1642–85', (two typescript volumes, 1983, copies held in WCSL), II, p. 314.

27 Ibid., p. 371.

28 PRO, SP 23/183, f.488.

29 For an example, see R.N. Worth, 'The Siege Accounts of Plymouth', *TDA*, 17, (1885), p. 232.

30 PRO, SP 23/214, f.603.

31 For a general discussion of the treatment of prisoners of war between 1642 and 1646, see B. Donagan, 'Prisoners in the English Civil War' *HT* (March 1991), pp. 28–35.

32 Coate, *Cornwall*, p. 197.

33 Wanklyn, 'The King's Armies in the West', pp. 122, 257–8.

34 Miller, *Grenville*, p. 138.

35 On Cornish distinctiveness in general, see Coate, *Cornwall*, pp. 1–2, 139, 147, 180; A.L. Rowse, *Tudor Cornwall* (2nd edn, 1969), pp. 20–30; J. Cornwall, *Revolt of the Peasantry: 1549* (1977), pp. 41–63; and P. Payton, *The Making of Modern Cornwall* (Redruth, 1992), especially pp. 54–65.

36 See M. Stoyle, 'Cornish Rebellions, 1497–1648', *HT* (May 1997).

37 See Chapter 4; and M. Stoyle, *Loyalty and Locality: Popular Allegiance in Devon during the English Civil War* (Exeter, 1994), pp. 232–41. As these works make clear, the overwhelming majority of ordinary Cornish people supported the King. The undoubted existence of 'a minority group' of Parliamentarian

supporters amongst the Cornish gentry (see Duffin, *Faction and Faith*, p. 192) should not be permitted to obscure this fact.

38 See, for example, *HMC*, Portland MSS, iii. 112–13; and C.E.H. Chadwyck-Healey (ed.), *Bellum Civile: Sir Ralph Hopton's Narrative of his Campaign in the West* (Somerset Record Society, 1902), pp. 24–47.

39 E. Warburton, *Memoirs of Prince Rupert and the Cavaliers* (3 vols, 1849), II, p. 257.

40 See Chapter 4; and P. Young and N. Tucker (eds), *Military Memoirs: The Civil War* (1968), pp. 12, 21.

41 See E. 37 (4), *The Military Scribe*, 5–12 March 1644; and Bod., MS Hope Adds 1129, *A Continuation of Certain Special and Remarkable Passages*, 29 February to 7 March 1644.

42 On the attitude of Royalist propagandists towards the Cornish, see Chapter 4.

43 Ibid.

44 See Miller, *Grenville*, p. 91.

45 Stoyle, 'Sir Richard Grenville's Creatures', p. 28.

46 Hyde, *History*, III, p. 425.

47 H.G. Tibbutt (ed.), *The Letter Books of Sir Samuel Luke, 1644–45* (1963), p. 71.

48 For Grenville's comparatively favourable treatment of the common people, see Miller, *Grenville*, p. 175.

49 Stoyle, 'Sir Richard Grenville's Creatures', pp. 28–30; and, on the Cornish Horse, see Granville, *King's General*, p. 95; and Bod., 4.M.68 Art, *Mercurius Aulicus*, 13–19 October 1644.

50 Carte, *Collection*, I, p. 77.

51 Stoyle, 'Sir Richard Grenville's Creatures', pp. 31–2.

52 Hyde, *History*, IV, p. 15.

53 Interestingly, Grenville himself alleged that he 'could not' draw his men beyond Taunton. See WSL, Salt MS 45 (Lord Clarendon's Book of Memoranda, unpaginated), entry for 11 April 1645.

54 Hyde, *History*, IV, p. 18; Miller, *Grenville*, p. 108.

55 E. Green, 'The Siege and Defence of Taunton', *Somerset Archaeological Society Proceedings*, XXV (1879), p. 40.

56 Miller, *Grenville*, p. 108.

57 Hyde, *History*, IV, pp. 18–19.

58 Ibid., p. 30. See also Bod., Clarendon MS 24, no. 1892.

59 Hyde, *History*, IV, pp. 99–100.

60 Ibid. p. 96.

61 Ibid. p. 61.

62 Bod., Clarendon MS 25, no. 1919.

63 Ibid., no. 1925.

64 Ibid., no. 1928.

65 For the proclamation of 24 July, see R. Metcalfe (ed.), 'Sir Francis Basset of Tehidy . . . his Letters and Papers', (5 manuscript vols, 1924, copies held in WCSL), III, p. 49. For subsequent usages, see *CSPD*, 1645–7, pp. 282–83; and Bod., Clarendon MS 26, nos 2065 and 2069. The King had granted Prince

Charles his livery of the revenues of the Duchy in 1644, with the specific aim of adding 'life and lustre' to the proceedings of the western royalists ('Basset Papers', III, p. 31; and Coate, *Cornwall*, p. 167).

66 P. Payton, 'A Concealed Envy against the English: A Note on the Aftermath of the 1497 Rebellions in Cornwall', *CS*, I (1993), pp. 10–11.

67 Hyde, *History*, IV, p. 69.

68 Stoyle, 'Sir Richard Grenville's Creatures', p. 35 and n.78.

69 Hyde, *History*, IV, p. 95.

70 See *CSPD*, 1645–7, p. 46; and Bod., Clarendon MS 2005, no. 11.

71 Stoyle, 'Sir Richard Grenville's Creatures', pp. 35–6.

72 Miller, *Grenville*, p. 127.

73 E. 266 (20), *Perfect Occurrences of Parliament*, 7–14 November 1645. Goring himself had by now taken ship for France, but the Royalist cavalry continued to be generally referred to as 'Goring's Horse'.

74 E. 266 (24), *Perfect Passages of Each Day's Proceedings in Parliament*, 26 November to 3 December 1645.

75 Stoyle, 'Sir Richard Grenville's Creatures', pp. 36–8.

76 Hyde, *History*, IV, p. 104.

77 Ibid., p. 105.

78 The full text of the letter was subsequently published by Grenville himself in his 'Narrative' (see Carte, *Collection*, I, pp. 103–6).

79 Ibid., p. 104.

80 Ibid., p. 105.

81 Ibid., p. 102.

82 E. 311 (11), *Mercurius Britannicus*, 1–8 December 1645.

83 Hyde, *History*, IV, pp. 105–6.

84 Ibid., p. 106.

85 Ibid., pp. 106–7.

86 For the gathering of the Cornish troops at Tavistock, see Hyde, *History*, IV, p. 110; *CSPD*, 1645–7, p. lx; E. 266 (37), *Perfect Occurrences of Parliament*, 27 December 1645 to 3 January 1646; and E. 314 (23), *The City's Weekly Post*, 30 December 1645 to 6 January 1646.

87 For Gatford, see *DNB*; and *CSPD*, 1661–2, p. 65. For his sermon, see Bod., Clarendon MS 25, no. 1932. This undated manuscript was tentatively ascribed to July 1645 by the original cataloguer of the Clarendon MSS. However several pieces of internal evidence show that the sermon must have been written some months later. Gatford states, for example, that Prince Charles would lead the Cornish soldiers forward in person. The Prince's council had only agreed to this desperate expedient on or around 24 December 1645 (see Clarendon MS 25, nos. 2057, 2059, fos.104, 108; and *CSPD*, 1645–7, pp. lx–lxi.)

88 Bod., Clarendon MS 25, no. 1932, f.56.

89 Ibid. f.57v.

90 Ibid.

91 Ibid. f.63r-v (my italics).

92 E. 314 (23), *The City's Weekly Post* (30 December 1645 to 6 January 1646).

93 Hyde, *History*, IV, pp. 113–14, 128–9; and Miller, *Grenville*, pp. 131–2.

94 Carte, *Collection*, I, p. 107.

95 Hyde, *History*, IV, p. 132.

96 Ibid., p. 135.

97 Ibid., pp. 132–5; Carte, *Collection*, I, pp. 107–8.

98 Miller, *Grenville*, p. 134.

99 Ibid., pp. 163, 179.

100 Hyde, *History*, IV, p. 132.

101 Many attributed the Cornish people's subsequent desertion of the Royalist cause to Grenville's arrest (see Carte, *Collection*, p. 108; and Hyde, *History*, IV, p. 135).

102 For the final stages of the war in the West, see J. Sprigge, *Anglia Rediviva: England's Recovery* (1647), pp. 182–231. Also Miller, *Grenville*, pp. 139–40; Coate, *Cornwall*, pp. 199–220; and J. Wardman, *The Forgotten Battle: Torrington 1646*, (Torrington, 1996), pp. 54–61, 100–74.

103 Coate, *Cornwall*, p. 180.

104 For Goring's pleas that the Cornish should join him—and his complaints about their unwillingness to serve with his army—see Bod., Clarendon MS 25, nos. 1920, 1925, 1928, 1974, 1984, 1990, 1993, and 1998.

105 Ibid., no. 1995.

106 The literature on this subject is vast. For a superb introduction see J.G.A. Pocock, 'The Atlantic Archipelago and the War of the Three Kingdoms' in B. Bradshaw and J. Morrill (eds), *The British Problem, 1534–1707: State Formation in the Atlantic Archipelago* (1996), pp. 172–91. On p. 181 of this seminal piece, Professor Pocock remarks that 'I could wish to know more . . . about what the . . . [King's] Cornish regiments thought they were doing and who they were'. It is hoped that this chapter has supplied some answers.

6 'The Gear Rout': The Cornish Rising of 1648 and the Second Civil War

1 I am most grateful to Lord St Levan and Michael J. Moore for their comments on an earlier draft of this chapter.

2 J. Bond, *Eschol, Or Grapes Among Thorns* (18 July 1648), p. 24; and *CJ*, 5, p. 576.

3 See, for example, S.R. Gardiner, *History of the Great Civil War* (4 vols, 1901), IV, p. 145.

4 R. Ashton, *Counter-Revolution: The Second Civil War and its Origins* (1994), pp. 363, 425–9.

5 See M. Coate, *Cornwall in the Great Civil War and Interregnum* (Oxford, 1933), pp. 237–41; and J.C.A. Whetter, 'Anthony Gubbs of Penzance: Sufferer in the Parliamentary Cause', in *OC*, 7 (1969–72), pp. 160–9.

6 See, for example, A. Everitt, *The Community of Kent and the Great Rebellion* (1966), pp. 219–20, 228–30 and chapter 7; I. Roots, *The Great Rebellion* (1988 edn), p. 127; D. Underdown, *Pride's Purge: Politics in the Puritan Revolution* (Oxford, 1971), pp. 94, 98, J. Morrill, *The Revolt of the Provinces: Conservatives and Radicals in the English Civil War* (1976), pp. 126–8; J. Morrill, 'Introduction', in J. Morrill (ed.), *Reactions to the English Civil War* (1986), p. 25; and J. Kenyon,

The Civil Wars of England (1988), p. 179.

7 See B. Lyndon, 'Essex and the King's Cause in 1648', *HJ*, 29 (1986), especially pp. 17–19, 27–8, 37–8; B. Lyndon, 'The South and the Start of the Second Civil War', *History*, 71 (1986), especially pp. 400, 405, 407; and, more generally, Ashton, *Counter-Revolution, passim*.

8 On Waller, see *DNB*; J. Adair, *Roundhead General: The Campaigns of Sir William Waller* (1997), pp. 4, 11; and M. Stoyle, *From Deliverance to Destruction: Rebellion and Civil War in an English City* (Exeter, 1996), pp. 127–35.

9 See *LJ*, 10, p. 268; and Bod., Tanner MSS, 57, No. 69, f.127.

10 M. Stoyle, *Loyalty and Locality: Popular Allegiance in Devon during the English Civil War* (Exeter, 1994), pp. 232–8, and chapter 3.

11 See Coate, *Cornwall*, pp. 221–4; S.K. Roberts, *Recovery and Restoration in an English County: Devon Local Administration, 1646–70* (Exeter, 1985), pp. 1–11; and Ashton, *Counter-Revolution*, pp. 120–1.

12 C.H. Firth and R.S. Rait (eds), *Acts and Ordinances of the Interregnum* (2 vols, 1978 edn), 1, p. 1053; Bod., Clarendon MSS, 30, f.273.

13 Bod., Tanner MSS, 57, f.127; DRO, ECAB, 1/9 (1647–55), f.8.

14 Plymouth continued to keep Waller's troops at arm's length for some months, see *HMC*, Portland MSS, 1, p. 466.

15 On Poyer's Rising, see Ashton, *Counter-Revolution, passim.*, especially pp. 416–22; P. Gaunt, *A Nation under Siege: The Civil War in Wales* (1991), pp. 66–71; and J.R. Phillips, *Memoirs of the Civil War in Wales and the Marches* (2 vols, 1874), 1, pp. 392–402 and 2, pp. 344–457.

16 *CSPD*, 1648–49, p. 37; and *CSPV*, 1647–52, p. 52.

17 S.R. Gardiner (ed.), *Hamilton Papers* (Camden Society, New Series, 27, 1880), p. 171.

18 Ibid., p. 181; and J. Morrill, 'Mutiny and Discontent in English Provincial Armies, 1645–47', in J. Morrill (ed.), *The Nature of the English Revolution* (1993), pp. 336, 343, 345, 350–1.

19 E. 436 (10), *The Perfect Weekly Account*, 12–19 April 1648; *CSPV*, 1647–52, p. 55.

20 *CJ*, 5, p. 525; FSL, XD.483, Bennett MSS, nos 12, 15; and E. 436 (10).

21 Gardiner, *Hamilton Papers*, p. 183.

22 *CJ*, 5, pp. 533, 536; W.C. Abbott, *The Writings and Speeches of Oliver Cromwell* (2 vols, Cambridge, Mass., 1937), 1, p. 597.

23 For Bennett, see Coate, *Cornwall, passim*; M. Coate, 'An Original Diary of Colonel Robert Bennett of Hexworthy', *DCNQ*, 18 (1934–5), pp. 251–9; and D. Underdown, *Pride's Purge*, pp. 308–9. For his command of the western garrisons, see Bod., MSS J. Walker, C.10, f.9. Photocopies of Bennett's papers may be consulted at the CRO in Truro (Bennett MSS, FS3/47)—I am most grateful to Mr Colin Edwards for this information.

24 FSL, Bennett MSS, no.15.

25 Ibid., no. 16.

26 Bod., Tanner MSS, 57, no. 69, f.127r.

27 R.N. Worth (ed.), *The Buller Papers* (Plymouth, 1895) pp. 101–2.

28 Bod., Tanner MSS, 57, no.69, ff.127r–128r.

29 Ibid., f.129; and *LJ*, 10, pp. 269–72. The dispute at Exeter has attracted far more attention than the Cornish rising, see R.W. Cotton and H. Woollcombe (eds), *Gleanings from the Municipal Records . . . of Exeter* (Exeter, 1877), pp. 134–7; M. Coate, 'Exeter in the Civil War and Interregnum', *DCNQ*, 18 (1934–5), p. 350; Underdown, *Pride's Purge*, p. 92; Roberts, *Recovery and Restoration*, p. 12; and Ashton, *Counter-Revolution*, pp. 66–7.

30 Worth, *Buller Papers*, p. 104; E. 445 (30), *A Letter from the Isle of Wight*, (1 June 1648) [hereafter: *A Letter*], pp. 3–4; and PRO, SP 23, 149, ff.587–88.

31 E. 522 (31), *Perfect Occurrences of Parliament*, 19–26 May 1648; and *A Letter*, p. 3.

32 PRO, SP 23, 149, ff.587–88.

33 PRO, SP 19, 148, f.5; FSL, Bennett MSS, no.20.

34 E. 444 (9), *The Moderate Intelligencer*, 18–25 May 1648 (my italics). See also E. 445 (4), *The Desires of the Countie of Surrey*, 27 May 1648; and PRO, SP 23, 149, f.588.

35 *A Letter*, p. 4.

36 *CJ*, 5, p. 606.

37 See Worth, *Buller Papers*, pp. 102, 108; *A Letter*, p. 4; and Bod., J. Walker MSS, C.10, f.97.

38 *A Letter*, p. 4; FSL, Bennett MSS, no. 18.

39 Ibid., no. 20.

40 For the rebels' numbers, see *A Letter*, p. 4; E 522 (31); and Worth, *Buller Papers*, p. 105.

41 *A Letter*, p. 5.

42 FSL, Bennett MSS, no. 20; Worth, *Buller Papers*, p. 105.

43 Ibid. Other sources give similar figures for casualties, but suggest that the fight was rather shorter. See E. 522 (23), *Perfect Occurrences of Parliament*, 26 May to 3 June 1648; *A Letter*, p. 4; John Keast, *The Travels of Peter Mundy* (Truro, 1984), p. 85 and CRO, DD.EN 2469 (Daniel Mss), f.50.

44 Worth, *Buller Papers*, p. 105; and David H. Cullum, *Society and Economy in West Cornwall, 1588–1750*, (2 vols, Ph.D. thesis, University of Exeter, 1994), 1, p. 5.

45 CRO, DD, EN 2469, ff. 41, 50.

46 BL, Egerton MSS, 2657 (Borlase's Parochial History of Cornwall), f.14; *A Letter*, pp. 5–6; Worth, *Buller Papers*, p. 105; PRO, SP 23, 149, f.588.

47 *A Letter*, p. 5.

48 Ibid.

49 FSL, Bennett MSS, no.19.

50 For the previous history of 'the Dennis', see Courtenay Vyvyan, 'Defence of the Helford River', *JRIC*, 18, part 1 (1910), pp. 62–102.

51 *A Letter*, pp. 5–6.

52 Ibid., p. 6.

53 R. Polwhele, *The History of Cornwall* (6 vols, 1803–8, reprinted Dorking, 1978), 4, p. 101.

54 Ibid.; and Vyvyan, 'Helford River', pp. 67–8. See also Joshua Sprigge, *Anglia Rediviva: England's Recovery* (1647), p. 231.

55 Polwhele, *History of Cornwall*, 4, p. 101; Worth, *Buller Papers*, p. 105.

56 *A Letter*, p. 6; Bond, *Eschol*, p. 31.

57 Worth, *Buller Papers*, p. 107.

58 John Walker, *An Attempt Towards Recovering an Accompt of the Numbers and Sufferings of the Clergy* (1714), p. 240.

59 Worth, *Buller Papers*, pp. 103–6; *CJ*, 5, p. 576; John Rushworth (ed.), *Historical Collections of Private Passages of State* (1721), 8, p. 1131; FSL, Bennett MSS, no. 20.

60 Coate, *Cornwall*, pp. 238–9.

61 Worth, *Buller Papers*, p. 102. For the previous military careers of the two Arundells, Basset, Harris, Jonathan Trelawny and Trevanion, see *RO*, pp. 6–7, 18, 177, 376, 377.

62 For Bogans, see Polwhele, *Cornwall*, p. 101; *CCC*, 4, p. 2549; and Vyvyan, 'Helford River', p. 80.

63 For Christopher Grosse, see Rushworth, *Historical Collections*, 8, p. 1306; Coate, *Cornwall*, p. 239 (this account confuses Christopher with his father, Thomas); FSL, Bennett MSS, numbers 20, 28 and 45; Worth, *Buller Papers*, pp. 104–7; BL, Harleian MSS, 6804, ff.197–98; and *CCC*, 1, p. 487 and 4, p. 2980.

64 For these individuals, see *A Letter*, p. 3; FSL, Bennett MSS, numbers 20–21; Worth, *Buller Papers*, pp. 104, 107; Whetter, 'Gubbs', pp. 162–3; and *CCC*, 2, p. 1935 and 4, p. 2866.

65 For Blight, see Worth, *Buller Papers*, p. 104; *CCC*, 4, p. 2731; and Stuart Reid, *Officers and Regiments of the Royalist Army* (Leigh on Sea, n.d.), p. 47. For Pendarves, see FSL, Bennett MSS, no. 21; *CCC*, 2, p. 1327; and Reid, *Officers*, p. 3.

66 Ashton, *Counter-Revolution*, p. 477. See also Lyndon, 'Essex', pp. 26–8.

67 For Glover, see FSL, Bennett MSS, no.19; and Keast, *Peter Mundy*, p. 85.

68 For Flavell, see FSL, Bennett MSS, no.19; Walker, *Sufferings of the Clergy*, pp. 240–1; M.A. Courtney, *Folklore and Legends of Cornwall* (Exeter, 1989), pp. 95–6; and E.G. Harvey, *Mullyon: Its History, Scenery and Antiquities* (Truro, 1875), p. 6.

69 Walker, *Sufferings of the Clergy*, pp. 240–1.

70 For the importance of Royalist soldiers in the disturbances elsewhere, see Ashton, *Counter-Revolution*, pp. 348, 456, 464.

71 For Pierce, see *A Letter*, p. 4; for Collins, see Newman, *RO*, p. 78; and M. Stoyle, 'Sir Richard Grenville's Creatures: The New Cornish Tertia, 1644–46', *CS*, 4 (1996), p. 39.

72 Vyvyan, 'Helford River', pp. 80, 74; *A Letter*, p. 6; PRO, SP 23, 149, f.587.

73 Worth, *Buller Papers*, p. 104; PRO, SP 23, 149, ff.587–88.

74 See, for example, Everitt, *Kent*, p. 229; Lyndon, 'Essex', p. 29; and Lyndon, 'Second Civil War', p. 400.

75 Bod., Tanner MSS, 57, f.127r.

76 See T.T. Lewis (ed.), *Letters of the Lady Brilliana Harley* (Camden Society, Old Series 58, 1854), p. 167; Keith Lindley, *Popular Politics and Religion in Civil War London* (1997), p. 211; David Underdown, *Revel, Riot and Rebellion: Popular*

Politics and Culture in England, 1603–60 (Oxford, 1985), p.177.

77 *A Letter*, p. 5.

78 Ashton, *Counter-Revolution*, p. 376.

79 See, for example, Coate, *Cornwall*, p. 241; and Ian Gentles, *The New Model Army in England, Ireland and Scotland, 1645–53* (Oxford, 1994), p. 246.

80 See Bod., Tanner MSS, 57, f.556.

81 See Worth, *Buller Papers*, p. 102; Ashton, *Counter-Revolution*, p. 417; E. 436 (14), *Colonel Powell and Colonel Poyers Letter*, 20 April 1648; and E. 435 (9), *The Declaration of Colonel Poyer and Colonel Powell*, 10 April 1648.

82 Ashton, *Counter-Revolution*, p. 450.

83 FSL, Bennett MSS, no. 20.

84 Ibid.; and Bod., J. Walker MSS, C.10, f.9.

85 See Ashton, *Counter-Revolution*, p. 399; and Everitt, *Kent*, p. 260.

86 *A Letter*, p. 3.

87 CRO, Arundell MSS, AM/15/153; John Taylor, *Wanderings to See the Wonders of the West* (1649), p. 17; and FSL, Bennett MSS, no. 21.

88 Worth, *Buller Papers*, p. 103.

89 FSL, Bennett MSS, no. 20.

90 Underdown, *Revel, Riot and Rebellion*, pp. 225–6, 230; and Anthony Fletcher, *A County Community in Peace and War: Sussex, 1600–1660* (1975), p. 273.

91 Morrill, *Revolt of the Provinces*, p. 130.

92 Worth, *Buller Papers*, p. 103.

93 E. 445 (4), *The Desires of the County of Surrey*, 27 May 1648; and FSL, Bennett MSS, no. 21.

94 See Chapter 4; and Ashton, *Counter-Revolution*, p. 221.

95 CRO, F2/39 (William Scawen's Cornish Manuscript), f.48.

96 See Chapters 1 and 4; and M. Stoyle, 'Cornish Rebellions, 1497–1648', *HT* (May 1997), *passim.*

97 E. 522 (32), *A Perfect Diurnall* (22–29 May 1648).

98 E. 436 (14).

99 Worth, *Buller Papers*, p. 103.

100 See Chapter 5.

101 Keast, *Peter Mundy*, p. 85.

102 Thomas Fuller, *The History of the Worthies of England*, (2 vols, London, 1811 ed.), 1, p. 209.

103 FSL, Bennett MSS, no. 20; Ashton, *Counter-Revolution*, p. 241; and David Underdown, *Somerset in the Civil War and Interregnum* (Newton Abbot, 1973), p. 91.

104 Lyndon, 'Essex', pp. 18, 26–9.

105 Norman Tucker, *North Wales in the Civil War* (Wrexham, 1989), pp. 131–46; and Stoyle, *Loyalty and Locality*, pp. 238–40.

7 William Scawen: A Seventeenth-century Cornish Patriot

1   P. Berresford-Ellis, *The Cornish Language and its Literature*, (London, 1974), pp. 78–85.

2   See, for example, W. Borlase, *The Natural History of Cornwall* (Oxford, 1758), pp. xi, 292, 306, 315; W. Pryce, *Archaeologia Cornu-Brittanica: Or an Essay to Preserve the Ancient Cornish Language* (Sherborne, 1790, unpaginated); D. Gilbert, *The Parochial History of Cornwall* (4 vols, 1838), IV, pp. 190–221; G.C. Boase and W.P. Courtney, *Bibliotheca Cornubiensis* (London, 1874–82), II, p. 629; H. Jenner, *A Handbook of the Cornish Language* (London, 1904), pp. 12, 16–17; Berresford-Ellis, *The Cornish Language and its Literature*, pp. 78–85; M.F. Wakelin, *Language and History in Cornwall* (Leicester, 1975), pp. 23, 91–2; A. Hawke, 'A Lost Manuscript of the Cornish Ordinalia?', *CS*, Old Series 7 (1979), pp. 45–60; B. Murdoch, *Cornish Literature* (Cambridge, 1993), pp. 1, 19.

3   J.L. Vivian, *The Visitations of Cornwall* (Exeter, 1887), p. 422; and WCSL, 'St Germans Parish Register' (2 vols, 1938–9, unpaginated), I.

4   Vivian, *Visitations* (1887), p. 422; and J.L. Vivian and H.H. Drake, *The Visitation of the County of Cornwall in the Year 1620* (London, 1874), pp. 198–9; A. Duffin, *Faction and Faith: Politics and Religion of the Cornish Gentry before the Civil War* (Exeter, 1996), pp. 52, 84.

5   CRO, F2/39 (William Scawen's Cornish Manuscript), f.35; and J. Foster, *Alumni Oxonienses: The Members of the University of Oxford, 1500–1714* (Oxford, 1891), p. 1323.

6   Vivian, *Visitations*, p. 422; and M.F. Keeler, *The Long Parliament, 1640–41; A Biographical Study of its Members* (Philadelphia, 1954), p. 335.

7   PRO, SP 23, 199, ff.89–90, 101.

8   Vivian, *Visitations*, p. 422; and WCSL, 'St Germans Parish Register', I.

9   Gilbert, *Parochial History*, pp. 195–202.

10 Ibid., p. 199.

11 H. Hulme, *The Life of Sir John Eliot, 1592–1632: Struggle for Parliamentary Freedom* (London, 1957), p. 383.

12 Duffin, *Faction and Faith, passim*, especially pp. 78–102.

13 J. Forster, *Sir John Eliot: A Biography, 1590–1632* (2 vols, London, 1864), II, pp. 639–40. 'Knighthood fines' were financial penalties imposed on landowners of relatively modest wealth for not having come forward to be knighted at the King's coronation. They were seen as archaic and were bitterly resented.

14 J. Adamson, 'Of Armies and Architecture: The Employments of Robert Scawen', in I. Gentles et al. (eds), *Soldiers, Writers and Statesmen of the English Revolution* (Cambridge, 1998), pp. 38–9.

15 Duffin, *Faction and Faith*, pp. 84, 88, 97, 108, 151–2, 171–2, 196, 209.

16 *RO*, p. 330.

17 Ibid., p. 119; and Adamson, 'Robert Scawen', pp. 39–40.

18 *CSPD*, 1640, pp. 41–2.

19 R.N. Worth (ed.), *The Buller Papers* (Plymouth, 1895), pp. 30–1.

20 Duffin, *Faction and Faith*, p. 178.

21 T.L. Stoate (ed.), *The Cornwall Protestation Returns, 1641* (Bristol, 1974), p. 241.

22 *The Humble Petition of the County of Cornwall to the King* (London, 1642), p. 4; and Adamson, 'Robert Scawen', p. 42.

23 *LJ*, V (1642–3), pp. 156–7, 177, 241, 275, 314–15, 361; and E.A. Andriette, *Devon and Exeter in the Civil War* (Newton Abbot, 1971), p. 71.

24 See Chapter 4.

25 C.E.H. Chadwyck-Healey (ed.), *Bellum Civile: Hopton's Narrative of his Campaign in the West (1642–44) and other Papers* (Somerset Record Society, 18, 1902), p. 23.

26 Scawen in fact appears to have been Edgcumbe's Major, rather than his Lieutenant-Colonel, at this time, see Chadwyck-Healey, *Bellum Civile*, p. 31.

27 CRO, Mount Edgcumbe MSS, DDME 2925.

28 Ibid.; and Chadwyck-Healey, *Bellum Civile*, pp. 29–31.

29 F.E. Halliday, *A Cornish Chronicle: The Carews of Anthony from Armada to Civil War* (Newton Abbot, 1967), pp. 63, 73, 104, 144–9.

30 E. Hyde, Earl of Clarendon, *The History of the Rebellion and Civil Wars in England* (W.D. Macray (ed.), 6 vols, Oxford, 1888), III, p. 236.

31 CRO, Mount Edgcumbe MSS, DDME 2925. See also BL, Burney Collection, 19A, *The Perfect Diurnall*, 7–14 October 1644.

32 Halliday, *Cornish Chronicle*, pp. 149–55.

33 A.C. Miller, 'Saltash and its Vicinity during the Civil War', *JRIC*, New Series 7, Part 4 (1977), pp. 283–4.

34 PRO, SP 23, 149, ff.383, 387.

35 R. Granville, *The King's General in the West: The Life of Sir Richard Granville, Baronet, 1600–59* (London, 1908), p. 80; and PRO, SP 23, 149, ff.385, 387.

36 A.C. Miller, *Sir Richard Grenville of the Civil War* (London, 1979), p. 86.

37 BL, Additional MSS, 15750 (Letters and Papers, Seventeenth Century), f.21.

38 BL, Harleian MSS, 6802, f.269.

39 That a garrison *had* been left behind is made clear by the correspondence of July 1644 reproduced in R.N. Worth, 'The Siege of Plymouth', *RTPI*, 1875–6, p. 282. See also *HMC*, Second Report (London, 1874), pp. 20–4. Sadly these documents, together with many others relating to Mount Edgcumbe during the Civil War, were destroyed in 1941.

40 Miller, *Grenville*, p. 91. See also Chapter 6.

41 BL, Harleian MSS, 6802, f.273; and Miller, *Grenville*, pp. 92–3.

42 CRO, F2/39, f.50.

43 PRO, SP 23, 199, f.95.

44 CRO, DDME, ME 2925; and Bod., Clarendon MSS, 2070, iii.

45 Clarendon, *History*, IV, p. 20.

46 E. 329 (2), *Master Peters Messuage from Sir Thomas Fairfax* (1646).

47 Clarendon, *History*, IV, p. 137.

48 R.P. Stearns, 'Mistress Phillipa Coryton, Master Hugh Peter and the Submission of Eastern Cornwall, March 1646', *DCNQ*, 18 (1934–5), pp. 355–61; Coate, *Cornwall*, pp. 206–9; and PRO, SP 23, 199, f.408.

49 PRO, SP 23, 199, f.415; and *Master Peters Messuage*.

50 F.T.R. Edgar, *Sir Ralph Hopton: The King's Man in the West, 1642–51* (Oxford,

1968), pp.185–6.

51 PRO, SP 23, 200, f.621.

52 Clarendon, *History*, IV, p. 137; T.E. Carte (ed.), *A Collection of Original Letters and Papers . . . Found among the Duke of Ormonde's Papers* (1739), p. 115; and PRO, SP 23, 199, f.413.

53 PRO, SP 23, 199, ff.89, 93.

54 PRO, SP 23, 199, f.413; Coate, *Cornwall*, pp. 226–7; and Stearns, 'Phillipa Coryton', pp. 358–61.

55 PRO, SP 23, 199, ff.413, 432, 447.

56 Coate's statement that Scawen was elected as MP for St Germans in November 1646 (*Cornwall*, p. 377) appears to be without foundation, see Keeler, *The Long Parliament*, p. 283, note 430.

57 CRO, F2/39, f.48.

58 Ibid., f.103.

59 *CSPD*, 1679–80, p. 62; and R. Polwhele, *The History of Cornwall* (6 vols, 1803–8, Dorking, 1978 edn), III, p. 102.

60 R.R. Pennington, *Stannary Law: A History of the Mining Law of Cornwall and Devon* (Newton Abbot, 1973), p. 225; *CSPD*, 1677–8, p. 502.

61 See Chapter 8.

62 Vivian, *Visitations*, p. 422; and WCSL, 'St Germans Parish Register', II.

63 Worth, *Buller Papers*, p. 30.

64 CRO, F2/39, f.35.

65 Scawen does not date this conversation, but Foster is known to have served as Judge of the Western Circuit in 1641–2 and again in 1660–3, see J.S. Cockburn, *A History of the English Assizes, 1558–1714* (Cambridge, 1972), pp. 272–5.

66 Gilbert, *Parochial History*, IV, p. 195.

67 CRO, F2/39, ff.51–53.

68 Ibid., ff.2–3.

69 Ibid., ff. 52–53. See also C.S. Gilbert, *An Historical Survey of Cornwall* (2 vols, 1820), II, p. 710.

70 CRO, F2/39, f.2.

71 For what appears to be a collection of preparatory notes, see CRO, DD, EN1999, 'Documents to Illustrate the History of Cornwall', ff.121–35. For Scawen's own master copy of the *Antiquities*, see CRO, F2/39 ('William Scawen's Cornish Manuscript, 1688'), ff.1–125. For a second version of the *Antiquities* apparently written by Scawen himself, see Royal Institution of Cornwall Library, Truro, 'Scawen MSS'. For Thomas Tonkin's early eighteenth-century manuscript copy of this latter document, see BL, Additional MSS, 33420, ff.106–40. For a late eighteenth-century abridgement of what appears to be a third variant of Scawen's manuscript (now lost?), see Bod., Gough, Cornwall, 12, *Observations on an Ancient Manuscript entitled Passio Christi* (1777). See also O. Padel, *Catalogue to Accompany an Exhibition of Manuscripts and Printed Books in the Cornish Language* (Redruth, 1975, unpaginated). I am most grateful to Dr Padel for providing me with a copy of this work.

72 CRO, F2/39, *passim*.
73 Vivian, *Visitations*, p. 422; and WCSL, 'St Germans Parish Register', II.
74 *Observations on an Ancient Manuscript*, reprinted in Gilbert, *Parochial History*, IV, pp. 190–221.
75 W. Hals, *The Compleat History of Cornwall* (Exeter, 1750), p. 143.
76 BL, Additional MSS, 33420, ff.133–34.
77 CRO, F2/39, ff.2, 15.
78 Ibid., ff.6–7.
79 Ibid., ff.6, 12, , 15, 22 and 26.
80 Ibid., ff.16–17.
81 Ibid., f.6.
82 Ibid., ff.6, 27.
83 Ibid., f.27.
84 Ibid., f.8.
85 Ibid., f.12.
86 Ibid., ff.16–17.
87 Ibid., f.25.
88 Ibid., ff.12, 25.
89 Ibid., f.5.
90 Ibid., ff.5–20.
91 Ibid., ff.15, 11, 10.
92 Ibid., ff.21, 12.
93 Ibid., ff.10, 26.
94 Ibid., ff.11–12, 21.
95 Ibid., f.12.
96 Ibid., f.20.
97 Ibid., ff.23, 27.
98 Ibid., f.23.
99 Ibid., f.48.
100 Ibid., f.42.
101 Gilbert, *Parochial History*, IV, pp. 191, 195–6, 209; and CRO, F2/39, ff.47, 5.
102 CRO, F2/39, f.51.
103 Ibid., ff.27–28.
104 Ibid.
105 Ibid., f.8.
106 E. 300 (15), *The General Complaint of the . . . Commons of England* (10 September 1645). Cf. J.P. Sommerville (ed.), *Sir Robert Filmer, Patriarcha and other Writings* (Cambridge, 1991), p. 34. I owe this reference to Mr Stephen Dean.
107 CRO, F2/39, f.8.
108 Ibid., f.26.
109 Ibid., f.27.
110 Ibid., ff.11, 27–28 (my italics).
111 Forster, *Sir John Eliot*, II, p. 640.
112 See Chapter 5; and *CSPD*, 1645–7, p. 317.

8 'A Monument of Honour': The Cornish Royalist Tradition after 1660

1   J. Nichols (ed.), *The History of the Worthies of England . . . by Thomas Fuller* (2 vols, London, 1811), I, p. 214.

2   M.G. Smith, *Fighting Joshua: A Study of the Career of Sir Jonathan Trelawney, Bart., 1656-1721* (Redruth, 1985), p. 8.

3   See, for example, N. Pevsner, *The Buildings of England: Cornwall* (London, 1951), pp. 21-2.

4   Though see M. Coate, *Cornwall in the Great Civil War and Interregnum, 1642-60*, (Truro, 1963), p. 128; and D. Bond, 'Sir William Killigrew and the Royalist War Effort in Cornwall, 1643-4', *CS*, Old Series, 14 (1986), pp. 55-6 for brief comments.

5   DRO, Tremayne MSS, 1499/M/4/3, 'Gratulacion to Cornish Men'.

6   J.F. Larkin (ed.), *Stuart Royal Proclamations, Volume II, 1625-46* (Oxford, 1983), p. 875.

7   M. Stoyle, *From Deliverance to Destruction: Rebellion and Civil War in an English City* (Exeter, 1996), pp. 5, 82-5.

8   I.G. Philip (ed.), *The Journal of Sir Samuel Luke, Volume II* (Oxfordshire Record Society, 31, 1950), p. 148.

9   Bond, 'Killigrew', pp. 56-8.

10 E. 669, f.7, 37, *His Majesties Declaration to all his Loving Subjects in Cornwall*, 10 September 1643.

11 Bond, 'Killigrew' p. 55. According to another source, the King intended that the letter should serve as 'a Monument of Honour to that Valiant Countrey'; see E. 67 (30) *Mercurius Civicus*, 14-21 September 1643.

12 R. Morton-Nance, 'John Keigwin's Cornish Translation of King Charles I's Letter of Thanks', *OC*, October 1926, p. 36.

13 E.68 (4), *Mercurius Aulicus*, 10-16 September 1643; E.67 (30), *Mercurius Civicus*, 14-21 September 1643; E. 669, f.7, 37, *His Majesties Declaration*; and DRO, Tremayne MSS, 1499/M/4/3.

14 CRO, B/LAUS/179/2/3, 'William Noble's Account'.

15 E.329 (2), *Master Peters Messuage From Sir Thomas Fairfax*, 22 March 1646.

16 J. Hammond, *A Cornish Parish: Being an Account of St. Austell* (London, 1897), p. 28; S.J. Taylor, *The Parish Church of St. Andrew, Stratton* (Stratton, 1991), p. 11; E.A. Beynon, *St Ewe: The Church and Parish* (Long Compton, 1937), p. 16.

17 See, for example, J.C. Cox, *County Churches: Cornwall* (London, 1912), p. 46.

18 G. Granville, *The Genuine Works*, (3 vols, 1736) II, p. 276.

19 DRO, MSP, Petition of J. Stevens.

20 J. Prince, *Danmonii Orientales Illustres, Or The Worthies of Devon* (Exeter, 1701), p. 568.

21 On Grenville's earlier political career, see J. Stucley, *Sir Bevill Grenvile and his Times, 1596-1643* (Chichester, 1983), pp. 12-62; and Duffin, *Faction and Faith* pp. 81, 84, 87-90, 97, 102, 104.

22 E.65 (6), *Verses on the Death of the Right Valiant Sir Bevill Grenvill*, (Oxford, 1643).

23 *DNB*, 'John Grenville'.

24 G.M. Trinick, 'The Great House at Stowe', *JRIC*, 1979, pp. 96, 98.

25 CRO, F2/39 (William Scawen's Cornish Manuscript), f.28.

26 Granville, *Genuine Works*, II, p. 230.

27 D. Lloyd, *Memoires of . . . Excellent Personages that suffered . . . for the Protestant Religion* (London, 1668), p. 469.

28 E.124 (29), *A Remonstrance or Declaration*, 21 October 1642; Bod., Wood Pamphlets, 376, *Sergeant Major James Chudleigh: His Declaration to his Countrymen* (Oxford, 1643).

29 E.79 (17), *The Weekly Account*, 20–29 December 1643; and C. Hammond, *The Old English Officer* (London, 1679), unpaginated.

30 E.300 (13), *A Copy of a Petition*, 10 September 1645.

31 Lloyd, *Memoires*, p. 469.

32 N. Tucker and P. Young (eds), *Military Memoirs: The Civil War* (Hamden, Connecticut, 1968), pp. 12, 28.

33 CRO, Tremaine Papers, DDT. 1767, 'The Services and Sufferings of Coll: Richard Arundell'.

34 CRO, F2/39, f.28.

35 Hammond, *The Old English Officer*.

36 K. Feiling, *A History of the Tory Party, 1640–1714*, (Oxford, 1959 edition), pp. 16–17.

37 G. Holmes, *The Trial of Doctor Sacheverell* (London, 1973), p. 37.

38 C.S. Gilbert, *An Historical Survey of the County of Cornwall* (2 vols, Plymouth, 1817), II, p. 714.

39 CRO, F2/39, f.27.

40 R.C. Richardson, *The Debate on the English Revolution* (Manchester, 1998), pp. 28–9.

41 E. Hyde, Earl of Clarendon, *The History of the Rebellion and Civil Wars in England* (Oxford, 1717), pp. 268, 276, 284.

42 R. Ollard, *This War without an Enemy: A History of the English Civil Wars* (London, 1976), p. 175.

43 Miller, *Grenville*, p. 147.

44 Lloyd, *Memoires*, pp. 472–3.

45 Granville, *Genuine Works*, II, pp. 220–1.

46 J. Polsue, *A Complete Parochial History of Cornwall* (Truro, 1867), III, p. 67.

47 *DNB*, 'George Granville'; and Granville, *Genuine Works*, I, p. 99.

48 Granville, *Genuine Works*, II, pp. 105–6.

49 *DNB*, 'George Granville'.

50 Feiling, *Tory Party*, p. 366.

51 Holmes, *Sacheverell*, pp. 238–9.

52 G. Holmes, *British Politics in the Reign of Anne* (London, 1987), p. 19.

53 A. Bray, 'Some Account of a Visit to the Battlefield of Stratton and the Tomb of Sir Bevil Granville, at Kilkhampton, Cornwall', *The Gentleman's Magazine* (July 1845), pp. 39–40.

54 Ibid., p. 36.

55 C. Petrie, *The Jacobite Movement* (London, 1959), pp. 222–4.

56 Ibid., p. 226; P.Q. Karkeek, 'Jacobite Days in the West', *TDA*, 28 (1896), p. 259; and H. Jenner, 'An Incident in Cornwall in 1715', *JRIC*, XX, Part 7 (1921), pp. 552–8.

57   There are some interesting parallels here with the situation in Wales, see M.G.H. Pittock, *Inventing and Resisting Britain: Cultural Identities in Britain and Ireland, 1685–1789* (Basingstoke, 1997), pp. 5, 7, 22, 24–5, 37–8, 40, 54–5, 106–8.

58   E. Cruickshanks, 'Lord North, Christopher Layer and the Atterbury Plot, 1720–23', in E. Cruickshanks and J. Black (eds), *The Jacobite Challenge* (Edinburgh, 1988), p. 96.

59   R. Granville, *The History of the Granville Family* (Exeter, 1895), pp. 272–3. An eighteenth-century drawing of this monument is reproduced in J. Wroughton, *A Community at War: The Civil War in Bath and North Somerset, 1642–50* (Bath, 1992), p. 103. See also BL, Egerton MSS, 2,657.

60   Granville, *Genuine Works*, II, pp. 185–248.

61   R. and O. Peter, *The Histories of Launceston and Dunheved* (Plymouth, 1885), p. 269; Polsue, *Parochial History* II, p. 174; and information supplied by Bill Stuart-White, Rector of the parish of St Martin and St Meriadoc, Camborne. I am most grateful to the Reverend Stuart-White for his help.

62   Personal observation in Philleigh and Landulph Churches.

63   J. Barry, 'The Seventeenth and Eighteenth Centuries', in N. Orme (ed.), *Unity and Variety: A History of the Church in Devon and Cornwall* (Exeter, 1991), pp. 83, 97.

64   P. Payton, *The Making of Modern Cornwall* (Redruth, 1992), pp. 64–5.

65   Prince, *Danmonii Orientales Illustres*, p. 323.

66   WDRO, 373/1, 'Danmonii Orientales Illustres, or The Wortheys of Devon: Volume the Second', Vol. 1, p. 255.

67   J. Prince, *The Worthies of Devon* (reprinted with additions, London, 1810), pp. 444–7.

68   Gilbert, *Historical Survey*, II, p. 546.

69   Ibid.

70   Bray, 'Some Account of a Visit to . . . Stratton', pp. 35–41.

71   C.E. Byles, *The Life and Letters of R. S. Hawker* (London, 1905), p. 542.

72   T. Lang, *The Victorians and the Stuart Heritage: Interpretations of a Discordant Past* (Cambridge, 1995), p. xi.

73   Byles, *Life and Letters*, pp. xv, 90, 146; and P. Brendon, *Hawker of Morwenstow: Portrait of a Victorian Eccentric* (London, 1975), pp. 96–7.

74   Byles, *Life and Letters*, pp. 24–31.

75   Brendon, *Hawker of Morwenstow*, p. 20

76   Byles, *Life and Letters*, p. 184.

77   Ibid., p. 461.

78   Although, ironically, the district around Stratton had been perhaps the *least* Royalist district of Cornwall during the Civil War itself! See M. Stoyle, *Loyalty and Locality: Popular Allegiance in Devon during the English Civil War*, (Exeter, 1994), pp. 150–1.

79   Ibid., p. 268.

80   R.S. Hawker, *The Cornish Ballads and Other Poems* (London, 1869), pp. 26–7.

81   Byles, *Life and Letters*, pp. 536, 545; and *All the Year Round*, 16 (1866), pp. 247–9. The paper was reprinted soon afterwards in Hawker's collected

essays, *Footprints of Former Men in Far Cornwall* (London, 1870), pp. 30–45.

82 Gilbert, *Historical Survey*, I, p. 165.

83 Byles, *Life and Letters*, p. 99.

84 Hawker, *Footprints*, pp. 39–40.

85 S. Baring-Gould, *The Vicar of Morwenstow: Being a Life of Robert Stephen Hawker* (London, 1899), p. 36. Hawker's account of the letters' 'discovery' was probably based on a very similar passage relating to some other, quite unrelated, manuscripts in D. Gilbert, *The Parochial History of Cornwall* (4 vols, London, 1838), IV, p. 375.

86 Byles, *Life and Letters*, p. 536.

87 This title was again a direct lift from Gilbert, see *Historical Survey*, I, p. 165.

88 See, for example, *DNB*, 'Sir Beville Grenville'.

89 A.H. Norway, *Highways and Byways in Devon and Cornwall* (first published in 1897, London, 1911 edn), p. 351.

90 See, for example, Stucley, *Sir Bevill Grenvile*, pp. 147–8.

91 See, for example, T. Deane and T. Shaw, *The Folklore of Cornwall* (London, 1975), p. 100.

92 H.S. Stokes, *Rhymes from Cornwall* (London, 1871), p. 80; and P.Q. Karkeek, 'Queen Henrietta Maria in Exeter, and her Escape therefrom', *TDA*, 8 (1876), pp. 471–3, 476.

93 J. Maclean, 'Notes on C.S. Gilbert', *JRIC*, VI (1880), pp. 344, 348; and Anon, 'A Short Account of Anthony Payne, The Cornish Giant: And the History of his Painting', *JRIC*, X (1890), pp. 275–9.

94 Coate, *Cornwall*, p. 32.

95 Though it continues to flourish in popular histories. For a splendid example, see A. Mee, *The King's England: Cornwall* (first published 1937, London, 1957 edn), pp. 14, 17, 93, 95, 99, 274–6. Mee assures his readers (p. 276) that 'it is as easy to doubt the purity of Galahad as the faithfulness of Anthony Payne'.

Conclusion

1 A.L. Rowse, *Tudor Cornwall: Portrait of a Society* (New York, 1969 edn), p. 10.

2 Ibid., *passim*, especially pp. 10, 305, 317–19.

3 R. Carew, *The Survey of Cornwall* (London, 1603).

4 CRO, F2/39 (William Scawen's Cornish Manuscript), *passim*.

5 CRO, SF 285/68, 69 (Account of John Ellis). I owe this reference to the great kindness of Joanna Mattingly.

Index

References in *italics* refer to plate numbers.

Admiralty, Court of, 142
Agincourt, Battle of, 36
agricultural practices, 12, 14–15, 68
Albion, 12
ale, *see* Cornish ale
All the Year Round (periodical), 177
Alley, William, bishop of Exeter, 43
Anderson, Benedict, 10
Angles, 149
Anglica Historica, 31
anglicanism, 25, 88, 166
animals, *see* bloodhounds, crabs, dogs, horses, moles, oxen, pigs
Anne, Queen of England, 171–72
'Anthony Payne: A Cornish Giant' (article), 177
anti-catholicism, 52
Antiquities Cornu-Brittanic, 6, 8, 145–46, 150–51, 153, 156, 182
Antony, co. Cornwall, 181
Arthur, King of Britain, 19–20, 38, 149
Arundell, John, 126
Arundell, Richard, colonel, 70, 126, 164
Arundell, Sir Thomas, 42
Ashton, Robert, 113, 126, 129
Atkyns, Richard, captain, 74, 164
Atlantic archipelago, 18, 51
Atlantic Ocean, 67, 148
atrocities, 75–78, 93–95

Babel, England equated with, 50, 61
Bacon, Francis, 45
ballads and songs, 43, 72, 171, 176–77
balls, *see* hurling balls
'barbarousness', 17, 34, 60, 78
Barnstaple, co. Devon, 71
Basset, Sir Arthur, 126
Bath, co. Somerset, 92, 162–63, 165
Bath, Earl of, *see* Grenville, John
Baxter, Richard, 52
Beaminster, co. Dorset, 87
beards, 127
Bedford, Earl of, 138
Behre, Hans, 61
Bennett, Robert, colonel, 116–17, 120–22, 125
Berkeley, Sir John, governor of Exeter, 101
Berkenhead, Sir John, editor of *Mercurius Aulicus*, 83
Blackheath, Battle of, 7, 21, 28, 34, 37, 152
'Blackmoores', 130
Blight, Neville, of Carnedon, 126
bloodhounds, 80
Bodleian Library, Oxford, 145
Bodmin, co. Cornwall, 70, 117, 140
   1549 rebels assembled at, 23
   near-riot in, 19
Body, William, archdeacon, 7, 21
Bogans, Hannibal, major, 124–27
Bond, John, Master of the Savoy, 113
bonfires, 122–23
Boorde, Andrew, 32, 34–35

253

'boorishness', alleged Cornish national characteristic 32–35, 38–40, 48, 54, 58
Boson, Nicholas, of Newlyn, 40
Bosworth, triumph of Henry Tudor at, 20
Braddock Down, Battle of, 140, 162
bravery, Cornish famed for, 83, 164, 169
Bray, Mrs —, 175
Bray, Vicar of, 153
Breage, co. Cornwall, 120
Breton language, 14
Bridgerule Bridge (River Tamar), 104
Bridgwater, co. Somerset, 142
Bristol, 162, 165
  storming of, 74, 164
Bristol Channel, 115, 131
Britain and the British, 12, 27, 31, 34, 58, 65, 67, 78, 147–49, 154
'British History', 3–4, 10, 18, 28, 50–51, 111–12, 114, 182
British Isles, 3, 10, 16, 33, 112, 148
'Britons', 13, 36, 54, 147–56
Brome, Richard, playwright, 8, 39
Brutus, King of Britain, 12–13
Buller family, of Shillingham, 139
Buller, Sir Richard, 70, 138–39
Burghley, Lord, 73
Bury St Edmunds, co. Suffolk, 128
butchers, 125, 132

Calenso, —, rebel scout, 127
Callington, co. Cornwall, 142
Calstock, co. Cornwall, 174
Camborne, co. Cornwall, 6, 174
Camden, William, antiquary, 6
Carew, Sir Alexander, 140
Carew, Richard, 7, 16–19, 41, 44, 67–68, 71, 79, 140, 181–82
Carleton, Adam de, archdeacon of Cornwall, 29
Carnedon, co. Cornwall, 126
Carrick Roads, 32
catholics and catholicism, 21, 24, 43, 52, 55, 72, 92
Cavaliers, see Royalists
Cawsand, co. Cornwall, 140
Chagford, co. Devon, 162
Chard, co. Somerset, 74

Charles I, 8, 4, 7–9, 25, 35, 52, 56–57, 59–66, 70, 82, 87, 89–90, 93, 96–97, 108–11, 114, 126–28, 131, 138–43, 152–55, 158–62, 164–65, 167–70
Charles I, 'declaration' of, 6, 7, 159–62, 174
Charles II, 143, 158, 163, 168, 171 see also Prince of Wales and Duke of Cornwall
Cheriton, Battle of, 79
children, 40, 46, 57, 75, 99, 136, 149
Chirwin, Thomas, 127
'Chough' (fictitional character), 37–40
christians, 147
Chudleigh, James, 164
Church of England, 55
Chynoweth, John, 44
Civil Wars, see First Civil War and Second Civil War
Clarendon, Earl of see Hyde, Sir Edward
Clowance, co. Cornwall, 4, 118
clubmen, 86–87, 130, 132, 164
Coate, Mary, 95, 111, 125–26, 179–80
'Cocknies', trounced by the Cornish, 60
Colchester, co. Essex, 113
Coleman, Robert, major, 126
Coligny Chatillon, Gaspard de, French ambassador, 42–43
Collins, —, colonel, 127
'Committee for Troubles', 125
common prayer, book of, 45–47, 131, 150
'commotions', see Helston Rising and Prayer Book Rebellion
Constantine the Great, 149
continentals, prone to rapine, 61
Corineus, 13
cormorants, 79
Cornish acre, 16
Cornish ale, unpleasant effects of, 35
Cornish Army, 5, 8, 158–60, 162–65, 167
Cornish chough (Pyrrhocorax Pyrrhocorax), 37–38, 78–79
Cornish chough (nickname for Cornish people), 37–38, 78–79, 87
Cornish County Committee, the, 118

'Cornish crew' (term of abuse), 36–37
'Cornish hop', see 'Cornish hug'
'Cornish hug', 80–81
Cornish language, 5, 14–18, 20–21,
    24–28, 31–33, 35, 39–40, 42,
    45–49, 68–69, 88–90, 96, 132, 134,
    142, 144–51, 156, 183
'Cornish mousetrap', 75
Cornish particularism, 50, 91, 97–98,
    103–04, 107–08, 132
'Cornish piskies', 82
Cornish Rebellion, of 1497, 4, 7, 9, 21,
    24, 26, 28–30, 40–42, 44, 48, 58,
    70, 88, 90, 96, 151, 159
Cornish Rebellion, of 1548, 7, 9, 21,
    23, 28, 30, 43, 48–49, 58, 90
Cornish Rebellion, of 1549, 4, 7, 9,
    23–25, 28, 30, 41, 43–44, 48–49,
    58, 70–71, 88, 96, 159
Cornish Rebellion, of 1642, 5, 8–9,
    24–25, 28, 71, 88, 157–59
Cornish Rebellion, of 1648, 5, 8–9,
    25–26, 28, 89–90, 113–33 passim
Cornish Record Office, 145
'Cornish Royalist tradition', 158–80
    passim
Cornwall, 1–9, 13–14, 16–17, 19–21,
    23, 25, 27–28, 30–37, 39–45, 48,
    51, 57–60, 64–71, 73, 75–77,
    79–90, 92–94, 96–99, 102–06,
    108–11, 113–17, 120, 126, 128–32,
    134, 136, 139–46, 148–49, 151–63,
    166–74, 176–77, 179–82
    archdeacon of, 29
    'county and province of', 31
    duchy of, 19, 23, 30, 44, 58–59,
        88–89, 153, 163
    Duke of, 8, 13, 19, 58, 103, 108–10
    East, 14, 16, 47, 104, 136, 142, 155
    Lord Lieutenant of, 163
    sheriff of, 31, 154
    West, 14, 16–21, 23–24, 28, 34, 40,
        68, 75, 89, 129, 142
Cornwall, Michael of ('Merry
    Michael'), 34, 108
Coryton, William, of Callington,
    colonel, 142, 155
Cotton, Sir Robert, 35
Council in the Marches, 54, 56, 58
Council of the West, 7, 42

courtiers, 35, 40, 138
courtliness, Cornish commended for,
    35, 40
crabs, 79
Crediton, co. Devon, 72
Cromwell, Oliver, 63, 116, 177
Cromwell, Thomas, Lord Privy Seal,
    21, 42
crosses, 182
Curnowe, —, butcher, 132

Daniel, Alexander, of Larigan, 122
'Dark Ages', 10, 150
Dartmoor, 94
Dartmouth, co. Devon, 85
    capture of, 84
Davies, R.R., 12, 19
Denmark and the Danes, 52–53
Dennis, the, fort near Helford, 116,
    123–24, 127
Devizes, Richard of, 34
Devon, county of, 2, 7, 10, 41, 68, 71,
    73, 75, 81, 84, 86, 93, 97, 99, 103,
    109–10, 114–15, 117, 120, 133,
    139, 142, 148, 151, 162, 164, 175
    East, 66, 103
    sheriff of, 93
    South, 95, 103
    West, 88, 105
dissent and dissenters, 166, 176
dogs, Scottish soldier baited with, 62
    see also bloodhounds
Dorset, 2, 66, 73, 87
Dover, co. Kent, 113
dress, styles of, 12, 14
Druids, 147–48
Duffin, Anne, 138
Dutch officers, 61
'Dutchesse of Cornwall's Progresse,
    The' (story for children), 40

East Anglia, 24, 66
East Looe, co. Cornwall, 138
Edgcumbe, Piers, 138–42, 155
Edward VI, 43
elections, see Parliament, election to
Eliot, Sir John, of Port Eliot, 35, 136,
    138, 154
Elizabeth I, Queen of England, 7, 33,
    35–37, 40, 43–44, 46–48, 151

Ellys, Roger, 127
elves, 82
England, 13, 16, 18, 28–32, 34–35, 37, 42, 45, 48, 50–56, 59, 61–64, 66–67, 69, 71–73, 83, 86–90, 92, 96, 107, 113–14, 132, 148, 151–54, 164, 172–73, 181–82
  crown of, 51
  king of, 152
  monarchs of, 33, 51
  North of, 63
English church, 55
English officers, 61
English Parliamentarians, 6
'Englishness', 5, 20, 24, 53, 68, 151
Essex, county of, 162
Essex, Earl of, 8, 59–61, 75–78, 80–82, 87, 94, 140, 158, 160
'ethnicism', 20
'ethnicity', 26
ethnie, 12
executions, 28, 140, 152–53
Exeter, 42–43, 66, 95, 111, 117–18, 133, 148, 165
  dean of, 42
  governor of, 101
  Marquis of, 41
  Perkin Warbeck's assaults on, 28
  permanent garrison at, 115
  rumours of trouble in, 128
  shopkeeper of, 74
exorcism, 127

Fair Quarrel, A (play) 7, 37–40
Fairfax, Sir Thomas, Lord General of the New Model Army, 80, 84–85, 104, 114, 116–17, 142–43, 154
Falier, Lodovico, of Italy, 32, 34
Falmouth, co. Cornwall, 32
'Falstaff of the West', *see* Payne, Anthony
Feiling, K., 166
First Civil War, 2–5, 8, 24, 30, 40, 45, 50–51, 53–54, 56–57, 60–62, 64, 66–67, 73, 80, 86–87, 89, 91–92, 95–96, 107, 111–12, 131, 136, 138, 141, 144, 152–54, 157–59, 162, 164, 166–72, 179
Flavell, Thomas, vicar of Mullion, 126–27, 130

Flemings, 34
Florio, John, 33
Ford, John, playwright, 45
Fortescue, Richard, colonel, 116–17
Foster, Robert, Judge of the Western Circuit, 144
Fowey, co. Cornwall, 136
  MP for, 171
  surrender of Essex's army at, 76
Fowey, River, 136
France and the French, 34, 42, 53, 61, 78, 87, 96
Frenchmen, alleged sexual proclivities of, 78, 87
forgery, *see* Hawker, Reverend Robert S.
Fuller, Thomas, 80, 157
Fyrste Boke of the Introduction of Knowledge, 32

Gardiner, S.R., 52
Gate Song of Stowe, The (ballad), 177
Gatford, Lionel, chaplain, 107–08
Gear, co. Cornwall, 124, 126, 182
Gear Bridge, 124
'Gear Rout', the, 9, 26, 113, 124–25, 182 *see also* Cornish Rebellion, of 1648
Gellner, Ernest, 10
George I, 171–72
Germany and the Germans, 53, 61
ghosts, 127
Gilbert, C.S., 178–79
Glasney, collegiate church of, near Penryn, co. Cornwall, 20
Gloucestershire, county of, 160, 164
Glover, —, rebel leader, 126
Glyn Dwr, Owain, 19, 57
Godolphin, Sidney, colonel, 162, 165
Golant, co. Cornwall, 136
Goldsithney, co. Cornwall, 130
Goring, Lord George, 99, 101–02, 104, 106, 109, 111, 142, 167
Granville, George, 170–76, 182
'Great Britain', 89, 103, 153
Grenville, Sir Bernard, father of Sir Bevill and Sir Richard, 92, 171
Grenville, Sir Bevill, *8*, 8, 92, 136, 158, 162–65, 169–75, 177–79

Grenville, Lady Grace, wife of Sir Bevill, 178
Grenville, Sir John, Earl of Bath, son of Sir Bevill, *10*, 163, 171, 178
Grenville, Sir Richard, *5*, 5, 7–8, 75, 88, 91–95, 97–112, 132, 140–41, 155, 163–64, 169–70, 173, 182
Grosse, Christopher, of St Buryan, major, 126, 128–30
Gubbs, Anthony, merchant, 118, 120, 122, 127, 133
Gubbs, Joseph, son of Anthony, 118
Gwaryes, 16 *see also* plays, in Cornish

Hall, Edward, of London, chronicler, 31
Hammond, Charles, captain, 165
Harris, Miss —, of Hayne, 177
Harris, Mr —, 120
Harris, Robert, 126
Hastings, Adrian, 3, 30, 45–46
Hawker, Reverend Robert S., vicar of Morwenstow, *10*, 175–79, 182
Hayne, co. Cornwall, 177
Hearth Tax, the, 144
'heathenism', 17, 60, 81, 89, 132
Hechter, M.J., 3
Helford, co. Cornwall, 9, 116
Helston, co. Cornwall, 25, 118, 120, 124, 127–29
   archdeacon Body murdered at, 7, 21
   'Committee for Troubles' moved to, 125
   Parliamentarian faction of, 123
   rebel forces gathering near, 122
Helston Rising, the, *see* Cornish Rebellion, of 1548
Henrietta Maria, queen-consort to Charles I, 179
Henry II, court of, 34
Henry V, (play) 7, 36; ('Captain Fluellen'), 36; ('Captain Gower'), 36–37; ('Ensign Pistol'), 36–37; ('Harry le Roy'), 36; ('Henry V'), 36
Henry VII, 7, 20–21, 34, 37, 40, 54
Henry VIII, 7, 32, 41–42
Herle, Edward, sheriff of Cornwall, 117, 120–23, 126, 128–29, 133
Hertford, Marquess of, 96

Heynes, Simon, dean of Exeter, 42
Hickes, John, 2
Hickes, William, 167–68
Highlanders, Scottish, 28
'Hilters Clift', St Keverne, co. Cornwall, 124
History of Cornwall, 178
History of Henry VII, 45
History of the Rebellion, *8*, 8, 91, 168–70, 172, 175
Holbein, Hans, *1*, 32
Holinshed, Raphael, 44
Hopton, Arthur, 32
Hopton, Sir Ralph, 70–73, 80, 87, 142–43, 164, 172
horses, 178
House of Commons, 104, 113, 116, 138
Humberstone, William, 39
hurling, 14, 16, 68, 80, 132
hurling balls, *3*, 16, 26, 68, 132
Hyde, Sir Edward, Earl of Clarendon, 8, 82, 91, 93, 98, 101, 103–05, 109–10, 168–70, 172–73

'Indians', 17
Ipswich, co. Suffolk, 132
Ireland and the Irish, 6, 14, 16–17, 31, 33, 51–52, 56, 60–61, 64, 74, 77, 87–88, 92, 96, 101, 112, 164 *see also* 'kerns'
Ireland, rebellion in, 52, 56, 77, 92
Isles of Scilly, 128, 148
Israel, ten tribes of, 107
Italy and the Italians, 31–33 *see also* Venice and the Venetians

Jacobites, 172–73
James I, 7, 51, 53
James II, 171, 176
James III, proclaimed at St Columb, 173
Jane, Joseph, 86
Jersey, 168
Jones, Mr —, 126
Judah, tribe of, 107–08
Jutes, 27

Keates, —, captain, 129
Kenegy, co. Cornwall, 121

Kent, county of, 27
Kent, Alan, 36
Kentish rebels, 27
'Kernow', 17, 132
'Kernowok', 17
'kerns', Irish, 87
Kerrier, hundred of, 21
Kett, Robert, 24
Kiegwin, William, 126
Kilkenny, Statutes of, 16
Kilkhampton, 92, 162, 174–75
Kilkhampton Church, 172, 175
Kneller, Sir Godfrey, 9

Land's End, 25, 40, 66
Langport, Battle of, 102
Lansdown, 163, 165, 175
  Battle of, 10, 74, 170
  Bevill Grenville killed at, 92, 162, 178
  monument at, 174
Lansdown Hill, 8, 173
Lansdowne, Viscount, see Granville,
  George
Larigan, co. Cornwall, 122
Laudianism, 176
Launceston, co. Cornwall, 85, 89, 104,
  106, 139, 161, 170
  copy of King's declaration at, 174
  Cornish county committee at, 118
  derivation of place-name of, 144
Launceston Assizes, 144–45
Leach, Simon, 95
leeks, symbol of Welsh pride, 36
Lenthall, William, Speaker of the
  House of Commons, 77
'Leostofen', 144, see also Launceston
Lincoln's Inn, 136
Liskeard, co. Cornwall, 43, 103, 141
Liverpool, 92
Lizard peninsula, the, 8–9, 21, 25–26,
  121, 126–27
Lloyd, David, 164–65, 169
Lluellin, Martin, 171
Loggett, Renald, 123
London, 32–34, 38–39, 42–44, 71, 75,
  77, 92, 116–17, 120, 140
  panic on the streets of, 56
  Welsh MPs in, 65
London pamphleteers, 59, 79, 83, 91,
  106

London press, 61, 76, 81
London stage, 37
Londoners, 30
Long Parliament, the, 56 see also
  Parliament
Looe, co. Cornwall, 121
Lord's Prayer, the, 150
Lostwithiel, co. Cornwall, 76–77,
  140–41
  defeat of the Earl of Essex at, 8, 59,
  93
  Great Hall at, destroyed in 1644, 136
Loyalty and Locality, 3
Ludlow, Edmund, 53
Luke, Sir Samuel, 87
Lydford, co. Devon, 94–95
Lydford Castle, co. Devon, 94–95
Lyme, co. Dorset, 74
  siege of, 74–75, 165
Lyndon, Brian, 132
Lyonesse, 148

MacGillivray, R., 91
Maddern, Martin, major, 126
Maidstone, co. Kent, 27
Mallack, Roger, of Exeter, 95
Marazion (Market Jew), co. Cornwall,
  118, 121, 129
Marseillaise, The, 176
Mary, Queen of England, 43
Mary, Queen of Scots, 152
Maurice, Prince, nephew of Charles I,
  74, 87, 93
Mawgan Church, co. Cornwall,
  123–24
maypoles, 'great combustion' caused
  by, 128
Menheniot, co. Cornwall, 136
mercenaries, 61, 63, 87, 96, 101, 149
Mercurius Aulicus (diurnal), 80–81, 83,
  87
Mercurius Britanicus (diurnal), 81, 83
'Merry Michael', see Cornwall, Michael
  of
Merthen, co. Cornwall, 1
Methodists, 174
Middleton, Thomas (playwright), 7,
  37–40
Millbrook, 139, 154–55
  garrison at, 140–41

surprise attack on, 140
treaty concluded at, 142–43, 167
Miller, A.C., 93, 95
Mirrour for Magistrates, 44
Modbury, co. Devon, 72, 80
Mohun, Lord Warwick, 165
Moilesbarrow Down, co. Cornwall, 70
Molenick, parish of St Germans, co.
 Cornwall, 136, 138–39, 151
moles, 79
Monmouth, Duke of, 171
Monmouth, Geoffrey of, 12–13, 148
Monmouthshire, 56
Montaigne, Michel de, 33
monuments, 163, 170, 172–75
Morrill, John, 10
Morwenstow, co. Cornwall, 175, 178
Mount Edgcumbe, 138–39, 141
 garrison at, 141
Moyle, John, 122, 124, 127, 132
MPs, 53, 56, 58–59, 65, 116, 125, 131,
 138–39, 171, 176
Mullion, co. Cornwall, 123, 126–27
mutiny, among the Old Cornish
 (1645), 102
 at Pembroke Castle (1648), 115
 at Pendennis Castle (1648), 115–16

Naseby, Battle of, 64
National Covenant, 143
nationalism, 1, 5, 12, 50, 59, 62, 108
Netherlands, the, and the Dutch, 53,
 61
New Cornish Tertia, 8, 98–106
New Model Army, 63–64, 80, 102–03,
 111–14, 142, 161, 164
Newbury, Battle of, 78, 80, 171
Newlyn, co. Cornwall, 40
Nicoll, Humphrey, of Penvose, 136
Nicols, Phillip, 46
Nighton, Thomas, 127
'Nonsense' (fictional character), 39
Norden, John, 16, 88
North, —, Lord Chief Justice, 145
Northern Lasse, the (play) 8, 39
Northumberland, 113
Northumberland, Earl of, 138

Offa's Dyke, 5
Okehampton, co. Devon, 103–04

Old Cornish Tertia, 102
oxen, 182
Oxford, 2, 62, 87, 92, 98, 136, 161
 elegies for Sir Bevill Grenville
 published at, 163, 171
 proclamation issued from, 159
Oxford Parliament, 62

pagans and paganism, 17, 81, 90, 147,
 149–50
Parliament, 24, 30, 44, 53, 56, 58–59,
 116, 118, 183 *see also* Long
 Parliament, Oxford Parliament,
 Short Parliament, Welsh
 Parliament
Parliament, election to, 136, 138, 171
Parliamentarians, 24–26, 53, 56–65,
 Ch. 4, *passim*, Ch. 5, *passim*, Ch. 6,
 passim, 138–43, 158–59, 163, 166
Pascow, Robert, 121
Passio Christo, 134, 144, 146
patriots and patriotism, 53, 90, 95–96,
 134, 155, 168
patronymics, 16, 68
Payne, Anthony, 9, 178–79
Payton, Phillip, 3, 19, 103
Pembroke Castle, 115–16
Pendarves, William, of Roscrow, 126
Pendarvys, —, captain, 126
Pendennis Castle, co. Cornwall, 106,
 115–17, 143
Penrice, co. Cornwall, 136
Penryn, co. Cornwall, 17, 20–21, 126
 demonstration at, 7
 rebels humiliated at, 26, 132
Pentreath, Dolly, 8
Penvose, co. Cornwall, 136
Penwith, co. Cornwall, 130
 hundred of, 21
Penwith peninsula, 69
Penzance, co. Cornwall, 26, 34, 132
 Perkin Warbeck lands at, 21
 rebellion at, 8, 25, 89, 113, 118,
 120–22, 126–30
'peoples', 12, 19–20, 26, 30, 33
Perkin Warbeck (play) 45
Perne, John, of Marazion (Market
 Jew), 129
Personal Rule, of Charles I, the, 52,
 138

Peters, Hugh, 85–86, 89
petitions, 48, 56, 59, 110, 139
Pierce, John, 127
Philleigh, co. Cornwall, 7
pigs, 35
Pike, Thomas, captain, 121, 126, 129–30
Pindar, Martin, colonel, 77
Piper, Hugh, of Launceston, 170
place-names, 151
plays, in Cornish, 16, 20 see also Gwaryes
plays, in English, 14, 36–40, 45, 171
Plen an Gwaryes, see Gwaryes
plots, 52, 128, 140
Plymouth, 71, 74–77, 81, 94, 97, 99, 133, 163–64, 175
  desertion from trenches before, 167
  Parliamentary garrison of, 95, 115, 139–40
  Royalist attack on, 80
  siege of, 93, 98, 141, 165, 170
Plymouth Sound, St Nicholas Island in, 140
Pocock, J.G.A., 18
Pole, Reginald, cardinal, 43
Polwhele, Richard, 124–25
popish plots, 52, 56
Port Eliot, co. Cornwall, 136
Porth Leven, co. Cornwall, 121
Portsmouth, co. Hants, 77
posse comitatus, 70, 139
Poyer, John, 115–17, 128–29, 131, 133
Prayer Book rebels, 2, 48
Prayer Book Rebellion, 7, 23, 70 see also Cornish Rebellion, of 1549
Prince, John, antiquary, 162, 175
prisoners-of-war, 92–95
Privy Council, 43
propaganda and propagandists, 5, 25, 56–57, 59–62, Ch. 4, passim, 157
protestants and protestantism, 24, 43, 46, 52–53, 55, 131, 181–82
proverbs and sayings, 69, 134, 152
puritans and puritanism, 24, 55, 69, 72, 138–39, 164, 182
Pym, John, 138

Queen's College, Oxford, 136
Quiller-Couch, T., 3

Quirini, Vincenzo, of Venice, diplomat, 32, 34

Reading, co. Berkshire, 77
rebelliousness, Cornish reputation for, 4, 29, 40–41, 45, 71, 151, 157
'Redshanks', 14
Reform Bill, of 1867, the, 178
Reformation, the, 45, 48, 55
'Reges Anglie', 152
religion, 21, 23, 41–43, 45, 53, 55–58, 81–82, 88, 148–50, 183
Reskimer, John, 1
Reskimer, William, 1
Reskymer, —, 32–33
Richard II, wife of, 16
'roaring', 38–39
Rome and the Romans, 147–49
Roscarrock, Edward, colonel, 169
Roscrow, co. Cornwall, 126
Roundheads, see Parliamentarians
Rowley, William, playwright, 7, 37–40
Rowse, A.L., 3, 181–82
Royal Institute of Cornwall, 179
Royal Oak, Order of, 144
Royalists and Royalism, 2, 3, 5, 25, 45, 57, 59–64, 67, 70–76, 78–89, 91–99, 102–12, 114, 116, 123, 126–33, 139–43, 152–55, 156–80, passim
Rupert, Prince, nephew of Charles I, 61

St Aubyn, John, of Clowance, 118, 120
St Aubyn, Thomas, colonel, 4
St Buryan, co. Cornwall, 126
St Columb, co. Cornwall, 8, 173
St Germans, co. Cornwall, 35, 139
  constituency of, 138
  death of William Scawen at, 146
  parish of, 136
St Ives, co. Cornwall, 25, 83, 118, 120, 128, 167
St James Park, London, 106
St Keverne, co. Cornwall, 26, 90, 123–25, 127–28, 130, 132
  insurrection at, 7, 21
  rumours of rising at, 41–42
St Mawgan, co. Cornwall, 127

St Michael's Mount, co. Cornwall, 38,
106, 120–21, 129–30
garrison at, 118
governor of, 116
St Nicholas Island, in Plymouth
Sound, 140
Sacheverell, Dr. Henry, 171
Salmon, Edward, lieutenant-colonel,
117–18
Saltash, co. Cornwall, 117
ejection of Parliamentary garrison at,
97
garrison at, 140–41
Sawle, Alice, wife of William Scawen,
136
Sawle, Nicholas esquire, of Penrice,
136, 138
Saxons, the, 10, 14, 17, 19, 58, 67, 147,
149–50
Scawen, Isabella, mother of William,
136, 138
Scawen, Robert, father of William,
136
Scawen, William, antiquary, 5–8, 42,
46–48, 134–56 passim, 163, 165,
168, 182
Scawen, Robert, brother of William,
138
Scawen, William, son of William, 136
Scilly Isles, see Isles of Scilly
Scotland and the Scots, 4, 12–14, 28,
31, 33, 51–53, 60–64, 88, 112–14,
148, 153
Second Civil War, Ch. 6, passim
Sennen parish, co. Cornwall, 182
sermons, 45–46, 107–08, 113, 177
Shakespeare, William, 7, 36–37
Shillingham, Buller family of, 139
Short Parliament, the, 138
Siculus, Diodorus, 148
'Sir Tristram' (Arthurian knight), 38
Slanning, Sir Nicholas, 162, 165
slings, 16
Smith, A.D., 12, 20
Somerset, county of, 2, 66, 73, 99,
130, 164
Somerset, John, 132
Spain and the Spanish, 43, 52
Speight, Helen, 23
Sprigge, Joshua, 85

Stamford Hill, co. Cornwall,
monument on, 172, 175
stannaries, 16, 19, 21, 30, 58–59, 68,
73, 82, 88–89, 94, 136, 144, 153,
163
Stannary Court, 94
Stonehenge, 149
Stout Cripple of Cornwall, The (ballad), 72
Stowe, co. Cornwall, 92, 162–63,
174–75
Stowe Barton, co. Cornwall, 178
Stratton, co. Cornwall, 83, 142,
178–79
Battle of, 73, 154, 162, 165, 170
monument at, 174
parish of, 172
town of, 175
Stuart, James Edward, the Pretender,
172
Sudeley Castle, Gloucestershire, 160
Suffolk, 53, 128
supernatural phenomena, see elves,
exorcism, ghosts and 'Cornish
piskies'
Survey of Cornwall, 7, 17, 41, 181
Sussex, county of, 113
Symonds, Richard, 82

Tamar, River, 1–2, 10, 14, 31, 45, 48,
60, 66, 69–71, 75–76, 82, 84, 93,
96, 99, 103–04, 106, 109, 117, 120,
136, 139–42, 151, 153–55, 158,
172, 176, 179
Taunton, co. Somerset, 101–02
desertion from trenches before, 167
Parliamentary garrison of, 99
Tavistock, co. Devon, 106–08, 117
gaol established at, 93–94
taxation, 115, 130, 132–33
tin-mining, 19, 21, 58, 67–69, 72–73,
81–82, 90, 94, 174
tin-pits, defeated rebels hide in, 125
Tintagel, co. Cornwall, 136
Tories, 5, 144, 166, 168, 170–73
Torrington, co. Devon, 104
Battle of, 84–85, 110
Totnes, co. Devon, 103
tourism, 175
Towednack, co. Cornwall, 121
Tower of London, the, 136, 173

Tower Hill, London, 140
trained bands, Cornish, 84, 103, 106, 127, 139–43, 155
Treaty of Millbrook, 8
Tree Inn, the, at Stratton, co. Cornwall, 175, 179
Tregonwell, Dr John, 42
Trelawny (ballad), 176–77
Trelawny, [Sir] John, 126, 176
Trelawny, Jonathan, 126
Trelawny, Jonathan, bishop, 176–77
Treleage, co. Cornwall, 124
Trerice, home of the Arundell family, 127
Tresillian, Mr —, 126
Trevanion, Charles, 126
Trevanion, John, colonel, 162, 165, 171
Trevilian's Barn, near Gear, co. Cornwall, 124
Trevisa, John, 67
'Trimtram' (fictional character), 37–39
Troy and the Trojans, 12–13
True Relation of the Sad Passages Between the Two Armies in the West, A (news-pamphlet), 77
Truro, co. Cornwall, 24, 68, 70, 93, 104, 125, 140
Tudor, Henry, *see* Henry VII
Tudor Cornwall, 181

Ulster, 31

vagrancy, 72, 74
Venice and the Venetians, 32–33, 115
Vergil, Polydore, 31
Vicars, John, 82, 85

Wales and the Welsh, 5, 12–13, 17–19, 27–28, 31–33, 36–37, 42, 46–47, 49–51, 53, 60, 64–65, 68, 78,

81–82, 84, 87, 112–14, 115–17, 131–33, 148–50, 152
Wales, Prince of, 8, 54, 56, 58, 88, 99–111, 142, 169
Wales, rebellion in, 28, 57, 115, 152
Walker, Edward, secretary to Charles I, 82, 127
Waller, Sir Hardress, colonel, 114–18, 120, 125, 128, 133
Waller, Sir William, 60, 74, 78, 80, 92
Wanklyn, M.D.G., 95
Warbeck, Perkin, 7, 21, 24, 28
Welsh language, 14, 27, 31–33, 42, 46–47, 54, 131, 150
'Welsh Parliament', rumours of, 57
Wesley, John, 174, 177
West Briton, The (newspaper), 6
West Midlands, 62
West Penwith, co. Cornwall, 122, 127
Westcote, Thomas, antiquary, 41
Western Men, The (ballad), 176
Westminster, London, 56, 131, 138
Westminster, Matthew of, 18
Westminster Hall, London, 61
Whigs, 172–73
Whitehall, 44, 106
'whitepots', 39
William of Orange, 171
Williams, Roger, 17
Wiltshire, 73
women, 16, 38–39, 53, 57, 74–77, 84–85, 93, 99, 136, 144, 148–49, 177–78
Worcester, Earl of, 56
Worthies of Devon, The, 175
wrestling, 14, 35, 66, 80

Yolland, Walter, soldier, 95
Yolland, —, widow of Walter, 95
York, 52
Yorkshire, 27
Youings, Joyce, 24